Gang-rape, Sodomy, Female Genitalia Cutting, Social Injustice, Kidnapped on a Foreign Soil.... These are a Few of the Horrific Atrocities Exposed When These Wounded Yet Thriving Visionaries Blow the Lid Off Their Stories of Resiliency, Relentless Determination, and Unyielding Strength.

FEARLESS VISIONARIES™ Vol 2

Tear the Veil!

GLOBAL EDITION

D1521911

FUMI HANCOCK
BESTSELLING AUTHOR

Psychiatric Mental Health Doctor of Nurse Practice, TEDx Int'l. Speaker, *Your Global Vision Midwife*™ *&* *LifeRehab*™ *Ambassador*

STORIES WRITTEN BY
Chanelle Washington, Markita D. Collins, Onyinye N. Chukwunyerenwa, Dr. Debby Olusa, Ramona E. Jones, Dana Priyanka Hammond, Dr. Eveangel Hines Savage, Chichi Edna Njoku, and Teri Charles

FOREWORD BY
Olori Iyabowale Mariam Adebayo
Queen, Elemure of Emure Ekiti Kingdom, Nigeria

DR. HANCOCK IS GIVING A FREE CHAPTER OF HER INSPIRATIONAL LIFE NUGGETS VIDEO SERIES - EXCLUSIVE TO HER VIP READERS GROUP:
http://bit.ly/millionaireinfluencersecrets

TEAR THE VEIL

FEARLESS VISIONARIES!

Gang-rape, Sodomy, Female Genitalia Cutting, Social Injustice, Kidnapped on a Foreign Soil. These are a Few of the Horrific Atrocities Exposed When These Wounded Yet Thriving Visionaries Blow the Lid Off Their Stories of Resiliency, Relentless Determination, and Unyielding Strength.

GLOBAL EDITION

FUMI HANCOCK

BESTSELLING AUTHOR

Psychiatric Mental Health Doctor of Nurse Practice, TEDx Int'l. Speaker, *Your Global Vision Midwife™ & LifeRehab™ Ambassador*

&

Chanelle Washington, Markita D. Collins, Onyinye N. Chukwunyerenwa, Dr. Debby Olusa, Ramona E. Jones, Dana Priyanka Hammond, Dr. Eveangel Hines Savage, Chichi Edna Njoku, and Teri Charles

Tear the Veil,
FEARLESS VISIONARIES!
Gang-rape, Sodomy, Female Genitalia Cutting, Social Injustice, Kidnapped on a Foreign Soil. These are a Few of the Horrific Atrocities Exposed When These Wounded Yet Thriving Visionaries Blow the Lid Off Their Stories of Resiliency, Relentless Determination, and Unyielding Strength.

GLOBAL EDITION

More Books in *Your Vision Torch* ™ Series
365 Daily Vision Nuggets
Wise Quotes for Life, Home, & Business
Wake Up Girl: YOU ARE WORTHY!
AVAILABLE ON AMAZON

Fumi Stephanie Hancock, DNP.
The Princess of Suburbia ® Brand
Psychiatric Mental Health Doctor of Nurse Practice
TEDx Int'l. Speaker, *Your Global Vision*™ *& LifeRehab*™ *Ambassador*

EMAIL(s):
askdrfumi@webpsychnp.com
successlaunchbp@theprincessofsuburbia.com

WEBSITE(S):
https://bit.ly/millionaireinfluencersecrets
www.drfumihancock.com / www.theprncessofsuburbia.com

MASTERCLASSES:
www.storytellerbistro.com

BLOG(S):
www.yourinneryou.com

FACEBOOK(S):
https://www.facebook.com/fearlessvisionaries/
http://bit.ly/fearlessvisionariescommunity

WATCH & SUBSCRIBE TO MY POPULAR TV SHOW
https://www.facebook.com/IAmPrincessofSuburbiaTV/
https://www.youtube.com/c/princessofsuburbia

DR. HANCOCK IS GIVING FREE INSPIRATIONAL VIDEO SERIES, LIFEREHAB™ NUGGETS. THIS IS EXCLUSIVE TO HER VIP READERS GROUP:
http://bit.ly/millionaireinfluencersecrets

DO YOU WANT FREE INSPIRATIONAL LifeRehab™ VIDEO NUGGETS?

'I am **ready to position** myself as an expert in my industry. I thought of writing a book or perhaps co-authoring with a bestselling author but I don't know how to start! **Can You Help Me?**

SUCESS BEGINS WITH INSPIRATION
Get your FREE 6-part inspirational video series!

"I Am An Advanced Nurse Practitioner.
Books & Documentaries Are My Legs to the World."
-Dr. Fumi Hancock

CREATE YOUR OWN OPPORTUNITIES. FIND OUT!
Receive my video series, empowering podcasts, practical tips & tools, inspiring 'vision rehab'™' delivered directly to your inbox!

First Name

E-mail

+1 United States ▾	Phone Number

SEND ME MY 6 VIDEOS!

http://bit.ly/millionaireinfluencersecrets

No matter what people say or do, remember that the power to change the trajectory of your life is solely in your hands!

DAILY VISION NUGGET™

DR. PRINCESS FUMI HANCOCK, DNP.

amazon.com

DEDICATION

To all the women across the globe suffering and itching to #TeartheVeil but are unable to; I salute you and declare that your day has come to push past fear… your time has come to release yourself from old-age secrets. The time has genuinely here when victims transition into ex-victims and begin to tell their truth.

To all who have gone silently in pain before us; taking these groans with them yet leaving unsurmountable pain for generation s behind them to display… we say, we stand and push beyond your secrets and we dare to stand.

I dedicate this to all the women and children globally who because we dare to tear the veil will be inspired, motivated, and empowered to walk their truth journey without the guilt, shame, and fear of repercussion or persecution.

I dedicate this to our men who stand by us… protecting us and ensuring that we are heard. Those who have decided to g against the grain of society to say, "No More!". No more will you weep in silence. No more will you, and my sisters carry shame like a torch of life. No more will you lie helpless, desperately looking for a savior who will come out to deliver from atrocities committed against you.

This journey is dedicated to you, our men who are standing solidly for us and with us - bearing our pain and tearing down the walls of disappointment.

Lastly, a big thank you to all my storytellers in this book You came, and you conquered. The beginning of this journey was quite rocky. We had no idea where this journey would lead us. We just knew we had to share our stories with whoever would dare to listen. Little did we know that as we genuinely tore the veil, the gloves were coming off, the masks are falling off our faces, we were peeling shame off as we were solidly behind one another, cheering each other when one person's story triggers the other.

"These women are writing from a place of strength as they decide to tell their truth and set themselves free once and for all."
~ Dr. Princess Fumi Hancock, DNP.

CONTENTS

FOREWORD

When someone is inspired to gather a group of women to write about their lives, child kidnapping/abuse, female genitalia cutting, sexual violation, domestic violence, unjust sexual accusation, failed relationships… all leading to mental illness or mostly on how to overcome life's obstacles; it is not meant to be an attempt for scholars' glorification but, a platform to contribute to solving social problems as being experienced throughout the world today.

This was with a view of providing a genuine opportunity for future generations to learn from how such women overcome their challenges in life.

My choice of being nominated for writing the foreword to this well-researched work may certainly surprise many people particularly being from Nigeria, Africa.

I was fortunate to know the Author- **PRINCESS FUMI OGUNLEYE HANCOCK,** shortly after my husband ascended the throne of his forefathers as the King and Paramount Ruler of Emure Kingdom … some years back as my sister-in-law and President of **ADASSA ADUMORI PROJECT** (The Princess of Suburbia® Foundation, Inc.) based in the United States of America – a non-profit Organization, bringing quality education to the less privileged in Nigeria. Since then, she has accepted me as her sister-in-law, friend, Confidant, Close Associate and a Queen in her Royal family **(ADUMORI ROYAL FAMILY OF EMURE – EKITI)**

I have also seen her as a Philanthropist, (Adassa Adumori Scholarship/yearly Bursary Award), a Mother, Mentor, Competent, Reliable and Trustworthy Princess and an Achiever of our time.

Logically, she is humble, respectful and entirely committed to hard work.

The whole essence of the book provides quality reading materials about today's life challenges, loaded experience, useful and helpful Companion for those in distress who desire to learn a lesson in delivering life solutions for people committed to making a living for themselves, despite all odds.

Having gone through the book, I am impressed by the simplicity in the presentation and language. I believe that it will make a good consolation and companion to many who are significantly in distress and ready to drink from the experience of the author (& co-authors) with an idea to be strong even at the peak of human distress and challenges but, with an ultimatum to become a total person in life.

Without necessarily taking the chapters of the book one after another, **PRINCESS FUMI OGUNLEYE-HANCOCK,** our African Princess living in Diaspora has presented this Book of Missions™ to outline the challenges facing many homes and families regardless of culture, tradition, creed.

This is a must-read for families and certainly one I hope the media will rally around for massive impact, therefore, recommend it as a companion in homes and for families.

Queen Iyabowale Mariam Adebayo

Olori Iyabowale Mariam Adebayo
Queen of Elemure of Emure – Ekiti
Ekiti State, Nigeria, Africa.

INTRODUCTION

THE ROLE AND IMPORTANCE
OF AFRICAN QUEEN

Oxford Advanced Learner's Dictionary defines a "Queen as the female ruler of an independent state that has a royal family".

The African concept of a queen (consort) refers to this as the wife of a king who resides in the Palace with her husband (king) throughout his life/reign. At the demise of her husband, she equally retains that title till death.

Paradoxically, in the Nigerian setting particularly Yoruba race, all the wives of Male children in the royal family are equally addressed as queen but, with limited role or function in the Palace except, if the incumbent queen co-opts them into her Cabinet for the smooth running of her administration

THE ROLE AND IMPORTANCE OF AFRICAN QUEEN:- African queen (Nigerian) for example, has a very significant role to play in the day to day administration of the empire, state or community or kingdom. Thus, her importance or role complements that of the king (husband). Her role or importance can also influence the decision of her husband on certain state or kingdom issue:- Just like the Biblical King Herod judgment on the condemnation of Jesus Christ when He was brought before Herod but, his wife (Queen) advised him not to be involved in the trial. This is equally peculiar in Nigerian (African) societies today. Suffice to say that her role is unique and can be described as the pillar, budget planner, game planner, game player and game changer in the Palace. Among her other roles/importance are- Head of king's kitchen Cabinet:- The queen is the head of a king's kitchen cabinet. She prepares and serves the food of the king. She keeps and supervises the wardrobe of her husband, selects a particular attire to match the function or occasion. Such dress and above it all, accompany her husband to such ceremony as tradition/culture demands.

Since Palace is her permanent house, she receives all visitors and entertains them on behalf of her husband. She addresses issues brought before the king if such does not necessarily demand the attention/presence of the king.

Head of Female Administration: - By African Culture and Tradition the queen is in charge of all female activities in her husband's domain. She influences the selections and appointments of female Chiefs and heads of various women organizations especially, the ones that relate with Culture and Tradition.

She holds regular meetings with the various segments of the female organization including wives of the traditional Chiefs.

Issues relating to domestic abuse, child abuse, failed relationships, how to manage family affairs and societies challenges are also part of the programs she puts in place for the success of the husband's administration.

African queen is seen and viewed as a symbol of peace and unity hence, she organizes and leads prayer meetings to seek God's favor for her Community, Local government, State and the Nation at large.

Equally of her importance is the keeping of the culture/tradition and teaching the young ones especially the females.

Apart from the queen in the Palace setting, notable African queens like **Queen Amina** in the Northern Nigeria, Aba women Riot of 1929 in the East and **Moremi** in Southwest are recorded in history for championing the liberations of their respective communities during the wars.

By and large, an African queen is the wife of a king in a particular kingdom, state or empire. Her role and/or importance is enormous, and these could not be easily pushed aside hence, she is the pillar of her husband's administration as enumerated above.

Since these stories are shared by our powerful women who have survived incredible life challenges, it is only befitting that the

Queen would choose this book to be her very first endorsement.

King Emmanuel Adebayo

His Royal Majesty,
King Emmanuel Adebayo
Elemure of Emure Kingdom
Emure Ekiti Kingdom, Ekiti, Nigeria
THE ROYAL HOUSEHOLD: ADUMORI NIGERIAN ROYAL FAMILY

A *LOVE LETTER* TO THE WORLD FROM YOUR GLOBAL VISION MIDWIFE™ & LIFEREHAB™ AMBASSADOR

by
Dr. Fumi Stephanie Hancock, DNP.

We are not a feminist movement neither are we a "religious move" but strictly an empowering vehicle… a book of missions™ under one umbrella. With one focus in mind… to inspire, motivate, and empower other women and children… We share our difficult and triumphant moments to save our future generation, both male and female regardless of creed, culture, traditions, religion."
~ Dr. Fumi Hancock

Allow me to clear the air as I usually would in my books, to those who are wondering why now? Why would these ladies choose to release their burdens? Why are they choosing this moment to tear the veil? Why of all times have they decided to bare it all, risking societal shame and uproar? Why are they wanting to risk their family ostracizing them and guilting them into another wave of silence? You ask again, why have these women chosen to unlock their silence to finally share their stories? Let me help you out! This journey is not about you.

This is a journey that every woman in this book of Missions™ has taken years to think about. It is a journey which is releasing and freeing them from time-bombs they have on for years... secrets which have affected every area(s) of their lives: Home, Business, Careers, and relationships. These incredibly brave women have finally understood the dangers of keeping silent. They are ready to break the curses off their boys and girls. They know it is time to empower our mothers who are still in hiding to use the tool they have, their voices, to share their stories. They understand that they no longer must suffer in silence and alone but that they can reach out to their sisterhood to help them through moments of PTSD, anxiety, depression, suicide ideation, and whatever imprint or residue their past experiences may have left behind. In fact, as we write many are still in therapy dealing with their thoughts /emotions and the effects of atrocities committed against them.

Sharing their stories have empowered them enough that they too are ready to enable others. These stories are not just another set of stories told ahead of us. These stories are triggers to success. While you our readers may not identify with all the stories, e guarantee that at least one will cause you to get up and be counted! If you are one of those that's never stood for anything, these stories will first prompt you to shutter, then encourage you to help be part of a global solution.

We are not just a group of women ranting and raving about sexual abuse... our stories are diverse. We bring solutions alongside our stories, inspiration for our men to reconsider specific thought patterns; equipping our mothers and daughters with tools to release themselves from toxic secrets... #PowerofUS using our viable tools to save our families.

I invite you to come along with us if you so, please. We move in unity... knowing that this is our moment to #releasethetoxins. Just as these stories have given us the wings to soar like eagles, we challenge you to push past fear... it is time to blossom where we are planted, and we will not be carrying life baggage on our backs.

This is the #PowerofUS, putting that the heavy back bags we have been carrying on behalf of ourselves, generations who died with their secrets and generations to come who have no idea why they may be feeling tortured by events they know nothing about.

WHAT THEN IS FEARLESS VISIONARIES TEAR THE VEIL™

Fearless Visionaries: Tear the Veil is an evidence-based work highlighting real-life role models and leaders that have overcome sexual abuse, mental illness, human trafficking, and gender inequality to live normal lives as mothers, doctors, lawyers, engineers, filmmakers, international business owners, and educators.

The path to rescue, recovery, and hope starts with Fearless Visionaries: Tear the Veil as the voice for gender equality and empowerment of women and girls is heard loudly throughout all 19 stories. The journey continues once these women enter the Fearless Visionaries Community and an ongoing support is delivered through the Fearless Visionaries Global Taskforce.

As each woman reads this book of Missions™ and joins the Fearless Visionaries mission, they will:

Understand the necessity of breaking the silence of secrecy around sexual abuse, mental illness, human trafficking, and gender inequality and instead challenge the culture to create real solutions and interventions based on that community's needs

Experience healing from the trauma of their past and move into areas of more confidence and courage to stand up for their human rights and fair treatment.

Help to remove the stigma of female genital cutting and sexual assault to encourage communities to increase safety for women and girls.

Turn their recovery from emotional, physical, and mental trauma into a roadmap that helps other women and girls find hope and help and come out of their challenges.

These are the 4 pillars which trend in our stories and what is currently causing people who encounter our stories to be steered into action, no matter how stoic they may have been in the past. These pillars and the vehicles we have chosen to help others…evidence-based practice storytelling is what set us apart from others. Our goal is not just to unleash our horrific stories on you but to give you tools and point you in the direction of available resources to help with whatever is being triggered. WE DARE TO SAY TO YOU… YOU ARE NOT ALONE.

How do we seek to empower YOU … our reader?

WHEN A MOTHER IS TRAINED, A DAUGHTER HAS A GREATER CHANCE OF ACHIEVING SUCCESS.

Our stories will bring healing and recovery. It will empower the faint at heart to push beyond the pain. When mothers are steered, children are positively affected. When children are positively affected,

23

our nations become healthy and when nations are healthy, the global communities rip the benefits. This is a ripple effect of what our stories are about…. Being steered to find sustainable results to all that is ailing our society at large. Either a young girl is raped in Nigeria or America, rape is the same! Whether a young baby was stolen in America or India, the ripple effect on that child when he or she grows up is the same; whether a mother dies from cancer in Kenya or in Camden New Jersey, the effect the death will have on a young family is same… loss and grief look the same way. A woman is beaten to the point of almost dying in East Africa or here in North Carolina… domestic violence has its face … the pain, the feeling of betrayal is the same across board. A woman who is contemplating suicide several times because of hopelessness in Ghana or in Wyoming USA… suicide is an evil force which is running rampage through our global communities. Many are taking that route because they feel they have no other recourse.

Fearless Visionaries Tear the Veil ™ is not just a conversation starter, it is also a foundational or rudimentary pathway to finding solutions acceptable to the global communities.

Why? We represent the fabric of our global communities: From Saudi Arabia, Dubai, UAE, Algeria, South Africa, Nigeria, London United Kingdom, and USA.

Fearless Visionaries™ is a social cab™ bringing resiliency, healing and recovery to our global audience in the areas of education, health and wealth. We unanimously concur that a healthy mind is a wealthy being.

"We are fearless visionaries on a mission of hope for humanity to every girl and boy, woman and man. Nineteen women have embraced their pain to tell their story and together we are healing. It has been an amazing journey as a student under the leadership of the Dr of Nursing Practice with a specialization in Psychiatric Mental Health, Master Storyteller, Indie Film & Hollywood African Oscar Award Winner, Princess Fumi Hancock. Today, our stories became Amazon bestseller. Thank you to all who have joined our mission to speak POWER to our truth around the globe."
- Dr. Eveangel H. Savage

Let healing begin ….

THE PRINCESS OF SUBURBIA © COPYRIGHT 2016

CHAPTER 1

ONE EVENT CAN CHANGE YOUR LIFE FOREVER!
by
Dr. Fumi Stephanie Hancock, DNP.

I sit in my white Ford car on Verrazano Bridge, New York, everything I have to my name... all gone! My money is gone, the house my father paid off and gave me collateral for business...gone and husband I thought loved me...gone! Here I am, a very young twenty-something-year-old mother in a strange country with boys who are 3 ½ and 2 years old. The shame and disgrace I just encountered in the "loving arms" of the one who promises to love me for the rest of our lives are beyond what my little mind can fathom.

People are famous for a lot, but here I am on this quaint island, famous for being thrown out of her own business in broad daylight! Here I am standing as the greatest fool because I chose to trust despite what every part in me was telling me.

I hear echoes of the judge deep tone as I rev the car pushing harder, closer to the edge of the bridge. Mrs. T, judges are not the devil. There is a thin line between Christianity and Stupidity. I am afraid you crossed it! You crossed the line when you chose not to come to court early enough before you lose everything. You crossed the line when you were thinking only about yourself and not about the children you have in your hands. Now, you stand before me, and everything you could have used to take care of yourself and your children is gone!"

With tears rolling down my eyes and my breathing profusely labored, I look ahead at shimmering waters below the bridge. I know if I hit the accelerator hard enough, my car will push against the railings and plunge feet's down the bridge. Echoes of me questioning myself merges with that of other voices in my head. A family friend who is also a business partner visits and tells me do not expect him back home. He is never coming back! My bottom drops! With all, he had done... the emotional abuse and the physical one day where I roll down the stairs, why would I still yearn for him? Why do I still desire someone who has not been kind to me? Why am I craving the one who brings a secretary or assistant into our marital bed? Why am I rooting to have someone who has taken a lot from my family and I yet denying nothing like that ever happened? His disapproving voice, "You are nothing! You will never amount to anything! You are a wealth depleter! Don't mind her mummy, all of them want to reap where they did not sow!" Here I am holding down two jobs while he is back in college! Why is my soul yearning for more pain by wanting him? Here I am, dragging y family name down the mud because I choose a man with motives beyond loving me. Why am I willing to take him back after sleeping with someone else and didn't apologize for it? What was in me that decides to accept all the abuse?

How can I go back home to my royal family in Africa to tell them I was a failure? How can I face them with the emptiness I feel on the inside? What will I tell them? How will I reconcile the fact that few of them had predicted that the marriage would not last and they are right? His friend who had visited and had wondered why I was taking the abuse, how could I say they are right? I rev up the accelerator again as the noises in my head increases. As soon as I removed my feet from the clutch, suddenly appear in front of me is a film reel! I see my two boys crying in the arms of another woman! I see them hungry and not taking proper care of. Another voice yet again interrupted my experience... is this the legacy you want for our children? The legacy of suicide! Do you want your children always to think they were not enough for you to live for? Do you want them to blame themselves for the rest of their lives, that they were responsible for your death? Would you believe that this pain you are feeling, you can turn into victory lap? While I was to convince of the latter statements, I knew right there I had to live for my two boys. These boys had not asked to be born into chaos. Why will I choose suicide over them?

I reverse off the edge and drive right back home. Funny, all the while on the bridge, not one car surfaced. It is now 12 midnight, and I decided that I didn't have to lie for myself but for my children.

My name is Dr. Princess Fumi Stephanie Hancock. I am an African princess living in Diaspora. I am also a Psychiatric Mental Health Doctor of Nurse Practice, a 21 years bestselling writing veteran, celebrated international speaker and award-winning filmmaker and this is my story.

While I do understand that certain persons may feel slighted about sharing my story, this is my truth. This is but a teaspoon of what I encountered in the "loving arms" of my beloved. I return home that night determined to live to tell the story.

I remember walking into the cold 3-bedroom house so afraid of what the future holds. I was afraid of what tricks I would be dealt with.

Determining to live did not preclude me from all that happened after that! It was indeed a raise that if truthfully did not allow GOD to guide me, I wouldn't have survived it.

With all the noises in town about my then husband and I, I knew I needed a fresh start, but I had no money and no one to discuss this with. After much deliberation and having been warned by my banker that he had called them and insisted they foreclosed on me… after another banker calls yet again, thinking I was Mrs. T who came with her husband and delivered a $9,000 down payment on a house in another part of the state. The same money I had seen move from my business account, and we had argued over! It was time to put a distance between the shame and figure out how to live my life without him. For three years, my children and I slept on the cold floor of an apartment in New Jersey while he paraded himself in a sports car whenever he picked them up for visitation. I will never forget one day when he sets up a meeting at a McDonald's shop. Even with all I had been through, I still wanted the marriage to work. Somehow, I concluded that if I prayed hard enough, he will change his mind and come home. What I left out of the equation was his will power and him continually telling me that I can pay all I want he is no longer interested. While I was busy praying for the marriage to be restored, he was busy doing his own thing… dating and trying to figure out ways to take the children from me! When he tells me to walk down the road to the restaurant to meet him and didn't care to pick me up was a clue I missed! When he decides to meet me at the neighborhood franchise restaurant instead of one worthy of someone will love was yet another clue I missed. I remember sitting in front of him, tired from going out to find a job and when he opens his mouth, it was more than a threat! He brings his contract out and insisted I signed it so he can have full custody of the children since I was now "jobless."

I excuse myself, quickly find my way to the bathroom and wept! I wept at the marriage I thought would last a lifetime! I left at seeing what length my beloved would go to prove to his family that he was right, and I was wrong! I came out of the bathroom and garnered the courage to say a resounding "NO!" My children were my lifeline! Without them, I would not be a life to face another day! Why will I the hand them over just like that! I walk into the cold, watching him drive his sports car right past me. There and then, I knew what I had gone through was just a tip of the iceberg. I knew I was in store for the most significant fight for my life… to hold on to my boys!

In all of my experiences, what was most painful is my mother-in-law serving me with the final divorce papers! I remember going to pick up my boys, I was invited in as if everything was okay. I was at ease because I thought since she was there, she would make things right. You see, I knew what my parents tried to do! I knew how much sacrifice they made for my marriage. After all, against all the odds my father was the same one who took most of what he had at a tie placed it in a brown bag, handed it over to me and asked me to give my then fiancé so he could travel! Just imagine you being invited into the house, you going downstairs where your children are playing, you praying with them, you hearing someone call you wicked, screaming at you and accusing you of coming down to pray over your children, imagine her then turning around smiling and saying "your husband told me to give you this envelope." Now, imagine you opening an envelope which you were made to believe was a letter for something else and you find out that you were just served divorce papers by someone you thought if anyone could influence your beloved to fight for his marriage, was the same one who helps you! Now, imagine you in the courthouse and looking right back at you is the affidavit she signs stating she served me, and I knew I was being served…. Just imagine!

While I have chosen to share this piece of my life, it's been over 25 years! My truth is in no way written to shame anyone but to release myself of toxic thoughts and experiences. The fact is we were young and had no clue what marriage is Those who were supposed to help us be responsible about it chose to turn deaf ears. Many decided to pick sides instead of picking our marriage. I was made out to be evil and a money squanderer. Those I thought was even called to see if I was alright, chose to be silent. I was raised to understand that once I was married, we were all ONE. My family showed me in man ways when I would see my mother purchase things and deliver to my mother-in-law in my name. During this war, because it was a war. I finally understood that e had two families and not one. It was painful because those I loved deeply, let me down.

As I write this chapter, I do the final release of the residual of pain in my life. So, I ask that if by some reason, they read this book… don't allow hatred to rule but let truth prevail. This is my truth, and it is all about my final push to healing. God has restored and allowed me to recover by giving me the greatest love of all… LOVE! Hat special kind of love which will lay his life down for me if need be… the one which is not anchored on money because he ha given it all…Now I know what real love looks like and can share with generations coming behind me what it looks like, feels like, smells like, acts like. I can genuinely say, I may not be a billionaire yet, I will never trade the love I have now for anything in the world. First, God's endless love that He chose to save me on that fateful night on the Verrazano bridge; the love of my wonderful husband, Dr. David A. Hancock who has spent over 15 years teaching me how to trust and love again; and my boys….whew… who have grown into incredibly young men, there unfailing love toward me, continually reminding e of how proud they are of me; my family… the Ogunleye's' (siblings and their spouses, my parents, and the Adumori Royal House and Alale families) who cheer me on with everything I do.

As I introduce these wonderful women who have triumphed over extraordinary circumstances, I ask that you be open. Rather than be angry, be in gratitude as these women are living... letting go of their past regardless of the pain it caused them.

Together, we are fearless women inviting other fearless women and men who are ready to encourage and support us. We are powerful, resilient, determined, committed and we raise a resounding #TeartheVeil! We are encouraging and empowering other women (and men alike) to tear their veil! We can no longer continue to perpetuate the culture of secrecy; where generational curses are being passed down the bloodline because we chose to be silent. Truth is that this is not about anyone who may feel insulted or exposed. These are our stories and others may have been characters in our plays of life. It is not our intention to belittle anyone. We are merely choosing to love and free US.....

CHAPTER 2

♥

DREAM BIG: FROM CAMDEN, NEW JERSEY TO CAMBRIDGE UNIVERSITY – CAMBRIDGE, ENGLAND
by
Dr. Debby Olusa

As I walk through the door, I instantly feel my stomach lock up in excruciating pain… a pain so muscular most would faint! As I look to the left and the right, the six stain glass windows on each side of the room filled with scenes of hope, faith, and comfort now fail to support me. The enormous stain glass windows that ordinarily serve as a soothing distraction would not open this evening… not on this night. I look for my little sister and grab her hand. I look around then lower my head and quickly say, "Dear GOD, please help ME!!!! Hear my cry." That's what my Mommy said would always help. Then I say to myself… whatever you do, don't collapse. As I look up again, the room that usually felt so large is now super crowded… not an empty seat in a place that holds around 300 people. The aisles are filled with people standing, and I feel as though they are closing in on me with their intense stares, tears, and uncontrollable sobbing. At this moment, I feel like a small doll soaked in lighter fluid walking through an inferno. My Daddy is walking in front of me, and I am forever grateful for his looming statue, as it is delaying what lies ahead.

I am still standing. I am walking slow, and measured steps. I am not looking left or right at the people sitting or standing in the two remaining aisles. As we walk by their sobbing increases, transitioning to wailing. There is a wave of gut-wrenching, twisting pain following our progression. First, in the back of the room as we enter, then with each row of seats the sobbing and wails become more piercing. I grip my sisters' hand tighter as people begin to touch us as we are walking by. They are saying things like "I Love YOU... I'm SORRY" then sobbing and wailing. My sister, who naturally cries, begins to fall. I steady her arm to keep her erect, looking down at her, touching her chin to look deep into her bloodshot, terrified eyes. I wipe her tears, nod my head, and she nods back to me. I squeeze her hand, and she returns my squeeze. We turn and continue our walk. We walk, looking straight ahead...

I am pushing through the WORST... more people are touching us saying, "Look at THEM', "They are So YOUNG," "Oh My God," "I don't know how they are doing THIS." The pain in my stomach NOW feels like my intestines are being butchered as we walk. More people are talking to my sister and I as we walk by ... the WORST is the never-ending people touching our arms, kissing our cheeks and foreheads or pinching our cheeks... THE WORST!! The touch of each person makes me feel like an object, not a person taking the LONGEST walk of my life... it feels degrading, not supportive. In no way are my sister and I the recipients for pity or charity... we are just children. My Daddy, just ahead, is the only comfort I have. His strong 6'6" presence is my source of much-needed strength, along with the sound of familiar gospel hymns.

Suddenly, my Daddy is not in front of us anymore and there we stand... in a room that usually feels hot, but now feels cold as the Arctic and my STOMACH is so TIGHT. I am not feeling my legs, but I am still holding my sisters' hand, and yet I can't feel her hand. I am now forced to look at what's in front of me... my Mommy is laying in a beautiful cream and gold coffin, wearing a white dress and white satin slippers. She just looks like she is sleeping. It is impossible for me to get too close to the coffin so COLD. The cold is coming from the coffin.

For a minute, I think she will wake up, then I say to myself, she is dead, and she is NEVER coming back. Tears are streaming from my eyes, yet I am telling myself not to cry. My sister falls to the floor, and I almost fall on top of her. I am kneeling on the floor over her body, I rub her back and whisper in her ear, we must go... we can't stay here with Mommy... she's gone, but she still Loves us.

"She's my Mommy." "Yes, and she will always belong only to Us. Let's go… come on." We begin to rise off the floor, and a funeral attendant attempts to assist us. I wave him away with my right hand, taking my sister's hand as we stand in front of the casket. I squeeze her hand as she squeezes my hand and we turn to the right and walk away from the coffin to our seats near Daddy. My Daddy is sitting looking straight ahead with glazed eyes and tears streaming down his cheeks like a waterfall.

People begin to walk by us and share their condolences with the family. My Daddy stands and greets the friends and family. I stand too… and now my excruciating pain in my stomach is beyond description… I am sweating. I am drenched in sweat, still holding my sisters' hand. A mix of perfumes possibly jasmine, citrus oils, vanilla, and rose… along with tarragon, offering a sassy, sharp yet sexy scent from the women that hug and kiss our faces. The mix of colognes from the men are possibly iris, lavender, bergamot, cedar, and leather, offering a lingering brash, masculine scent. The combination of the female and male fragrances, the constant hugs, tears, sobbing, and wails are leaving me….

~~~ *** ~~~

I'm 9 years old, sitting on the floor, playing with dolls and looking up at my Mommy admiring her beauty while enjoying the smell of fried chicken, greens, rice & gravy swirling from my grandmother's kitchen. My sincere hope is that my grandmother will surprise me with homemade yeast rolls topped with warm butter and a hint of sugar. My Mommy, looking in the mirror, was dressing to attend a gala with Daddy and she says to my grandmother, "Mommy, I have this lump in my right breast." My grandmother replies, "Don't worry about that… .You look beautiful!" "Go to the gala and enjoy your husband… we will talk about that later… This is the end of my childhood!

~~~ *** ~~~

My mother is diagnosed with breast cancer and is undergoing treatment. As a 9-year-old, I learn how to clean and season meats and vegetables. I am frying chicken and Mommy is making it all look like an exciting game. Mommy always says with her soft, soothing and encouraging voice, "Let's play the Chef Game?" "What does that mean, Mommy?" The Chef Game is learning to wash, clean and season meats and vegetables. Cooking is completely fascinating to me… the different textures of vegetables and meats and especially the cutting up of an entire chicken. I LOVE, LOVE the excuse to splash water during each Chef Game and love even more my mother's smile and help cleaning up the water on the floor and countertop. The smell of each newly introduced seasoning is a magical experience because I am a curious child… the smell and feel of black or ground pepper makes me sneeze, but I made a game out of that, and my goal is not to sneeze or hold my breath. Somehow, mastering the technique of holding my breath has not been successful, but I remain hopeful. LOL! The Chef Game is quickly progressing to learning to cook rice, potatoes and various types of pasta. I had so much fun during our "Chef Game" because, I was doing "BIG GIRL" stuff. Each time a new Chef Game is introduced, my Mommy starts with an electric smile, and a wink and says, "You ready little girl"? Mommy has this wonderful way of making everything fun, from learning how to cook, clean, and wash clothes, to learning how to talk to bill collectors on the phone.

The lump in her breast is noticeable through her clothing, and I am becoming concerned. I quickly console myself with the thinking "Mothers don't die and leave their children. That just doesn't happen to kids." As a 10-year old, this line of thinking is what helps me rationalize the decline I see in my Mothers health… She is undergoing radiation treatments, and I am assisting her in and out the tub. I am nearly 5'2' at 10 years old, and I am developing techniques where I use my body to support my Mother. I fold both arms tightly and position my 10-year old body next to the right side of the bed, she uses my arms to pull herself up, sit on the side of the bed, then stand. I stand to her right in case she stumbles or starts to fall as she turns to the right to begin walking, I use my body to break the stumble or fall by leaning in to keep her upright or quickly catch her body with my left side then turn in toward her chest to stabilize her, preventing a fall. I study my Mommy constantly to provide support and comfort. All my techniques are developed without discussion with an adult, especially my Mommy… I don't want her to feel any worse. Always thinking ahead and developing creative and effective techniques to support my Mommy… that is my razor focus… and the other is my sister. In my 10-year old mind, she is my Mommy, and it is my responsibility to provide care while my Daddy is at work. Mommy is a very private person, I never wonder why no family members or friends come to assist with her care... I see the problem and create solutions. When family members or friends call on the phone and ask how everything is going, I always say fine. I never discuss my reality with family, friends, teachers, or my Daddy... nobody. She is my Mommy... my Mommy. I go to school each day and earn excellent grades. I come home and cook dinner, give my sister her bath and do her hair for the next day. I clean the kitchen and complete my Homework. I never ask questions or think to do anything differently. This is my reality... the life I have come to know... the Mommy I love sooooo...

Mommy's upper body is covered in black, red, yellow and green lines and numbers. Her body looks like a ruler. As I am washing Mommy's back, I hauntingly notice the colorful magic marker entries across her back, and the front of her body is not disappearing. I mumbled aloud, "Why won't the magic marker go away." Mommy says, "The different colors, the numbers, and the markings will disappear over time. They are created to guide the doctors as they provide my radiation treatments." This is very disturbing. For the first time, since she was diagnosed with cancer, my tears are falling as I wash her back. For the first time, I am feeling angry. This just isn't fair, a body that looks like a color charted ruler, shortness of breath, stumbling and/or falling. Still, sharing my home-life experiences with others was not an option...it was our family secret until Mommy demonstrates otherwise... not because I am sworn to secrecy, I am following Mommy's lead and perfectly accepting her decision.

During a breast X-ray, the technician drops the X-ray machine on Mommy's breast... the breast filled with cancer. A woman that is fighting to stay alive on an average day is now experiencing even more pain due to his gross negligence and, not to mention, the technician begins screaming at Mommy after causing the injury. For what seems like three weeks or more, Mommy is discussing the additional soreness and associated pain. The black and blue bruising marks are a constant confirmation of her further pain.

I am feeling rage... I think again "This is just NOT fair!! This injury is taking a lot out of my mother, the force of the X-Ray machine hitting her breast sounds extreme. "Do you feel the technician dropped the X-Ray machine on purpose?" "It sure feels like it." My once blossoming, smiling, regal queen is fading before my eyes, but consciously I don't acknowledge the deterioration. I continue my rigorous chores and homework regime. On a rare occasion, my reality begins seeping in, and I comfort myself with my belief "Mothers don't die and leave their kids!" This thinking always jolts me back from my brief and torturing plunge.

I am bringing home my Honor Roll certificates, Certificates of Achievement in Leadership and family and friends always remark "Debby is such a Big HELP"! My Mommy always smiles and winks as she gives me my signature compliment "Debby is smart and a star." "Oh Yeah!", "My star is going somewhere!" I am working super hard at school because I know how much my school achievements mean to Mommy. On her worst days, my grades, certificates, letters of acknowledgment or even a phone call requesting permission for me to lead another school club always cause a cherished twinkle in her eye.

My mother is 6'2" tall, gentle and exceptionally kind almost to a fault. She created a prison ministry and provided services each Friday. In two years, this effort is expanding to a maximum security state prison. In her quest to provide some normalcy for the prisoners, she is providing a Thanksgiving dinner donated by community members, local and regional churches, restaurants, policeman, fireman, politicians and beyond. Mommy is an innovative thinker totally before her time. She is creating a Prison Ministry, before it is popular, in a city, state or national scale in the 1970s. Before and during her illness, Mommy is holding meetings to solicit financial and other donations needed to make this event successful. Additionally, she is visiting restaurants and political events to secure the necessary funding and resources. Mommy is always carrying me to her frequent restaurant visits and political events. I look up and smile as my Mommy begins her chat soliciting funding, volunteers, etc. "It's a wonderful day or evening, and the world is a better place because of people like you and/or your organization." The person is always listening smiles and, in no time, they are writing out a check, giving cash and/or volunteering services.

~~~ *** ~~~

Our first visit to the …. my legs are hanging from the chair, and my sister and I are sitting side by side. Our heads are swaying from side to side as we are looking at the room full of approximately 100 men wearing beige jumpsuits with white undershirts underneath and black boots. I immediately note the men are wearing jumpsuits that are expertly ironed and their white tee shirts are exceptionally white. I wonder to myself, "Why are all of these men dressing alike," Why are we somewhere that has many men dressing alike? Why are most of these men so BIG and others just as small yet all are wearing the same clothes? Some men seem happy and are talking and smiling while others are quiet and appear to be worrying. A lot of the men stare off in space… no sign of happiness. Where are we, I wonder? We are wearing Sunday church clothes, but we are definitely not at church. I finally stop looking at my surroundings and notice there is a table with sodas. The sodas appear to be free and available. Both my parents are in the front of the room. I have my sisters hand, and we are walking to the table. About eight men are standing behind the table draped in a white tablecloth. As I am approaching the table, two men hide behind the others and I thought, this is odd. After studying the table filled with approximately 20 different sodas, I begin asking for two grape sodas, and the man stood there looking at me with a blank stare. He is not moving. "Can I have two grape sodas?" He is not moving to give us a grape soda …just a blank stare with a hint of nervousness as he is touching his chin. I am snapping LOUDLY at the man while holding my, sisters hand and asking for two grape sodas. Another man is stepping in front of the man that didn't give us a soda, "He can't read and handed me two grape sodas." I then say "I am sorry for being demanding and short." As a child, I have no idea that not being able to read as an adult is even possible…

The man I previously asked for the sodas is visibly shaking now, and another man is moving him to the side as he trembles. The remaining men are watching with a look of sorrow, mixed with regret, that my sister and I are having this experience. Until this moment, I thought all adults can read and read well. In my nine-year-old mind, all adults are super smart. I find this experience confusing, as it defies all the things I assume about adults, parents, school, and teachers. I think to myself, we will not be sharing this encounter with our parents. Later, I was asking our parents "Where did we just visit?" They said, "We were visiting the State Prison that we visit each week and it was a social ministry event."

~~~ *** ~~~

While stumbling around the small, crowded apartment, filled with boxes of fresh vegetables, fruits, desserts, cases of sodas, water and juice in every room, I am thinking maybe… just maybe… Mommy may have too much-donated food. In the hallway, the boxes are stacked much taller than me on each side. As I was falling asleep, the doorbell never stops ringing with food and cash donations well into the evening. My Dad and mother took turns cooking vegetables on our small stove at home. The next day, two churches in our community will be donating the use of their large kitchens. The salads, turkey, stuffing, chicken, roast beef, ribs and spaghetti will be cooking along with the remaining vegetables. Teams of people are lining the tables in each kitchen preparing the food in an assembly line formation with one cook stationed at each stove. I find the food preparation process intriguing to watch, and I enjoy comparing and contrasting my observations at each church. Because I am a 10-year old child, no one is paying attention to my walking around each kitchen nor my full review of their effort. It is moments like this that engulf my attention and serve as a break from the gut-wrenching horror that awaits me when we return home.

~~~ *** ~~~

My Mommy is slipping away much faster than the public realizes. By all appearances, she looks like the picture of health. Her hair is thick, long and growing. Her skin color is radiant, and her weight remains the same. She always maintains that dazzling smile while in public and shows no signs of being in discomfort. Regularly, while attending church, my sister and I hear church members, neighbors, and community members whispering, "Isn't their mother supposed to have cancer?", "Are you sure their mother has breast cancer," "She looks beautiful or is that their mother the really tall lady with breast cancer?", "Isn't she supposed to be dying from cancer?" Over and over again, I want to turn, jump into each person's face and SCREAM "MY MOMMY IS DYING ARE YOU HAPPY!!!!!" I can never understand how so MANY people can make such heartless comments… as though my sister and I are deaf or invisible. The only reason I never respond is that my sister will have yet another crying and collapsing episode. Each time, I take my sister's hand and walk away before she can hear the comments and collapse crying.

The doctors explain to my Daddy that my mother is suffering from a type of cancer that manifests strangely in that she will never appear ill. Her skin color, hair, weight or otherwise will not reflect typical signs of cancer disease. The doctor emphasizes that we should NOT look at Mommy's appearance as her true condition… she is a very sick woman and slowly dying!

Mommy climbs five steps and then sits down… climbs three more and sits down for 15 minutes and continues this pattern until she climbs all 12 steps before entering our apartment. Daddy is sitting on the steps with Mommy and holding her arm. A month later, Daddy supports her body as she is climbing the steps to enter the apartment. I am always standing at the bottom of the steps and feeling a deep sense of helplessness that I cannot do more to help my Mommy. As I am looking up the narrow stairwell with worn fading wallpaper and a peeling wooden rail, the memory of each comment people has made makes me more FURIOUS! … they play vividly in my tormented mind. I am constantly amazed by how my Mommy maintains her public appearance so well. Time and time again, I watch my statuesque Mommy in sheer awe, pride, love and admiration as she engages the public… in church, the community or neighbors. She walks by, and heads turn with lingering gazes, her stride is strong while walking, her words are always soft and encouraging. Her impact on others is both mesmerizing and intoxicating… my Mommy… defying public perception at every turn…

~~~ *** ~~~

My entire family is attending the Thanksgiving Prison Dinner, along with 200 inmates and 100 other attendees, all who have been invited by my parents. Again, I am sitting on a chair holding my sister's hand and studying the people in attendance. The event is held in a large super clean room with long tables draped with white table clothes. Donors are delivering the food in U-Haul trucks, restaurant vans, the attendee's cars and more. Prisoners are lining up behind tables placed around the perimeter of this large room and serving the food.

I am navigating the large crowd, fixing my sister's plate as well as my own, returning to the table and we are eating our meal. The room is filling with laughter, chatter and a spirit of joy are visible from almost all attendees, including the prisoners. Approximately 35 prisoners are serving the food and then cleaning during the event. It is fascinating… the organized fashion by which the prisoners perform their assigned duties. All empty dishes on the buffet line are immediately filled with replacements, all trash cans are promptly emptied, and a replacement trash bag is neatly inserted. All desert and beverage stations are superbly maintained as well. The remaining prisoners are mingling with the guests attending the event. At no time are any prisoners shackled or handcuffed. I am cleaning the table of our empty plates and cups, taking my sister's hand, emptying our trash, navigating this now really crowded room with five Prison Guards sparingly stationed around the perimeter of the room with approximately 300 attendees. I eagerly return to our seats and continue swinging my legs as they dangle above the floor. During this visit, there are so many prisoners, invited guests and politicians that I feel swallowed up like a pebble in a tsunami. Too much movement, too many people… I am tired of smiling and greeting people. Mommy taught me well. As each person greets my sister and I, I am on my feet, stretching out my hand to shake their hand with a bright smile and firm eye contact. Almost at the same time, I say a quick comment to cause a smile and leave a positive lasting impression before the fast interaction ends. As always, I shield my sister from most of the engagement…this is all just too MUCHHHHHH, yet I have a tremendous feeling of safety. While I am swinging my legs and observing my surroundings, I am thinking they will NEVER run out of food," and I am right! There is food left over after the event.

~~~ *** ~~~

"If I had parents that tall, I would never do anything wrong" is a comment I frequently hear in every setting. Not that I am an unruly kid… people are often initially surprised by the height and statue of my parents, especially at school. The next frequently heard comment is "They are giants"! Mommy is the President of the Parent Teacher Association (PTA) at my Elementary School and continued her volunteer duties through the first year of her illness. She never shares she is sick. Again, she is maintaining a stoic public presence while suffering in silence.

Look at my Mommy singing with that beautiful voice of hers and my Daddy playing the piano. I am sitting in the library of my school, and it is filling with other parents, the principal, district

Supervisors, and Assistant Superintendents along with community members. Mommy has organized a PTA meeting featuring a food tasting (my Daddy is a professional chef), music and an agenda. The meeting is going to address parent-teacher and district observations, concerns or developments. The emphasis is on FUN in a positive sharing climate. I am observing this event and thinking, "Earlier this morning, Mommy was rolling out the bed and fell on the floor." Mommy thought she was standing, but her feet didn't move. I remember seeing Daddy helping Mommy off the floor and her sitting on the side of the bed. She was not able to see me off to school and forgot to hug me or wish me a wonderful day... I didn't get a wink from Mommy this morning. But look at her now... I am smiling because there is NO sign that anything happened this morning at home! My teacher is commenting, "You have a special Mommy" after Mommy finished singing. "She is a special person with a special heart for others and beautiful voice as well." "I know... I know!" More mornings like this one occur, and many visits to the doctor are becoming an almost daily event...

~~~ *** ~~~

Mommy is now living with my grandmother because there are fewer steps to climb and a smaller apartment to navigate to reach the bathroom. Its two years later in January of 1978, two years since I was sitting at my mother's feet as she was looking in the mirror adjusting her clothes and saying to her mother, "Mommy I have a lump in my right breast"... just two years. I am sitting in the room in silence, this small room always represents comfort, peace, reflection, and love. A place where I have enjoyed drawing many pictures on the floor, playing with glue, clay, and dolls. It is a place where I began reading my favorite books out loud to my sister or silently to myself. I am sitting still on a small wooden stool-like chair, looking at the colorful curtains, beige walls, one of which has a picture of Jesus and his disciples at the dinner table and the other a picture of Martin Luther King, Jr. Crispy white ironed sheets with a blue, white and yellow comforter are providing a soothing bed for Mommy. Mommy is talking to me, "Don't leave me," "I want to spend as much time as possible before I fall asleep," "Only leave to go to the bathroom and get meals," "Promise me." "I promise, Mommy, I promise."

At this time, my conversations with Mommy are with her eyes closed. Initially, our conversations made sense but increasingly she is rambling with her eyes closed, and I am asking "Are you sleeping?" When she is snoring, and she immediately says "I am NOT sleeping. Why would you say that?" "Because your eyes are closed, and you're not making sense." Long silences are common now, and Mommy is more frequently asleep, but she jolts upright and calls my name as I play with dolls on the floor. I leap to her side and say "I am here Mommy... always touching her left shoulder with my right hand. I move my hand across the top of her shoulders until my right hand is now touching the top of her right shoulder as I use my left hand to support her body and ease her slowly back down into the bed where she instantly begins snoring. I am talking in almost a whisper as I now touch Mommy. I am feeling her body relax, "I'm here Mommy... Your Debby is here... It's ok. Go to sleep."

As I am sitting on my wooden chair-like stool, reading a book, Mommy leaps from the bed and is running straight past me into the wall with such force her entire body falls back straight as a board, and I am directly below. I jump to my feet... I am 5'5" now... I turn to the right to try and break her fall, quickly facing front as her legs buckle and I am screaming for my grandmother. I successfully break Mommy's fall using my body and the bed. My grandmother finds us on the floor with my back against the bed and my legs wide open with Mommy sitting between them leaning back against me and both my arms around her waist. I am still talking in a whisper to Mommy, "Where are you running too?" I am stroking her forehead. With her eyes still closed and slumped in my arms on the floor, "The pain hit me... It hit me... I just want to get away." My grandmother directed me, "Leave the room and call your Daddy." I am running to call Daddy. "Daddy, you gotta come NOW... it's BAD... real BAD Daddy!" As I am hanging up the phone, my grandmother is talking to my Mommy, and she is resting in bed where my grandmother and I have placed her. The next thing I see is my grandmother on her knees screaming a prayer to God. "Father I stretch my hand to thee... NO OTHER HELP I know, for if you were to remove my hand from me WHERE WOULD I GO?" The sound of my grandmother's prayer is becoming drowned out as I realize my heart is pounding, my stomach feels like its swimming and I am sweating profusely. Sweat is dripping from my forehead like a faucet, my face is wet, and I'm soaked underneath my armpits. My heart is beating so fast that my body feels like it is swaying, and my head feels like it's on a roller coaster and its plunging down… all these feelings are happening simultaneously. I sit down… and Daddy arrives lifting Mommy from the bed and taking her to the car, then to the hospital. Mommy is now in a deep sleep, and unaware Daddy is transporting her to the hospital. This is the last living memory of Mommy.

~~~ *** ~~~

Daddy explains that cancer spread to Mommy's lungs and heart. Mommy's lungs were filling with fluid faster than the doctors can drain them and she never returned home. March 23, 1978, my Mommy died.

I hear my Dad's keys outside… I have always had a keen sense of hearing, and I am running to the window. I am right. Why is Daddy at my aunt's house at 7:30 in the morning? I ask my cousin "I don't know." "STOP lying!" "Every time something is wrong you don't know NOTHING!" Daddy is entering the room wearing mismatched shoes… hugs my sister "Mommy is GONE." "She's with God, and he can take better care of her than the doctors."

~~~ *** ~~~

Clink, Clink, Clink… Shuffle, Shuffle, Shuffle!!! I am inhaling through clenched teeth and turning in complete SHOCK!!! To the right, as far as I can see, there are 50 men dressed in beige jumpsuits, white tee shirts, and black boots. All with haircuts and shaved… perfectly groomed. Each prisoner is handcuffed and shackled standing in a perfect line in silence. The prisoners are all facing front, inching along with their hands near their chest as they lift the shackles to SHUFFLE along until their turn to view my Mommy's body in the coffin. The line of prisoners extends the entire right side of the church, along with the back of the church, down the church vestibule and out the church onto the street. As I am turning and see the prisoners, some funeral attendees are GASPING out LOUD in horror. Upon noticing the presence of the prisoners, the sounds coming from a large group of funeral attendees sounds like it was orchestrated by a choir director on cue. I see some women grab their purses, couples move from the right side of the church and leave the main sanctuary. The basement of the church is full with an additional

150 funeral attendees. They replaced the funeral attendees that left due to the prisoner presence, and the right side of the church is quickly filling again. I am feeling shame that the prisoners are received in this manner! Aren't we in Church? Doesn't God love everybody? I am holding my sister's hand and find it amazing that no prisoners are acknowledging the funeral attendees or even looking in their direction. The prisoner's presence is like a military presence but with shackles. Clink, Clink, Clink. Shuffle, Shuffle, Shuffle. Over and over again, the prisoners drop their head and tears flowing from their eyes. Almost all demonstrate this behavior. I am thinking WOW! These prisoners LOVE my Mommy as much as I do!!!!

One correctional officer is stationed on each side of the casket. The Correctional Officers are looking straight ahead and are very patient. At no time do they rush the prisoners as they are viewing Mommy's body. How can they feel so deeply about my Mommy? They are not in my family. I am really feeling honored by the prisoner's presence and behavior but most of all for their LOVE for Mommy. As they walk by the family, the prisoners are acknowledging Daddy with a nod but no words. Most, but not all prisoners, are doing a quick scan to locate my sister and I. Their gaze at my sister and I is SHEER sadness and a look of concern. I am feeling their words through their eyes.

After the prisoner procession, I am standing to greet funeral attendees and to keep them from engaging with my sister. By now, my sisters face, hands, arms, and fingers are red, and she is still crying well past an hour. Before my standing, people are trying to hug her too, despite her crying and visible pain. I am tolerating the continued hugs, pinches on my cheek, kisses on the cheek and forehead and much more. My clothes are beginning to smell like a combination of putrid fragrances from the many hugs with a mixture of the funeral attendees' tears and sweat. Naturally, I HATE people to touch me, so my volunteering to shield my sister from further contact with the funeral attendees is an act of sheer LOVE!

I am looking over at my Daddy, and he has the unfortunate responsibility of greeting ALL funeral attendees. I think because he is such a large man a lot of women are especially seizing the opportunity to fall into his broad-reaching arms. It's super impressive how some women are notably chatty during their procession to the casket. Daddy is looking weary, polite and totally not interested in the extended comments being offered by some of the women.

The funeral service is coming to a close, and they are closing the casket. I think I am standing up and screaming "NOOOOOOO!!!!" I realize I am still sitting, and my sister is now on the floor sobbing and wailing. I get her back into her seat, and I am holding her hand. The casket is closed. My Mommy is dead, tears are strolling down my face, and I am shaking. I DO NOT want another person to touch my sister and me or make promises to "Always be there," "Just call me and I will come," "I will do anything for you guys," "You will see me EVERY Christmas, Easter and on your birthday… you will see," "You are NOT alone… trust me, your Mom meant the world to me." My memory is fading… the exiting from the church, the burial and repast are a complete blur despite being in attendance. I CONTINUE to dread people hugging me while crying, sobbing and making promise after promise…my sister is collapsing into retreat from reality even more than I. I am alternating between people hugging me, sobbing, wailing and gathering my sister from the floor sobbing and wailing…

~~~ *** ~~~

It is feeling COLD… I mean physically COLD… I am feeling a COLDNESS inside my body while my Daddy is opening the door to the apartment and we are entering after the funeral. I am shaking inside. I look back because my sister is falling down the steps crying. I am sitting on the floor next to her and watching her cry, rolling on the floor, sobbing and wailing. I am sitting on the floor, with my back against the wall in this narrow stairwell, wearing my beautiful white dress and heels, watching my sister sobbing, wailing and rolling around the floor. She is wearing a beautiful white dress, lace stockings, and white Mary Jane patent leather shoes. I am staring alternately at my white heels and ahead at the worn, tattered teal, cream and red wallpaper on the wall in front of me for about 45 minutes… in silence.

While we are in the stairwell, Daddy looks down the steps. His face is beet red with tears streaming down as he is gripping the side of the wall looking up almost like he is saying a prayer with his eyes open. He goes into his room and closes the door. This is a Daddy I never met. A new Daddy I am trying to understand. What happened to my old Daddy? My 6'6" giant Daddy needs a hug, but I choose my sister to care for this time.

After approximately 45 minutes, I am reaching for my sisters' hand, she is grabbing my hand and is holding it tight… we walk up the 12 steps together and enter the apartment to begin living our new life. There were no tears from me… just looking ahead… without Mommy.

My little 8-year-old sister, with the big brown saucer cup eyes, long brown hair with slight waves and fair skin. Her beautiful wide smile with a gap between her two front teeth is contagious but ended two years ago when Mommy began treatment for breast cancer. She is collapsing and crying more and more each day. She is crying and collapsing anywhere, anytime. I get her off the floor in the grocery store, the mall, at school in the classroom and on the playground in front of friends.

I begin my role as the FIXER and caregiver of the family at age 9. By age 11, I am exceptionally skilled. I am Emotionless and create my first unconscious mental box to place painful experiences after the funeral. The box proves to be hugely beneficial to my survival as a child and later as an adult but then…

~~~ *** ~~~

Tick, tock… Tick, tock… Tick, tock!!!!!!! This is the constant sound that echoes day in and day out. The only other sounds are the sound of running water for baths, me cooking meals and yes, the deafening silence… in a home that was once filled with laughter, games, plans, and DREAMS! Each family member is in their bedroom and only emerges to bathe and eat. The television and radio are not turned on… No one thinks to turn on the television or radio.

I am looking around, and I see flowers on stands, flowers in huge vases, large arrangements of flowers draped across living room tables, flowers that are filling every inch of the window sills. Some flowers span most of the remaining walking space in the living room. The smell of roses dominates the apartment despite the presence of lilies, violets, orchids, baby breath, eucalyptus flowers and more. For the first three days after the funeral, the flowers are somewhat comforting. Comforting because I love flowers, the range of vibrant colors and the flower types are visually spectacular. As a young girl, I am especially mesmerized by the red, dark and light pink, white, and light purple roses. Until the funeral, I am thinking roses only came in the color red. Bizarre because who brings funeral flowers home from

50

a funeral. After two weeks, it is insanity because ALL the flowers are dead, and my Daddy is not allowing me to throw any of the flowers away. The smell and sight of a room filled with decaying flowers translate into an entire apartment that smells of DEAD flowers. After a month, Daddy throws the flowers away. The flowers become yet another searing reminder my Mommy is DEAD!

It is as if we are all semi-FROZEN. We share a PAIN so profound words and almost living itself escapes us! This home life continues for about 1 month. My Daddy is going to work and returning to his room upon his arrival home. He is uttering Hello and manages a faint smile. I am thrilled he stopped wearing mismatched shoes after a while. My sister and I get dressed, go to school, return home and never talk about anything... only meal choices. I am holding her hand, we walk to school in silence, she cries every day as we walk to school and the entire walk home. I just function on autopilot, no tears, mostly no engagement, other than my Daddy and my sister. I am answering and handling all phone calls. Initially, family and a few friends frequently call and are asking, "How are you? How is everybody doing? I always respond, "Fine." Can I speak to your Daddy? "Oh, he's busy... Can he call you back or He's not home right now? I will let him know you called." I tell Daddy each time someone calls, but he is not responsive. My most enduring thought is "Why am I so COLD?", "Why do I feel COLD in the house and outside?" This is something NEW... no time to think about this plague of feelings and gruesome change!

Daddy gives me his shirt to iron, and because his stature is so massive, not obese, just massive, his shirt covers almost the length of the ironing board and almost touches the floor on both sides of the ironing board. I am crying. How can I possibly iron his shirt perfectly? Where do I start? I have to figure it out... He said I did a wonderful job and went to work. There are many more experiences like this. Even though my Mommy has prepared me for many things, there is much more to learn.

~~~ *** ~~~

I walk through the door into a place of clean and glossy floors, halls filled with smiling student and adult faces... my shoulders immediately relax each day. A slight smile creeps across my face as I enter my elementary school daily. The halls are warm and inviting and filled with student work. Our school day is highly structured, and I am challenged to meet high academic expectations and a rigorous curriculum. I LOVE everything about my school environment, from Kindergarten to Grade 5. Indeed, school is my sanctuary. It is the one place that I enjoy having six uninterrupted hours of relative peace. A place where cancer doesn't exist and my only responsibility is to learn, and I am excelling. School is validating, empowering and inspires me to be my BEST me! My safe place... my happy place is school.

As I hear myself being introduced as a curious, brilliant, creative and overall exceptional student, I think Wow and Ok... I am not that extra special... I am just Debby. I am standing, smiling and hugging the principal, turning to the podium, adjusting the microphone, looking out at the crowd of approximately 150 people and beginning my Introduction Speech without pause. As the Fifth Grade Graduation Student Representative, I am reading the entries for half of the Grade 5 graduation program. I am given a huge certificate of achievement as an academic award along with $50. I am smiling inside and out upon receiving this award, which is a rare occurrence since my mother's death three months prior. It is June 1978, and this is my first memory of happiness. While walking back to my seat next to the district administrators and principal, I am thinking for a second that Mommy is smiling and winking at me from the audience, my eyes tear and I shut those thoughts DOWN and push the tears back. My Daddy and grandmother are in the audience. I am accepting my reality... end of story!

~~~ *** ~~~

It's August, our unairconditioned home is serving as a constant reminder that we are living in an urban tropical rainforest with concrete instead of grass. My sister, father and I are the objects being barbequed each day in the layers of humidity and heat. The heat is so stagnating that my sister and I wear our underwear for most days until the cool breeze arrives each evening about 7:00pm. We drink water, place ice on our foreheads and sit in front of fans that circulate searing heat and fail to yield a cool breeze.

~~~ *** ~~~

There is a knock at the locked, but open screen door... open to allow for a summer breeze to pass through the house. Standing on the other side of the locked storm door that rattles at the hinges with each knock is a beautiful tall-ish, forty-something woman with velvet skin the color of a black pearl with salt and pepper hair, closely cropped and a well-manicured afro-fro with a long slender white cigarette hanging from the right side of her mouth. As I approach the screen door, she is uttering, "How yall"? "How is your Daddy?" "Did the church send some money around here?" I reply, "We are fine... Daddy is getting better... he is in the bed resting." "The church sent some money." She asked, "How much money?" I replied, "About $250" and quickly lowered my head as I wait for her reply. "OPEN THE DOOR," and I quickly unlock it as she continues with "I'm gonna call them MotherFuckers down there... they got plenty of money down there... Yall got lights?", Puff...puff. "Yall got food?" Puff, Puff, Puff (I am looking up and looking respectfully in her eyes) "YES." "Let me see!" She briskly started walking through the downstairs of the house opening the refrigerator and turning the light switches on and off, flushing the toilet in the powder room to make sure there is running water and the sewage bill is paid. I follow behind her with my head lowered respectfully, promptly following all directions. While Ms. Pat's mannerism and voice send sharp chills through my body, it is clear she cares deeply for our neighborhood and advocates for anyone that needs any level of support! I find it fascinating how she is speaking and smoking her cigarette. The cigarette almost never leaves her mouth, and smoke slides out of the right side of her mouth like a movie star in a movie scene. Watching Ms. Pat's talking and smoking routine is definitely an art form. Daddy is returning home from his second heart attack and has not been to work for six weeks. His color is just beginning to return, he was pale as a ghost for weeks. Ms. Pat more than delivered on her promise for additional money with another $250 being donated to our family and groceries for two more weeks. We are grateful.

My immediate neighbors all work in chicken factories, hospitals, or schools as maintenance or kitchen workers. Several, work as nursing assistants or LPN's. They are all hard working people with families that shower our neighborhood with LOVE and Care. The same practice is shared by the children of the neighborhood and the community at large. If you have a problem, your friends have a problem. Most often there is little to no discussion other than someone asking "What's Wrong" and they silently turn and immediately begin to fix your problem. Sometimes this involves charitable efforts, and at other times they are addressed with violence. It is common for someone to knock on the door and ask for a cup of sugar or flour, a slice of bread and more… you eagerly give what you can to provide help.

~~~ *** ~~~

"Keep still!!!!," "That Hurts," "STOP IT," "Shut UPPPP I mean it… You better sit down!!! It's HOTTTT." My sister is throwing herself on the step, and I am beginning the difficult task of combing her long, thick hair. As I am parting her hair to begin another braid, she jumps up and runs to her left and up the street. I jump backward with the comb still in my hand on the step. The loud sound of crashing glass paralyzes me, and it was this noise that sent my sister blindly running with no destination. Directly across the street from our house, a neighbor is throwing his girlfriend out the window on the first floor. The force of his hitting her body thrust her entire body out the length of the window. As a direct result, the well-fortified window pane that separates the top and bottom window is breaking. I am seeing the back of an upright female body coming through a window backward… this is not what I thought my summer day would be like! To see how long it takes for the boyfriend to come out of the house to check on his girlfriend is morbid. Neighbors gather… cars stop on this one-way street, and the drivers all rush to aid the female victim of Domestic Violence… a term that did not exist at the time of this incident. The ambulance is called but not the police. The girlfriend returns later that night. I am thinking she came to get her clothes and RUN for her life. The next day, I am walking down my front steps on my way to the corner store. Directly across the street from me is the girl who was thrown through the window the day before, cuddling on the step with her boyfriend with the backdrop being the window she was thrown through, which was all boarded up with nails and duck tape. In this MOMENT, I am learning I will NEVER be treated in this manner by any man… especially someone who is supposed to LOVE me.

I place one foot into Ms. Dee's house, and she is snapping sharply, "DON'T wear your shoes in my house, I just finished mopping my hardwood floors!!!" These floors are so shiny I am sure astronauts on the moon are blinded by the glare. I think… this is my first and last time coming to this house!!!! I am confused by Ms. Dee's invitation to come to her house. All the kids on the block say she is GLOW IN THE DARK MEAN. I am used to difficult women, especially attending church so often. I must admit Ms. Dee did have a certain special kinda tense behavior. She is a thirty-something, small frame with clothes, hair, and nails always perfectly in place. Everything is always perfect and on time about Ms. Dee almost to the point of being overly rigid. Dinner is served at the same time every day, the same meals each day of the week, a spotless house just like the neighbors say. She is asking me to be a babysitter for her sister. Ms. Dee said I will be "perfect" for the job and the couple is willing to pay me top dollar. She feels that I manage my house well and my sister is well groomed and mannerly. I think Ms. Dee must be talking to someone behind me. I had no idea she is paying that much attention to my family or me. As usual, a group of neighborhood friends are sitting on my step a place the neighborhood frequents. Rocket says, "she gone," I said, "Who gone," he said "Ms. Dee." I said, "She gone down South?" He said, "No…you know… she has gone." I said, "Gone like died. NOOOOO?" "You always so GOOFY!" he said, "She gone to jail." My mouth is dropping open, I am leaning against the metal railing, wiping sweat from my forehead, became silent and froze for a while. "You Ok," "Like she's in jail downtown in City Hall?" "No!!!! Like she's in jail for 18 months in maximum state prison for women. I know it's hard to imagine with her perfect outfits, routines, and rules." I say, "but she is a wife, mother and nice at heart once you get to know her." Rocket said, "That's what did it to her!!!! What did it to her?" "Her husband… he had an affair with a woman three blocks over. She wasn't the first other woman." "Ms. Dee cooked dinner, cleaned the house that you know is already spotless, walked out the door and went to the other woman's house and rang the doorbell. When the other woman opened the door, Ms. Dee slashed her face with a box cutter over and over again." Beefy walks up to my porch, and the conversation between Rocket and I immediately ends. I am flashing back to her children that are left with no mother and one under 10 years old. I am thinking of her husband who is notorious for dating other women throughout the neighborhood, and he continues this practice while she is incarcerated and even after her return home. Again, I learn another hugely beneficial life lesson before my dating life began. No one is worth my freedom… primarily a man who does not highly value or appreciate me…

The wind is blowing, I am feeling a draft inside the house. I look out the window and think that Antarctica can't be colder than it is here today. As I glance to the left, I see the gas and electric truck pulling away from the curb. Just as the gas and the electric vehicle is turning left at the corner of the one-way street, I am seeing Mookie running up the road, leaping on the pole in front of my neighbor's house and climbing to the overhead electric wires. I begin smiling as he is taking out his tools and I am closing the curtain. I am thinking Sandy's lights and heat are turned off again. Thank God for Mookie! He is the neighborhood electric man. He is a handyman by trade and keeps the neighborhood with electricity when you cannot afford the bill. Billy turns the cable on when your service is shut off… same routine. As soon as the cable company representative is halfway up the street, Billy (a technician for the cable company that lives in the neighborhood) is on the pole to turn the service back on.

Remarkably, I have yet to find a community that has such incredible lawyering skills. A designated few will listen to someone's problem, explain what type of lawyer they need, offer a settlement estimate, which is almost always correct and provides a lawyer referral. Usually, the people providing the lawyering advice are heavily addicted drug addicts who by all appearances look homeless or mentally ill. Occasionally, these same people win their life-long fight with addiction and rejoin society as contributing citizens and gain employment, housing, cars and all the trimmings of a productive life. Only to return to their lives of addiction, homelessness, depression and beyond. A cyclical process that leaves me being a cheerleader, in times of recovery, and a helpless spectator in times of relapse. It is not uncommon for people in the neighborhood to receive settlements and some sizeable, and to receive loans against a pending settlement and more…

~~~ *** ~~~

As I walk up the steep 20+ stairs to enter High School, I smile with deep pride and accomplishment, "I can officially say I attend the legendary Camden High School. The pride of the community… the Castle On The Hill!" At Camden High, many sections of the city attend the school. I have made many life-long friends, broadened my exposure to many more cultures, even levels of poverty, as well as pockets of thriving families.

Who is she? As I am walking across the ramp connecting the main building to the D-building of Camden High, I am stunned by a beautiful, full-length mink coat with a fox collar that a student is wearing. She walks with grace, class, confidence, and purpose. My friend replies, "she's a model... that's the one that goes to New York on the weekends and does photo shoots for magazines." As I look more closely at the hundreds of students that pass in the hallways between classes, a lot of male students are dressed in suits, carrying briefcases, while others are wearing tailored pants and shirts. The girls are dressing in outfits or designer jeans, wearing heels or designer sneakers, and much more. The message is simple... you are attending Camden High, and you are expected to perform well academically, dress both professionally and casually with distinction, and above all, have respect for yourself, others and provide support to your school community when needed.

Where is Brian going after graduation? He got a full four-year baseball scholarship to... What about Sammy? He has a full four-year basketball scholarship to... And Iris... you know she is smart, "She is going to Swarthmore," "Biddy is going to Yale and Kiddy is going to Sarah Lawrence." Wow! "You just have to talk to the Guidance Counselors... they will help you." MeMe knows everybody and everything. She is in 9th grade with me, but she's a social butterfly on steroids. All the upper-classmen are greeting her by name as we are sitting on the edge of the school enjoying lunch. I am trying to process how this school of approximately 1,200 students function both academically and socially. Without question, I am definitely at the right high school, with an emphasis on your academics, your appearance, commitment to the school family and others at large. My sense of community more than doubles during these years and remains unparalleled today. Much like my neighborhood, friends, classmates, and school attendees frequently say to me, "You're different," "You don't belong here, You're nice, and everything but you can go anywhere you want in life." These words and many like them are repeated to me over the years... I am always thinking I am just like you.

Yes, Camden is a fiscally poor city, but the unwavering community support and genuine care for others are beyond expression. I always felt safe in a town known nationally for violence.

As I am turning right at the corner of my street, I see five young men that grew up with me sitting on my porch. All greeted me with a quick smile and kind words as I am walking by... "Hey Deb," "What's Good girl?", "Awww There she goes," "Debby Deb What's UPPPP?," "My girl Deb," "Looking sharp as usual." Next, I am hearing an unfamiliar male voice speaking to me in a way I am not used to, "Yeah, I'd like to get to know Debby Deb with that." BOOM, BAMM, LOUD THUMP!!! I am so startled by the unfamiliar noise that I look back with my shoulders raised.

Oh My God!!!! I am turning, and I see a substantial blow to that young new male face who I didn't know... his lips are shaking, and blood is gushing out, his body falls limply to the ground where all five young men are screaming various things like "It's Debby, This is Debby," "Keep her name out ya mouth," "She's better than YOU," "Dumb Mother-Fucka," "Respect HER... you Hear Me!," "Respect Her!", As they all are kicking, punching and spitting on him. No one ever talked to me again in that manner in the neighborhood or anywhere else.

The next day, on my way to school, I walk past the same childhood male friends standing there and smiling with their standard greetings, but they are adding encouraging phrases, "You Ahh Star Deb," "Don't Forget, You Going Somewhere," "You Alright Deb," "Keep Hittin Them Books Girl," "That's What I'm Talkin Bout," "We HERE Deb... just Say The Word. I know these five young males are my friends and I have only known them to be fun-loving, jokesters, caring and supportive. They transformed on my behalf in a way I could have never imagined and sent me to school emotionally frozen. While I do not condone their method of correction, I am eternally grateful for the protection. These five young male childhood friends, teachers, principals, neighbors, ministers and many others are clearing a safe and supportive path for me to exist without fear and thrive. I am forever #camdenproud because I am proudly #camdenmade.

I surf through high school and gain acceptance to Hampton University, a top-tier Historically Black University (HBCU) at the completion of High School. This is a huge feat given I am a product of Camden, New Jersey (USA). Camden, a city that is nationally recognized more than three times as the number one city in the United States of America with the highest levels of poverty and crime.

~~~ *** ~~~

I am tired, very tired, and my eyes are red, and I am seeing so many people moving so fast and purposefully in a thousand different directions. The noise level is high, the facility is notably clean, and almost everyone I engage speaks more than two languages. I am looking out at the sea of people representing many countries across the globe. I am thinking Oh My God! I am really far away from home. I will definitely not find anyone from my neighborhood here or many people from my original socio-economic background. I am quickly regrouping and decide that I am not here because of my skin color or socio-economic background... besides no one knows my true story because I have meticulously taught myself to code-switch, blend well in any socio-economic setting and across cultures. My plunging into self-doubt is ending because I hear my Mommy's voice, "Nobody is better than you, and you're not better than anybody else." My shoulders are beginning to relax... the crowd and bustle are not now feeling so suffocating. The unfamiliar demands associated with navigating a place this enormous feels much less intimidating. I, like the people surrounding me, are looking at the arrival and departure monitor in Heathrow Airport in Longford, England and arranging and/or locating their connecting form of transportation.

I am especially intrigued by the youthful look of many of the females in the airport because they have bodies like they are 19 or 20 years old but aged wonderfully and are approximately 40 or 50 years old. One woman stands out from the crowd. She looks younger than her teenage daughter with her quick smile, smooth, wrinkle-free fair skin along with a childlike twinkle in her piercing green eyes and brownish-red hair. She is wearing a simple white-tee, stonewashed jeans, and black sandals with a slight heel. To accent the outfit, she is wearing silver jewelry on her hands, wrist and a swinging necklace that moves like a long silver pendulum. She is speaking English and French to her children and husband. I know she is speaking French because I studied the language for two years and I am excited to use my knowledge in a setting other than middle school. The children never stopped smiling the entire time they engaged their mother. Her husband is reaching to hold her hand each time they begin to walk. I think ... what a super happy family and such a carefree woman!!!!

At the same time, I notice a very talkative English male toddler with blonde hair and blue eyes wearing a white oxford shirt and navy-blue shorts with gold buttons. He is running freely through the crowd, approximately 12ft ahead of his notably calm parents, who appear unconcerned that they are unable to see their son due to the crowded airport. All communication with their toddler is in between the parents holding hands, exchanging soft kisses, and bouts of laughter. I am amazed by the parents being comfortable with not being able to see their son for extended periods and remaining so relaxed. I am definitely on a different continent… light years away from my upbringing. I welcome these mental images in a sea of organized airport chaos. This is my first time traveling alone. Until now I have always traveled with my sister, my cousins or my best friend. I have traveled nationally and internationally, but never alone. For the first time in my life, I am alone…

~~~ *** ~~~

As the bus is driving along the highway, then winding narrow roads with two lanes, we arrive two hours later in a quaint city filled with small restaurants, local stores, and a small theater district. As the bus is approaching the huge fort-like black brick walls that are surrounding the premises of my destination, I gasp aloud. The bus stops in front of the two gigantic black fort-like doors that dwarf the Security Officer. I gasp because I feel like a ghost floating in a movie in the 1400s… like I was going back in time. The weight of the doors is clearly a challenge for the Security Guard, but he is relentless and alternates between adjusting his hat and energetically pushing the doors open over 10 minutes. I exit the bus, and behind the fort-like black brick walls and doors, I see luscious green manicured lawns, striking pink, purple, green, white and black flower beds, as well as, a superbly concealed surveillance systems nestled into the beautifully diverse landscaping.

During my walk to my destination, the guide points out waterways that surround the buildings and suggests we go "punting on the backs." Punting On The Backs is an essential part of exploring the exquisite River Cam in England via a boat and a wooden pole which is used to navigate the waterways of the world famous Cambridge College "Backs." King's College Chapel, The Wren Library at Trinity College, and the Bridge of Sighs are just a few famous landmarks featured during the 45-minute tour. I think that after my long journey and dizzying exhaustion I am not capable of doing anything but sleeping… it's a miracle I made it to my destination… a sheer wonder! My sister and I have well-defined roles…travel and navigation is her area of expertise. I always followed her lead. Just imagine she stopped crying and collapsing, and I no longer have to hold her hand. Boy, did I miss her now… I miss her dearly.

~~~ *** ~~~

The room is huge, dark yet semi-lit with 20 candelabra centered down a 1500's wooden dining table that seats up to 50 people but then, who knows? There is an enormous gray and black flat granite stone fireplace built into the wall that exceeds 7ft in length and width that provides a relaxing, but warm, crackling fire. A two-hour ten-course meal is served by females dressed in gray dresses with white blouses underneath and a black bonnet with black shoes. All discussion is in a heavy English accent and the meal served is traditional English food options, Course One: Hors d'Oeuvres made bite-sized served with cocktails. I find the handheld pieces of food art meticulously crafted, captivating and served on small pieces of fried or grilled bread. Course Two: Soup… clear broth or cream of asparagus is offered to prepare our digestive systems for the meal. Course Three: Fish is offered as hot or cold options, with bones. Additional bread is provided to avoid any inadvertent consumption of fish bones proactively. Course Four: Entree of glazed duck, green beans and carrots are provided. By this time, I am completely starving and having visions of a fried chicken wing. I am declining the duck, and the server replies "No Duck Yah"… I repeat "No duck, Many Thanks." She told the other server I said, "No duck." Other students look up and tell their servers as well, "No duck." The servers all echo that about 20 students don't want the duck. They are clearly upset and baffled by our not wanting duck. I think, Oh No! I didn't come over here to start a duck revolt. Oh great, just what I need. I close my eyes and imagine I smell a fried chicken wing somewhere in their far away kitchen. Fantasy over… Reality check... On to the next course. Course Five: Removes - this is the part of the meal used to exchange the side dishes out in preparation for the roast course. Course Six: Sorbet is served to clean the pallet and is usually citrus-flavored, and this segment of the meal usually progresses quickly as the table is prepared for the roast course. Course Seven: Roast Beef, potatoes, mushrooms, turnips, celery, and many more vegetables. Course Eight: Avacado salad, beet salad and a bed of greens with light dressing. Course Nine: Sweets… small portion sized jellies, pastries, and puddings with a large variety of options. All offered "sweets" lacked any taste of sugar, butter or vanilla. Essentially, I am being served the American version of beautifully designed sugar-free and fat-free deserts in England. Once again, I thought of a largely glazed donut soaked in butter, sugar and powdered sugar. Fantasy over, next course. Course Ten: Fruit and Cheese. This is the final course and used to aid in digestion. I am thrilled to see something I could eat two long hours later. Classical Beethoven is softly filling the room yet allows for conversation with others throughout the dinner. The furniture, clothing worn by the servers the ornaments that adorned the room, the dimly lit environment all creates a feeling of being in the early 1400s. I am attending a Welcome dinner at Cambridge University – Cambridge, England - Kings College. I am studying abroad during the summer of my Master's program in Educational Leadership & Supervision. Cambridge University – Cambridge, England - Kings College was founded in 1441 by King Henry VI. The Founders provided for a Provost and 70 poor scholars. Many lifetimes later a brown girl from Camden, New Jersey attends this prestigious institution. How ironic! Oh, how life is filled with unforeseen twists and turns…

~~~ *** ~~~

Despite sheer exhaustion, I try to attend every event. I overslept, and my group is going to the designated Chinese restaurant. I have the address. I am feeling confident I can locate the restaurant with little to no effort. Logically, I am approaching an armed Security Guard dressed in a black and gold- trimmed uniformed with a black hat and boots. I politely ask for directions to the restaurant, and the Security Guard is standing still quietly, and his eyes track left then right and repeat in a normal rotation twice before darting frantically back and forth in what is appearing to be desperation! His cheeks turn red and not long after his hands are trembling, and they turned red as well. "Please follow me, Mum." "I know where the restaurant is located, but I just can't remember." He took off walking so fast and asking me to follow him and uttered several other things I cannot understand because he is so SORRY he couldn't remember. We arrive at the Security Headquarters, and he removes a huge map located on a large scroll with black wooden rolls on each end. While he is wildly pouring over the map of Cambridge, England, and profusely apologizing for not being able to locate the restaurant I repeatedly tell him "It is Ok… I understand. I will just walk out the two large black double doors located in the back of the campus and turn right because the group discussed the restaurant being in that direction." He became even more upset, "IT'S NOT OKAY… IT'S NOT OKAY" and trembles and apologizes even more each time. Then he drops the scroll, featuring the map, and became again animated with his apologies. I decided that as long as I am standing here, he will feel compelled to continue apologizing and may very well collapse from a heart attack or worse. I am thinking… wait a minute… this place must be much more impressive than I want to really accept. Who the HELL are these people that attend this school that the Security Guard acts in this way because he can't provide directions? I walk out the gates onto the narrow winding street filling with people and luckily locate the restaurant just as the group was discussing. They were waiting for me, and I am HUNGRY!!!! No fried chicken wings on the menu. Oh No! Chicken and Broccoli is my dinner choice until a fried chicken wing can be located.

~~~ *** ~~~

I study at Cambridge University, Kings College School of Education - Cambridge England, my lectures are in the lecture halls, and we tour public schools in Impington, Frumpington and London - England. I am exceptionally impressed with one principal I met in Frumpington, England as he holds a school-wide morning meeting each day in the gymnasium, including the diverse extensive special education population that requires wheelchairs and rugs placed on the floor for disabled students to attend. Also, nurses and medical machines accompany each student that require support. Students with severe Autism and Asperger's Syndrome are present. Frequently these students run around the gymnasium or make loud and disruptive outbursts during the morning meeting but are accepted and calmed in a supportive manner. The principal, all staff and students at the microphone… all continue discussing their topic and the attending students remain focused on the presenter and not the behaviors of 3-5 disruptive students with special needs. I am thinking that it's been my pleasure meeting a principal who is that passionate about creating an equitable school-wide community that is tolerant, diverse and supportive. After interviewing the teachers, it is evident they like their daily morning meeting practice as a welcomed routine. Equally, each teacher completes a written survey and they all sincerely feel it is their duty to create the school-wide climate. It is a refreshing experience to see teacher dialogue, action, planning, and implementation of practice that is student need driven. Refreshing indeed!

~~~ *** ~~~

In my quest to find a fried chicken wing while studying abroad, I order chicken wings at an equivalent to our Appleby's in the United States. I see the waiter approaching my table and I say to myself that he can't be coming toward me with golden brown, fried chicken wings with large white feathers emerging all over each wing. Because I am super sensitive to not being home in America, I pay $35 for the meal I didn't eat. I order fried chicken wings in a Pub. Again, the waiter delivers a plate full of golden fried chicken wings with large white feathers emerging from each piece. Determined to get a fried chicken wing, I decide I need to go to a high-end restaurant and make certain no white feathers are served with my meal. I am relaxing, confident and leaning back comfortably but appropriately in my seat when the waiter places a plate full of chicken wings and vegetables with an extra amount of white feathers emerging from the wings… I cry…Ugh!!! Chicken wings. Chicken Wings. I sincerely believe I must CLUCK in my sleep… lol.

~~~ *** ~~~

The door opens, and I enter… the cabins are nearly full, but I find a seat near the rear of the train. With each stop, more and more passengers are exiting the train. The stop before my destination is an interesting experience. I notice one then two and three and four people's faces are progressively becoming red. When the doors open, several men are grabbing their briefcases and take large fast steps to exit the train. I'm on the local train in London, England. The train is now filled ONLY with people of black, brown and beige hues. I ask a lady sitting in front of me what just happened? Why did the people that exit at the last stop run off the train with faces filled with FEAR?

She says, "Oh because the last stop is Brixton and mostly Black people live in that community." I am thinking, No worries. Whatever they got going on I've seen it or lived it. I will be fine. I am walking out of the subway and smile. I am home... the streets are clean and filled with many people of color from all across the globe. As far and as wide as I can see are people that look like me and greet me like I am used too back home in America. I walk past groups of Bi-racial people born in the UK, Africans from various countries, Jamaicans, Haitians and more.

Oh, and I found golden brown fried chicken wings without FEATHERS... Yeah, Baby! The last week of my studying abroad experience I find chicken wing heaven. LOL!!!!

As a group studying abroad at Kings College from The United States, we are seated each day on a raised section of the dining hall at a long table that seats approximately 30 people. As I sit looking around the dining hall, I think this place can seat 150-200 people. One day, a man enters the dining hall, and I am captured by his posture, stride, calm yet confident presence, that commanded immediate respect and regard. Who is this man? Most people don't evoke that level of curiosity from me? I discover his father is the president of a country and his mother is a foreign Ambassador. I quickly recall the trembling Security Guard that could not provide me with directions to the Chinese restaurant... his apologies made much more sense. I keep things simple. I am a simple person... you are a person, and I don't get too impressed. Keeping things simple is my perspective serves me well and allows me to navigate many landscapes.

I have fulfilled my mother's greatest wish that I continue to excel at school. I think studying abroad in Cambridge, England satisfies her many pleas that lead up to her death.

~~~ *** ~~~

Look at you. Wow! Tonight, you look like Mommy. Those are my thoughts as I look in the mirror preparing to attend a gala. My tall, curvy figure with an accent on my small waist. YES! Thanks, Mommy! Your shape sure is appreciated. I am looking deeper into the mirror and reflecting on both parents, their statue, the lingering glances that reeked of admiration as they were entering a room together, their unyielding commitment of service to others and the impact of their collective community service. How fortunate am I to have such grand examples for parents!

I returned to the present and allowed myself, for the first time as an adult to say to myself, "You have done GOOD!" Thank You, Mommy. I listened! Rest Easy....

Just like an onion is peeled and one finds so many layers there are always more...

Dr. Debby Olusa, CEO of Olusa Associates, LLC is a seasoned educational and organizational leader with a passion for advancing International Business Strategy, Economic Development and 21st Century global learning. Additionally, Debby Olusa is a compelling Inspirational Speaker that draws audiences into an engaging journey steeped in unique personal and professional experiences that span the globe. Notably, she is recognized for providing "Impactful and Practical" Inspirational Speeches that provide audiences with immediate and actionable steps toward achieving their fullest potential. She is a model and was recently featured in two Eye For Ebony ad campaigns (2018) and the Editorial Beauty Model for the Launch Edition of Compulsive Magazine (2018) and will be featured in future issues. In an effort to support others in an interactive manner, she launched the FaceBook & Instagram Page Inspirational Square: A space centered on Inspiration, Wellness, Health & Beauty with an emphasis on Empowerment. She holds a B. A. in Elementary Education and Psychology from Rowan University, a Masters degree in Educational Administration and Supervision from Cheyney University where she studied abroad at Cambridge University – Cambridge, England and a Doctorate in Educational & Organizational Leadership from the University of Pennsylvania.

Feel free to contact her using the following:
Email: dolusa@olusaassociates.org
FaceBook: Inspirational Square
Instagram: Inspirational Square

CHAPTER 3

THE LIONESS AWAKENED
by
Dana Priyanka Hammond

The never-ending life of India, where dirty roads are the place of travel and still not paved with cement, the cities are full of life and always active. Crowds of people going around with rickshaws, mopeds, and bikes. Billboards everywhere, big and small, advertising films and movies that are 2 to 3 hours long, with actual meaning to the stories that grips and changes the lives of people and their views when they watch it. Gathering together for festivals and holidays that sparked the clouds with fireworks and colours in the times of every important event.

It is now 1988 at my early age of 4. It's the year I see myself carried in a sack. I see myself opening my eyes inside this brown woven hemp bag. I recognize this bag as an industrial size rice sack that Indians have when they want to bag up large quantities of rice. Surprisingly enough I see myself hidden in this big bag where I cannot see anything outside, but the beam of lights coming through the tight woven holes, indicating that it is morning time.

The silhouette of trees with its shadows passing over me, with the sun that is beaming bright, making me use my senses for awareness to recognize my surroundings. I can hear the morning birds chirping, cooing, and cawing. I feel myself hanging over on someone's back like a sack of potatoes but too afraid to move, slung over on a man's back, not knowing what's happening to me. Hearing this person's footsteps on a gravel road, walking, and understanding the strength of the footsteps as he steps down one foot at a time. As he lifts his legs walking, I'm able to discern that it's a man walking in sandals.

Where is he taking me to? Who is he? I do not know. I didn't want to move to give him any indication that I am awake. If only I can figure out what's happening to me? Moreover, where am I going to? I sure would love to know. Where's my family? Is this a family member? NO! I know something terrible is happening to me, not knowing what? However, something bad. I'm balled up in a fetal position, wanting to stretch and move. Cramped up and uncomfortable in the same area, in an extended period, getting a crick in my neck, joints tired of holding its same place, needing to reposition myself but I cannot. Not knowing what's going on, I didn't feel I should move or make a noise, just from having a fear of the unknown.

Thirsty, wanting some water, mouth feeling dry like a desert, like cotton mouth. Itchy with the bag poking me, feeling like little pins all over my body, wanting to scratch myself, hungry, hearing my stomach growling with the stomach juices churning, making noise. Tired still, my eyes still too blurry and hazy with film over my eyes, without clearly being able to see. I cannot figure out why I'm so tired? When it's early morning, what's causing me to feel so sleepy? It is not a natural sleep but one beyond regular rest. I can't recall what happened to me before finding myself lost in this rice sack, wondering how I ended up here? Wondering how I landed myself in this rice sack? I see myself going somewhere in the hands of this unknown bad man whom I did not know. What's causing this terrible fear to come over me? I sensed something terrible is taking place, as the hands of my destiny are ending very quickly, for being so young. I soon will find out very quickly.

The funny part is I cannot recall anything before this. I cannot remember my parents' faces; I cannot recall my home, I cannot recall what I could have been doing. I don't even know exactly where I'm from, what city, or state. But I know, I am not from the part of India that this terrible man is bringing me to, I couldn't possibly be! It is not my place of origin.

Too afraid to move, with this gnawing sleep that didn't feel normal, my hairline being sticky with sweat, with the residue of wetness on my forehead, feeling the significant wetness on my back, with my frock sticking to me from sweat. "It's hot in the bag," "I need fresh air to breathe," but my energy has dropped with my sleeplessness, still

70

drooping over me, I am struggling with no other choice, but to stop fighting my sleep, and allow myself to fall back to sleep. Huddling together, holding myself, my body's only heat keeps me warm when the temperatures dropped during the evenings and night, becoming cold throughout the night until early morning. Once the sun peaked its head open, it grew over 90% being scorching. I had to deal with the temperature adjustment as sweat made it even colder at night. When the temperature starts cooling, my body starts shivering with the wetness left behind, and it's chilly, even though this relentless sleep didn't want me to wake up for anything, my suffering of cold didn't last long once I dozed off to sleep. Trusting and hoping for the best that I wouldn't wake up to a nightmare of life; that I will be safe for those very moments of me being asleep.

It's my only moment of times, in between, I find myself waking up, recognizing with my ears, nose, to feel another place of my surroundings. Putting more etches in my mind that paints a picture of what is really happening to me. I only wore a frock, no sweater or shoes. A Lot of us usually go barefooted in my country.

Whether it is by day, afternoon, or evening when kidnapping happened from under my family's nose, any of those times are the possibilities! Suspecting that the abduction took place at night, I can't imagine what my parents have been feeling when they realized that their baby girl is missing from underneath them. The time of my disappearing, I can't believe how much grief and devastation my parents will be feeling. Allowing this tall man with a shirt, a pair of pants, and sandals to grab me when their eyes aren't on me, putting chloroform over my mouth, to knock me unconscious, and stuff me into a rice bag to carry me to the destination that he has chosen for me. Doing his job as a thief, this man must have been watching me for a while before he attempted to move — What's taking place in my life is also taking place in many children's lives.

I am 4, and I am wondering what could be taking place at this young age? There are a couple of speculations and possibilities that run through my mind, but the reality is hitting me! What hardships my body might experience, and wondered what I might go through? However, at the same time, I didn't want to know, and I didn't care to know. "I quiver at the thought of it!" So many children have endured things that I can't imagine myself going through, and this is my reality! That I may go through it also! Like many of the victims who have already been living the life of the scary world. It also seemed like my destiny is taking place, like it's been signed by the stars of my future.

The scary places that these thieves take little children like me, are either being made to sex traffick where they go through the process of being locked up in fear, threatened to be killed, not being fed, and forced into a room of darkness with no one to turn to, until the pimps and madams deemed to choose. When it's time for the child to get started as another one of their objects, to please every one of their clients, when they first begin their puberty, they undergo the brutal process of being abused and dressed in cheap clothing, to make them look grown as young women. Humiliating their bodies and putting them to shame, giving them the back-alley procedures, without proper care or treatment. Having to endure being cut in their privates in preparation of sexual servitude until they are brutally mutilated, causing various health problems, potentially having a high risk of infection due to using dirty glass, razors, or scalpels. While still bleeding and not given enough time to heal, they are seeing their first client who takes away their virginity, innocence, and virtue. Then time and time again seeing another person after another, entering in them with no break or rest to heal, shaming them of their value as another cash cow. The pimps and madams are putting so much fear in the child where the child has no option or choice to escape, and if the girl ever did, then it meant death. Leaving their bodies on the ground, on the streets of the cruel world where nobody cared. The dead bodies are turning into another unknown life. The victims are having a hard time making it in life from childhood to adulthood. That is if they do survive, barely breathing and barely living.

The other direction a child goes, is when the evil men force them to beg for money. Putting fear in the child's life and forcing them to become nothing. Some get tortured with abuse and pain and some often get a limb intentionally broken, cut, or brutally severanced, along with their eyes gouged to make them blind, and or acid thrown on their face and body to make them weak or feeble in the eyesight of ordinary human beings. Becoming hungry and starving, getting very desperate for money, if they didn't bring something, then it's another anguish of pain and torture, which possibly meant death also. They are broken with frightened and scared looks in their eyes. The last thing they need is for ordinary people to treat them like disgusting nothing. They didn't need to be called the untouchables or to be addressed like they aren't even human beings. It is not by choice to be where they are, especially when they're kidnapped. These child prostitutes and child street beggars are already going through enough torture in life by their own masters, the last thing they ever need is the whole world to be against them and have mistreatment coming from everybody. It's unfair; it's cruel. They need to have a voice also, they need to have a choice as well. Humanity is unfair, judgmental without the kindness of the heart, or understanding.

There becomes no empathy and no heart for the lost and the dying.

These two things have been the main reasons why little kids get stolen, and society has been blind to what's been going on around them to stop them altogether. Until one day someone finally decides to do something about it, yet still there hasn't been enough helping hands to help these children out, and enough hands that will volunteer to make movements to change lives of the devastated lost and dying.

These kids are forced into a slavery system that has been nothing but dirty money. The love of money is the root of all evil. What are the children to do? They have been forced into an unfortunate chance that has been no fault of theirs. They have no say, no voice, no knowledge of their well beings or their future. Some make it alive, but then some don't.

Crushing every child's hearts and souls from what they have had in life. They could have had a safe, secure, clean home, like every other child, with warmth and comfort, being able to grow up into a healthy childhood life, without worry, allowing them to be a kid, who have adults to protect them and provide for them. These kids deserve a great childhood, but sometimes destiny doesn't turn out that way. From the looks of it, as I said earlier, this is going to be my life! Not knowing what? It is one of these things that's taking place for me, but unexpectedly, I'm getting spared, someone comes and rescues me.

Everything awakened in me, the very first-moment traumatic situation starts happening to me. As soon as I get kidnapped, the stranger starts traveling by foot all night until he reaches the train, far away from my home, it's been a long journey in that rice sack.

Falling back to sleep, I eventually wake up to hearing a train slowing down with a shhh noise, the steam hissing, with smoke coming out, and the tracks slowing down to a complete halt from its squealing sound.

Hearing the hustle and bustle outside of the train with people around; having goods and items and things; talking in their language as if they have something important to say and somewhere important to go; bumping against one another; rushing and hasting to wanting to get on the train. It is like a crowd jamming in the entrance way but cannot get in, until the train engineer finally releases the doors to open. With anxiousness of getting their first seat, so they can land their hands on the seats before the place starts filling up with a crowd, before masses of people huddle in having no room to move.

Hearing the ruckus of a busy train station, I am glad to be at peace, where nobody's even bothering me. It is just another surrounding, another strange place I wake up to in the train. Touching and feeling my way around, I can feel the seat where I am at, feeling the energy of the train slowing down with no noise or sound in the subway. I don't know how long I've been on the train, but I just wake up from sleeping in the cold rice sack. Scratching my hands around the opening of the bag to see if I can escape, feeling safe to do so, but cannot because the knot above my head is so tightly tied. I am cooped up, and I want out, looking above, I felt like a prisoner deflated in frustration. I tried to get out and see my surroundings to see where I'm at, not knowing what to do next, I just knew, my life's been in the fate of the hands that can behold me and lead me the right way to bring me in a good place. I sensed that I am no longer with the wicked man, his presence is no longer around, feeling a lot more at ease, I'm able to relax a little more, moving a little more to relax my muscles from tension. Being able to have the freedom to do so, without my life feeling like it's in endangerment. Being trapped inside, I just gave up and let it be, falling back to sleep with this little bit of sleep still left in me, feeling it wearing off, I am not as tired, but I can use a little more sleep.

I don't know how I came out of the train or who brought me out? However, eventually a train station Indian cop finds me at Pune Railway Number 1, at the train station in Pune, India.

Something must have taken place where things got mixed up with the thief who stole me, whatever took place, he no longer existed in my life. I never make it to my destination that he had chosen for me, whatever this thief initially planned, it didn't work out, which allowed me to be safe and sound. My future with a blink turned around, whatever meant for evil, turned around for good. Someone's been looking out for me; something's been protecting me, I wondered who? Whose been this unrecognizable force? I do not know? I am relieved, now I am found by a train station cop who rescued me to get me off the streets. It's a miracle, this is rare, I must have been special to have escaped death.

This is my last destination in Pune, India. It is the year where Pune has been prominent in sex trafficking before Mumbai, India became very big in sex trafficking. I'm so relieved that an honest cop found me and brought me to a juvenile facility in Pune, India. I escaped death for the first time, and I am glad to know I have a chance to live. Usually, cops in India work together with pimps and madams of prostitution to help put the kids in prostitution systems. The police in India are generally known to be just as dirty. It surprised me that an honest cop found me and brought me to a juvenile orphanage until the juvenile court can figure out what they wanted to do with me. Escaping death has never felt that much sweeter.

I stayed at the juvenile orphanage until they could find my family. They advertised me in newspapers and news for my family to come to claim me, since they had no information about me or my family from the time, they found me. Nothing has been left, no written report, no letter, nothing, from what the orphanage tells me. When they advertised on behalf of me, they ended up getting no answer; nobody came to pick me up, I've been a lost child from what I have been told. They gave it at least three weeks, then the court ruled for me to be abandoned. A certificate of abandonment gets created and I am now set by the court system to be placed as an orphan. The court gives a green thumbs up for me to be put up for adoption, who then transfers me to another orphanage. I am now at the second orphanage and this orphanage also attempts to place me in newspapers and newscast to find my parents one last time. No success at hand, and nothing to go off, they decide as my results to officially put me up for adoption, from what I get told as well. Somewhere between the lifespan, from the time I'm born, from the first orphanage to the second orphanage, from age 4 to 8 years old, I'm a resident of India until it's time for my adoption to take place at the age of 8. adoption being my only option, I finally get adopted by a family the orphanage chooses for me in America. It is now, finally time for me to go. The orphanage feels I'm too old to stay with them. I am now prepared to go to America.

~~~ *** ~~~

It is the year 1992. I am woken up by one of my house moms who takes care of all the little children. There are usually several rotating house moms who look out for various sized children, small, newborn, infants to 8 years old. In the middle of the night, very early in the morning, when everyone is fast asleep, about 3 am, I am woken up. I have been sleeping on the top bunk bed where I am sharing with another child. Too sleepy to wake up, my little body felt groggy, it isn't normal for me to wake up the hours I've never been woken up before. It isn't familiar for me. I'm able to climb down the ladder, stumbling all over, not knowing what I'm supposed to be doing. It is unusually different, and this is beyond new, what am I supposed to do? Why am I awakened? For what? I did not know! It is the day for me to leave India for good, this is the day that made my milestone to the next level. I recognized the house mom get another girl ready, helping her get dressed. Indicating to me in what I'm supposed to be doing.

She packs our unique bright coloured silk lehenga dresses the orphanage made for us for our special occasion. So, we can wear it one day to mark our traditions, with brand new colourful metal bangles that fit our tiny wrists perfectly, our new floral coloured Indian sandals, along with our travel toothpaste and toothbrush, photo albums of our new adopted family, Indian documents, and passports. Our bags are set to go.

Taking our time to brush our teeth, throw on clothes, brush our hairs, as soon as we finish, we are whisked away for the night. Having to rush out, we rushed out the doors, so we can make it to wherever we are going. I wanted to take my favorite dolly that I loved playing with so much but instead, I decided to leave it behind for the next child to enjoy. I purposely gave it with my giving heart and did not want to be greedy or selfish. I wished for another child to like my little dolly as much as I did, even though I did not want to depart from her. I loved my dolly, she was my favorite, and she was just beautiful to me. I felt good leaving her behind for someone else to be attached to like I did. In the orphanage, I took her everywhere, I did not want anyone else to have her while I was there. But now, I wanted another child to feel the love that I did.

As we were leaving, our house mother grabbed hold of our hands, one on each side and brought us outside of the orphanage through the outside doors. Entering out from the doors, we came down the stairs, and I felt the cold air hit my face as we are being led to our three-wheeled rickshaw. Our rickshaw driver remained anxious to take us, while he hasted us along.

We had our frocks, sandals, and sweaters on, feeling the brisk cool of the day, it is chilly! Our house mother guided us up to the seat, in the back seat of the rickshaw, as she sat in the middle, we both sat on each side of her. As the rickshaw moved fast, the brisk wind blew against our faces. I can feel my nose and ears going numb, soon as the cold hits my face. I am glad to have my neck and head somewhat covered with my silk scarf to protect me a little. I couldn't wait to get out of the fresh breeze that's been blowing in my face. With a fast-going rickshaw, we get to our destination. It's a building I have never seen before, and I soon discover, that it's the airport! As I find out new things along the journey, we make the deadline.

Finally arriving at our location, our house mother checks us in and gets our boarding passes. Carrying our little bags on our sides, we hardly had much with us, making traveling easy with nothing but our small valuable goods with clothes on our backs, this has been the only things that we brought with us.

Our house mother rushed us through security, bringing us to our exit. I have never stepped foot in an airport before; this is the beginning of my new journey: everything brand new, in a child's eyes, everything massive in a child's eyes.

As my wondering eyes get big, my curious eyes looked around, but we didn't make any waste to stop for us to see anything, the house mother made my head spin, it's been a lot to see, it's been so busy to see all the commotions and actions. So far, everything's been rushed as if she has been instructed to be on a mission, getting her job done as she's been commanded.

We went from Pune Airport to Mumbai Airport. We are the first ones to be seated having special accommodations for being little children, we went to the front to be seated and settled in before the plane gets boarded with crowds of people. Our house mother is with us all the way through the journey while we are in this new experience of flights, airports, and locations. From Mumbai we take the Delta Airlines and drifted over the skies, it's been three days of the journey before reaching the big city in America, which is New York. We land into their big airport comparing to what I have just seen in India.

We've been favored by the Delta flight attendant who kept their eyes on us while we've been in mid-air on our way to a new country, America. They gave us a doodle pad and coloring crayons and papers. I enjoyed the lovely flight attendants, always checking on us, we didn't feel bored. It did not hit me until this day, that I'm leaving my own country. I have been sad, recognizing that I may never see my homeland again, seeing the different looking people that looked entirely different from me, It's been a lot to absorb as a little eight-year-old kid especially for not knowing any English.

Our long journey of flight finally lands in New York, and I say bye to my friendly flight attendants who made me smile so much from how they made my trip so enjoyable. They hugged us giving each of us delta airline pins as our departure gift to remember them by.

As soon as we arrive New York Airport, it happens to be even bigger, with even more crowds from different countries. We had to pick up our feet, running, while our house mom walked fast to get to our next location. We could easily get lost in this airport, with the next flight to catch we caught a smaller plane this time to go to Chicago O'Hare Airport. It seemingly took maybe another couple more hours before arriving at Chicago O'Hare Airport. I started getting used to this flying from airports to the next locations. It is finally time for us to land, and our house mom took us on this long journey to finally arrive at the arrival area. It is our time to say goodbye!

~~~ *** ~~~

Our house mom stood there at the arrival area at the airport. I did not know why she's just standing there. All I know is that she is my last familiar face that I'm comfortable with, I didn't want to let go of her hand and so I stand by her side for comfort.

As soon as she let go of our hands, I hear, screeching, screaming, joy, and laughter. I see the girl who came with me get very excited and happy, jumping up and down in celebration, runs right into the open arms of her new family who approaches her. With acceptance, love, and delight, she's instantly attached to them. Feeling my heart melt for her and desiring the same thing that she is experiencing. You immediately feel the love in the airport for her.

Standing there like a bump on a log, not knowing what to do, waiting, not seeing anybody approach me. Turning my head back, seeing my house mom leave, seeking security to no avail. With no hesitation, she walks out of my sight to go back home, she must have recognized both adoptive families before stepping off. Finding it hard to swallow, feeling separation, anxiety! I couldn't help but feel scared and insecure. My house mom went back to the only home I knew. My concern rises as my house mom leaves without looking back. I didn't want her to leave!

Who's there to receive me? I did not know? I didn't recognize anyone, the airport's busy, full of people, and I didn't want to be left alone. She just left me there standing by myself. Feeling my feet glued to the floor, I couldn't move, I didn't want to move.

Reality is hitting me, and my life is changing at this very moment, left with total strangers with whom I have no connection or bond, never developing any association with the family the orphanage picked for me. Since the correspondence is weak, I didn't know whom to look for in this new place. Some of the kids at the orphanage developed bonds with their new families through phone calls, visits, and love letters. Moreover, the kids formed lasting memories of their new families who are familiar with their faces, voices, and most importantly, intentions. Never receiving any of those connections, not recognizing who's there to pick me up, I waited with heartfelt anticipation.

Recognizing my house mom isn't coming back, I'm left alone for the first time with an uncertain future. My country, my culture, the environment, food, smell, color, and the way of life, is gone from me. In this very moment, a place that I don't know anything about and never knew it even existed. Everything closed in on me, and I'm experiencing my heart beating fast with my hands sweaty, feeling jittery, my only security blanket removed from me. I want my family back, I want my country back, Help! I don't want to say goodbye! My whole life is torn apart, India just deserted me!

I can't do this, how am I supposed to deal with this? I feel numb! How am I able to deal with my real feelings, with frightened eyes and despair? Finally seeing an older white couple appear before me, standing there with a blank look on their faces, looking at me across the way. I am wondering if these are the people whom I'm going with? Them standing there, made it feel like an eternity, just staring at me. With no expected excitement for seeing me, there's no interaction, reaction, move, sound, or emotions, along with, no welcomed joy, hug, or kisses, no celebration or gathering of the whole family. My arrival didn't get celebrated like I witnessed the other girl. Having a bad feeling come over me, seeing them for the first time, something in my spirit and soul didn't want to leave. They seemed scary, not liking their vibe, frightened eyes, nowhere to turn, feeling like I'm being forced to go with them.

This awkward greeting turned out to be even weirder. Truthfully, they didn't know what to do with me. They made me feel eerie! A cold chill goes down my spine as darkness falls before me. There's something dark about them, feeling like the orphanage made a mistake, I thought these people couldn't possibly be it for me! These people couldn't be the ones that the orphanage matched me with! Feeling like the orphanage just threw me to the wolves, without even carefully considering my life! What kind of jeopardy did they just put me in?

With no hello spoken during this time of approach, the woman just takes my familial sandals away from me, putting on big clunkers on my feet, this is something I'm not familiar with. What are they? Moreover, why did I have to put them on? Not knowing they are called boots, with having never seen boots before, they then put on this puffy thing on me, zipping it up, I felt buried in this big thing. I did not know what it is and why I was put in this? It is my first time putting on a snowsuit with a coat. Buried alive in these garments, I feel like an Oompa Loompa.

No love or fire in their eyes, safety, and security is an issue with me. I didn't feel safe. Not knowing where I fit in, I couldn't get this uncomfortable feeling off me, I'm not happy or settled in my heart. There's been no bridge built between them and me, India to America. Wasting no time leaving the airport, it just became a business. Wanting the love that I witnessed other children receive from their new families, like the exciting reach outs, anticipation in the new family's hearts and voice of excitement of getting their child, phone calls, storytelling, new toys, cards, and travel visitations to India to see their child. It has been inevitable that these people would be strangers to me. The other girl's new family started disappearing from us, while going on their own way, we went our own way to our separate realities.

Arriving at the airport parking lot, approaching my new family's car, I get placed in the back seat of the car with the seatbelt put on. Feeling a lot colder than what I'm used to, not knowing it's called winter, I didn't even know what winter is! It's night, the city seems cleaner, brighter, and up to date than any city I have ever seen or known. The air is crisper, not dusty, and the atmosphere is different than what I am accustomed to experiencing. Driving away from the airport as I start seeing the airport get smaller this night, going to another unknown place. I see white stuff on the ground that I have never seen before, I come to learn that it's called snow. I gaze out into this new land and wondered about this new place, looking around and seeing a bright city with lighted roads, it's late, and my eyes become heavy, it's a long journey on the way, I can't keep my eyes open anymore, I fall asleep.

The journey ends at a house in a small town called West Liberty, in Iowa. I have never seen houses like this before; it's a stand-alone rambler, three bedrooms with a big finished basement. We arrive about 5 or 6 am, my new parents are taking me in with them to this new strange place I now call home. I'm scared, I'm alone, with no affection, the woman instantly undresses me and puts cute, warm pyjamas on me, this is a different kind of clothing, and I like them.

Soon after this, she guides me to my new bed in a big room. I have never slept by myself before and the silence is deafening. I desired more security or at least to be tucked in. The lights get turned off, and I hear my new, unfamiliar parents going into their room to sleep; I immediately get up in this strange place, cold, and afraid, wanting comfort. Everything's quiet and I don't know what to think. I go into the hallway, wanting some human interaction, with no one around, I stand there crying; wanting my need to be fulfilled, not wanting to be alone.

The elderly woman gets up, out of her room and pushes me to go into my room, walks me to my room once more without tucking me in and without any affection. She's standing there watching me get in my bed and then leaves with shutting the door behind her. I am admonished to lie down into this new room, in the daybed. I put covers over my head feeling scared. I have never felt this scared, everything is brand new, by myself for the first time, I'm outside of my comfort zone.

I have officially been isolated for the first time, with no other children to play with or have any relatable connection with. Separating me in the corner of life where everything seems lonely and big. No time for introductions to this new world or even understand the transition, I now find myself forced to accept a different way of living where there is a vast cultural difference.

My adoptive mother takes care of my daily needs temporarily. She baths me, feeds me bland food, enrols me in a school. Summing up most of her responsibilities to me, causing the beginning stage activities to be short-lived. Neither of the parents does any parent-daughter activities along with either of them taking the time to interact with me, which leads me to question, why they even adopted me in the first place? Learning anything about the qualities of life, so far, has come from school and not from home.

Moreover, there has been no structure, no foundation, no meaningful time invested in teaching me the do's and don'ts, the right from the wrongs. I've been left alone and neglected. It has been a crucial part of my life to be protected and loved, entirely covered by an adult who will take their time to value me. I needed someone to spend time with me, someone to teach me things, someone to hold me and tell me that everything is going to be alright. Mistakes are mistakes, and I can try to do better. I wanted and desired to be nurtured by someone. From my observation, my schoolmates received that quality time from their parents, and I wondered why I never did? It's been getting lonely being by myself day in and day out, without the real meaning of family. It made me numb to the whole world, leaving me to fend for myself. Becoming numb from anger, bitterness, and isolation. What am I supposed to do?

I couldn't imagine leaving a child helpless to defend and fend for themselves in this world, because a child doesn't have the mental capacity to survive on their own. Just the thought of it leaves me terrified! Some people shouldn't be given parental privileges of having children. My adoptive parents left me trying to figure things out on my own, having no clue, what I'm supposed to be doing.

Down the road, I discovered that my adoptive mother is a severely damaged human being. Growing up, she became the second mother to her younger siblings. She had many responsibilities on her shoulders to take care of her siblings while her mother was derelict in her responsibilities. Her father became intoxicated almost daily, abusing her mom physically as often as he drank. Unfortunately, my adoptive mom became next in line to suffer generational abuse by her father, thus, not having a quality childhood, taking on adult responsibilities and stress. She just coped by doing what she experienced. This pattern of behaviour she exhibited has completely been manipulative, intimidating, and abusive. Simply narcissist in nature, possessing and ruling over the home, controlling the finances and her husband, she became an emotional volcano, anything can set her off. If not liking something, she will badger until it wearies you out, everything always became dramatic. You couldn't be around her without being negatively drained.

My adoptive mother frequently demeaned, intimidated, bullied, and belittled me even though I am just a child, a child who didn't know any better, a child who didn't understand what is taking place. I never indeed received real security or covering that I longed for. The lack of empathy and egoism caused her to pay no attention to her natural motherly instinct. Whatever it is, she never received contentment from adopting me into the family. I do not know what she thought the outcome would be, moreover, if she thought she would feel complete after taking me, no one can fill that void, no child or any other human being can fill that emptiness in her heart.

In a narcissistic personality, being the center of attention is paramount, it's worse when all the care is taken off the person and is demanded to put into a child, who requires the attention and love. Whatever her shortcomings were, she felt entitled to oppressively punish for minor things. Her insecurities made her suspicious of my motives and behaviours and thus her reason to why she became angry with me frequently. I tested her nerves, without really understanding how I did that. Her bitterness became damaging, her anger became too much burden, and I became her reason for everything. Dumping everything on me like a garbage can, I became her punching bag also.

My adoptive father…. Impotent! He couldn't stop her because he is too weak and emasculated, not having a voice in his own house, he became ineffective and too feeble-minded even to say or do anything worth his weight in salt. He went along with everything she did, said, or wanted, and he pretty much worshipped her. I am a child never feeling the protection from him that I deserved either, he often sat there, watching his wife say and do all manner of abusive actions to me and wouldn't even utter a word or stand up to do anything.

I wondered if he's scared of her also. He often let her do anything she wanted with me, and it didn't even phase him. He didn't have anything to do with me, and we never had any connection. He let his wife take care of all my needs but even then, I never get what I truly need from either of them. I wondered how a human being lets another being mistreat a child so bad in front of their sight without protecting the child. There's something twisted about this, and it did not look right for someone to be a witness and yet not do anything about it. I did not receive security from either of my adoptive parents, neither of them cared for me in any way, it's been an unfortunate period for me.

My life is quickly spiralling down, feeling like the walls of my life are closing in on me. Things are becoming very dark, living in a watery prison where I can't breathe or see the sky. I'm too afraid to move, too scared to talk, ignorant on getting the help and verbalize to someone what's happening to me. I became confused about what's normal in families, and this treatment couldn't possibly be what every other child is going through! Physical, emotional, and mental.

Every time I make a simple childhood error, it's another slap in the face or to the body. Screaming and yelling directly in my face, hurting my ears. Spitting in my face, she threw spoken words to tear me down. Dragging me by the arms through the carpet, pushing and shoving me around. Violence, lots of constant violence.

No family to turn to, no one to understand me, feeling hopeless, not understanding what is happening to me and why bad things continue to befall me. I am not able to make any mistakes even if they have been accidents, I am not able to learn from them as well, even if it's been out of my control. I'm beat on and cornered repeatedly for any such things, as if mistakes aren't even an option for me to learn and grow from. Having a fear of making any errors or mistakes, the fears so great even to a point when I get older, as nature intended, I start my puberty, growing, going through body changes, I bleed in bed. Feeling like I am going to be beat for natural issues. From the first sight of blood, I thought I was dying, not knowing that it's a natural course that all girls go through. With no one to teach me about these changes, how can I have known? I am exhausted, alone, perpetually hungry, and want a place to feel safe and cared for.

From day to day there isn't any nutritional support, my adoptive mother never intentionally grocery shopped, the house is empty. I cannot eat regularly, where I can have energy and focus. My strength is always down, creating health problems, brain fuzziness, can't focus, why is my mind still blurry? I lack nutrition to give what my growing body needs. I am always hungry and starving, while my adoptive parents go out to eat, day in and day out. It never crosses their minds that I also am hungry! They couldn't see fit to bring me anything from their frequent trips to restaurants. Every once in a blue moon, they will buy food for both, staying home to eat, my mother always made themselves a plate, just enough for the two to have and never enough for me. Sitting in the living room eating away while watching tv, sharing food with the dogs. I wondered where my share of food is. Couldn't they see they took responsibility for another human being? A girl child that they " wanted"? However, failing to acknowledge, why is the behaviour intentionally pointed at me. Am I that bad for this kind of cruel punishment?

Moreover, why are the dogs being treated better than me? This isn't making any sense!

Food withheld at home, my only means of food is at school. During the summer, it's survival mode. It's me searching for food through the kitchen to see if I can find any means of goodies, anticipating and hoping that I will find something. Never seeing anything, I instead find a box of old graham crackers that I don't know is old. I climb up on the counter to grab it to eat, not realizing how old they are with bugs crawling in the box. Seeing the bugs, I get disgusted, I then understand why the crackers tasted sugarless and cardboard like. The bugs are eating the sugar from the graham crackers, forcing me not to touch it anymore. Fixating on my next mission to find someone who can feed me. Neighbour, friend, anyone, if not then it's a trip to stealing candy at a corner store to satisfy my hunger or simply go hungry for weeks.

The clothing I wear is either too big or too small. They are from sweaters, t-shirts, to straight legged jeans. Never making me look cute or attractive, I am used to having clothes that hide my figure, ashamed of my body of what's hiding underneath, the loose clothing makes me feel safe from showing anything. I get dressed in anything that plays me down, making me look unattractive and boyish. Growing out of my clothes is the only time my adoptive mom always bought clothes, anything outside of that, I never randomly get gifted with nice clothes or things. No quality clothes from the mall or high-end name brands that will make me feel good — nothing beautiful, or any gifted items that will value me. Never taking the value to buy me things decent enough, I felt the way I am treated, like nothing, nobody, and worthless. My growth spurt moments are the only times I am given any clothes, even when I get something, they are from second-hand stores like goodwill. Always feeling ugly in what she gets for me in the times when I outgrow anything. I am let go of and looking torn up.

Money withheld from me, never given any allowances, I didn't get any investments for my future, bonds, stocks, college funds, etc. Feeling jealous over my nephews who receive all the beautiful things from the mall as well as future investments for their colleges. I'm the black sheep whom no one thinks of.

Getting locked up in my own house like a prisoner, and if I did not stay in the house by certain time, I get locked out of my own home. I am invisible as if I never even exist in front of anyone. I can easily do anything in front of the parents and family and still get ignored. My movements and noise didn't faze anyone. I became dead and not existing!

No natural affection given to me, love isn't even in my adoptive parent's nature. Holidays have been lonely. I didn't get to spend much time with any family, majority of the time it's isolation for me. I didn't have anything to look forward to, including my birthdays.

I've never been provided with any money or any means for sports activities or games, and field trips, always left empty-handed. My traveling to school, or anywhere else is walking or biking; the parents never gave me rides. Whether it's cold (winters) with lots of snow, through the storm or heavy rains, I hiked and walked through my sickness, pain, exhaustion, and tiredness. It's my only way around. I often see my adoptive parents pass me by, with no hesitation, I seem to be a ghost. It made me wonder why they never had the heart to recognize me as their own? Moreover, stop to bring me along with them to go home? Still not understanding why I never get accepted as part of their family? I have always been treated like a stranger. I cannot rely on anyone for anything. Rejection has been a hard pill to swallow, and people who are my family, didn't act like my family.

Feeling dead, spiritually, emotionally, mentally. Like a rag that's been used repeatedly. I have been tattered, torn, and ran over — a piece of fabric that no one wants and have no use for. I have no value, no future; everything's dead in my life. My life, my purpose, I had none.

I am just awakened by the thoughts and the feelings that lie in me, the truth that I know hits me in my face consistently! The attacks make me bitter and angry. I get tired of the lifestyle that I am living. I feel like a non-human being, as if I am an alien from Mars that nobody understands.

After going through the trials with my adoptive parents, I come to realize my adoptive mother didn't know her boundaries or limitations, making me suffer from the constant narcissist abuse. I'm at a place I want out from the traumatic narcissistic injuries that makes me feel nothing but an abandoned orphan. My adoptive mother certainly made sure to injure my life, psychologically and emotionally, where I am severely trauma bound in my psyche. After going through everything, I have experiences of several episodes of severe suicides where I've thoroughly been ready to kill myself and die. I have also been living a life of severe mental depression where I am not able to get out of bed for weeks and months during the times of oppression. I want out and be free from everything, including being in the relationship with my adoptive parents! Where is my freedom? Not knowing how to deal with this severity! Restoration seems far from being recovered in my life, that is if there's any hope, it's undoubtedly through grace.

Not having or even seeing a bright future ahead, I need someone to give me a second chance. One faulty mistake from the orphanage allowed my life to be in shambles. The orphanage should have taken their time to investigate these people. A child who has been well deserving of a great life, a better future, has been given a turn for the worst that she never knew she would experience. Where's restoration? Where's hope? Where's life for me? I am the ugly duckling of this world that never became the beautiful swan. My life became so incomplete, so incapacitated, so disabling, I finally take the chance to do something. I finally come to a sense to take the chance to get my freedom, even though I'm feeling handicapped to do so.

Feeling so void of love, so void of compassion, where I did not know what love even is. Lacking love beyond anything where security and stability have not been the option for me.

~~~ *** ~~~

Walking with a little bravery in my heart, with my head swung up high, letting myself know I can do this. Seeking help, help from the nearest place I know, School! After going through neglection and improper treatments, I finally take my chance, many times, not knowing how to verbalize to the counsellor to let them know about my neglected situation.

After so many nights and months of crying, feeling weary of the life given to me, I needed to be free. Needing the right opportunity that will take me there. The right moment that causes me to have open doors to be free. Then, finally, that moment comes when I am 11 years old, taking into consideration what authorities such as a cop have told me. Needing signs and marks on my body to show evidence of abuse so I can be free. The night prior, all hell broke loose, and finally getting the evidence that I've been needing, giving me the perfect opportunity to show my marks at school.

I came home from my nightly game canceled due to the thick fog. The fog is dangerous to drive in; everybody scattered and hurrying up, rushing to go back home, parents, teachers, and children. I quickly make my way out the door, hurrying up in my sports gear, shorts, and jersey. With hardly anything on, I get in the cold and start walking, seeing my breath from breathing and pacing myself fast, I'm crossing the long school field to get home. Not being able to see through the thick clouds, I didn't know I'm walking in the wet, muddy ground. I step over a broken fence, and I'm almost home. Reaching a few more steps, I'm entering the front door. Feeling the warmth of the house as soon as I come in. Making myself into my room without noticing I'm tracking mud. Catching myself at the last minute, I walk back to the entrance way to take my shoes off. Anxiously hurrying to set things down, so I can figure out how to clean this mess I've created. Being tossed back and forth from wanting to get cleaning supplies and having to empty my bladder. I chose to relieve my bladder, and what happens next couldn't be my worst nightmare! Toilet overflows, water everywhere, now my attention is divided, from the bathroom to the mud on the floor, I don't know which one to do first! I'm torn!

Having two strikes against me, now, I'm scared for my life. Hearing my adoptive parents' voices in the basement, I knew they have been hanging mostly downstairs. Crunching for time, I can hear footsteps coming up the stairs. Having never been taught to clean, I knew I had been in for a new one! Feeling the conflict between the two, the overflow of the toilet and the mud on the floor, I couldn't get to either of the two on time before my adoptive mother came up.

My adoptive mother seeing the mess, instantly went off, yelling, screaming, and cursing. My circumstance became a lit match. I see demonic possession take over her, screaming, spitting, and cornering me in a small area where I can't move. Getting pushed, I almost fall on the dog who also wanted to take a chunk off my flesh. Fighting back, tired of the same abuse. She's still managing to be stronger than I can bear. She finally gets me between the doorpost of my room, I hang on, struggling to keep my strength. I cling onto dear life in between the doorposts, and she finally digs her nails into my skin, piercing pain goes through my skin, I can't hang on any longer, weakening me to let go eventually. She pushes and shoves me where I hit my bedroom floor. She locks me inside as I lay there feeling so hopeless and crying, I couldn't escape!

Nowhere to turn to, I keep my wounds fresh for the next day, the following day comes with school day ahead.

Anxiously rushing to go out the door, heading to school, I couldn't wait for those counsellor doors to open so that I can share the evidence on my arm. Passing by the halls, passing several times in between my first two classes, here and there, I kept an eye out for the time as to when someone will be in the office. Communication may not have been my thing of knowing how to express my real emotions and feelings, but I am determined to show on my body what I cannot speak in words.

I release myself from my second-period music class, pretending to walk out for a restroom break. I now can see the office light on and open. In desperation, I anxiously slip in the office so that I can show what's been scaring me for several years. Taking a deep breath, I breathe out a sigh of relief, sitting there breaking in tears. Uttering a couple of words that I can think of divulging......"I'm scared" and "please don't take me back."

Verbalizing words have not been as bad as it seems, finding (my roar) the power to speak. It is more than I have ever spoken before. Suddenly I didn't feel as mentally dumb. I am finding a little more freedom than before. Nothing is clamping me down or holding me, and I didn't become as fearful to speak my mind. Many times, over again, I felt so much anguish and didn't understand why I couldn't speak! Feeling the freedom of release, I soon speak out words, "I'm being abused" and "I'm tired," "please don't let me go home with them," "I'm scared." "Take me to a shelter," "anywhere but there!" then boom! I am finally feeling relief.

Feeling the burdens on my shoulders fall off. I don't think I ever felt this way before!

Experiencing the heaviness fall off me for the first time, the school counsellor wasted no time to talk to the principal regarding my matter — instructions given to her by the principal to call the Child Protective Services. She walks back in the door and informs me that she must notify CPS. She tells me to wait in a private room until their arrival. 2 to 3 hours later, CPS finally arrives to ask me questions.

Why didn't CPS ever arrive sooner in my life? Why didn't any teachers and counsellors take notice that something hasn't been right with me before? Weight lifting off of me knowing that I am finally going to be safe, I am so surprised that it has taken this long. All the burden that I have been carrying felt like it came crumbling down, I never felt this much lighter ever in my life, I am now able to breathe. CPS made me tell my story to them, and as soon as I get done, CPS moved, feeling like they have enough evidence for a case.

With the arrivals of the cops, CPS makes me go to my house with them, pulling me out of school, to question the parents that have adopted me. Filing a case, my mother never went to jail. The only slap in her hand was losing her job when the news lady reported the news in the newspapers for the whole town to read. It has been the very last time for my mother to become furious towards me. When she gets told about my accusations that I have made, she rushes towards me angrily, grabs my arms to insist on seeing the marks that she left on me. I holler with a loud shrilling voice, telling CPS to please don't let her touch me! I jerk back and sway closer to the police officer. I didn't want her to touch me, not wanting to see her face anymore, I am ready to go.

With the assistance of the cop, I get to pack my bags to leave, taking as much I can because I'm sure I'm not ever coming back to see a sight of anything, house, dogs, items, and things. It's shelter time; I'm on my way to leave. Driving off in the cop car, this is the last time I lay my eyes on this house.

While under the care of the state, the state arranges the parents to do visitation time to see me, hoping that they can rekindle the parent's relationship back together with me, but it didn't surprise me that both parents refused the states offer to come see me. This was a way for the state to keep the parents from having their custody rights revoked, which I did not understand why the state would go the length to keep relationships together especially, when I have expressed my life being endangered of terrible abuse and neglect. Both parents unwilling to cooperate for their custody rights, it made the state to revoke their rights after the state made several attempts of getting the parents to cooperate with them, no other option left, the state took over completely in my life. Since I have been in the state system, the adoptive parents were willing to give up their legal rights. Not making any sense in why they went through all the trouble to adopt me?

Wondering if it had anything to do with getting more money for internationally adopting me? As soon as you adopt a child from a foreign country, you usually get more money from the state for adopting someone from another country. It seems that could have been the possibility, where I have only been an asset in the adoptive parent's retirement plan, which seems like the most logical thing that made sense in my mind.

My most significant victory has been this release of bondage, knowing, I will never ever again struggle with abuse, food, or sense of sleep. In this very time and moment, my life will never be the same again! The evidence of trauma may be the only thing crippling me.

Going through the trials, I wondered how I lived. Wondering how I even survived. What awakened in me became more than just a phase, the reality of strength that resurrected, became more than just an ordinary life. I came to full awareness of the giant that slept inside, this has been just the beginning of the young lioness that came out of the deep sleep. Putting me through the fire to discover the heart of gold in me. I needed to press through the battle to mark my victory. Coming out as a warrior to bring the roar out of me. To know who I am, I had to go through the war to find me.

The Lioness awakened is about courage, strength, and dignity. Having the battle scars to show forth the brokenness. I became a Survivor, a Warrior, who found my voice. This has been my biggest weapon of my life.

My biggest weakness emerged as my kryptonite, but my biggest strength became my story. The young lioness arose, slew, and defeated her enemies. It's time to move forward to the next journey. Shutting the door behind the old life and appearing to a new beginning. Wherever it takes me, I am ready! Not able to change what was done to me, considering the facts of life to my next journey. The shelter life begins, and the rest remains to be told in a new story.

As I close this chapter, I want you to consider this, what if you were stranded on your own? What would you do if this happened to you? Would your life be any different than what it is now?

This is not the end of the story. The story begins here!!!

This chapter is about how i overcame my world and what started my drive. Going from nothing to something. Nobody to someone is my life pattern of what why my name is engraved to be remembered by. I lived and survived the trauma and hardship of life that threw nothing but bones in my life. I was meant to die but I lived and gave the devil a black eye because I still live. I have succeeded to overcome and destined to make something of myself. Through the warfare I did not know how I was going to survive but God kept me somehow, I can't explain how. I did not go crazy or out of my mind. I want to inspire people and show them them can do it and make it like I did. What became untouchable became touchable again. I was given a life, a second chance to be a voice for those who don't have a voice or could not speak. My hope is that my strength will inspire and encourage those to live and make it in life. Look to God for answers. Through it all, I graduated from high school, made it through getting and having my own with not getting paid that much. Now being a homeowner and a small investor I stride to succeed to be financially cushioned. I am doing something about it to change 1 life at a time.

CHAPTER 4

A MILE IN MY SHOES
by
Onyinye N. Chukwunyerenwa

Disclaimer
I have tried to recreate events, locales, and conversations from my memories of them. To maintain their anonymity, in some instances, I have changed the names of individuals and places, I may have changed some identifying characteristics and details such as physical properties, occupations and places of residence.

"Onyinyechukwu, bia dujem k'anyi jee bujere dede Ije Uwa ihe," mummy beckons on me. But I do not honestly want to come with you, mummy, I mutter under my breath, as I am reluctantly wearing my white background, and blue stripes 'bathroom slippers', with my very beautiful flowered long dress, with 'gather' right on top of my navel, a V-neck and three-quarter sleeves. I wish I have the boldness to tell mummy to her face that I do not want to go with her to visit 'mama Ije, a name we all fondly call my big aunt. I am always conscious that as the 'Ada,' I must show good examples to my six younger siblings and that includes running errands regardless of my feelings. Mummy, I am ready, and I have the 'basin' containing mama's 'ukwu anu' (the hip/waist part of the goat/cow, which is a special treat for the 'Ada- the first daughter). I am comfortably seated in the front seat of mummy's 80s cream pick up van, and we are driving to mama's house. I am getting excited because I will see sister Ego oyibo and she will give me that dress she promised me the last time she visited us in Enugu. I observe that the roads are jam-packed, and I say it to mummy, and there are so many masquerades. It's Christmas season, are you forgetting? Be prepared to see many more as we approach 'mama's 'village, mummy replied.

The truck pulls up in 'mama's 'house. I am feeling a bit uneasy, but I am working towards the corridor to give mama her basin of 'ukwu anu,' and to receive her blessings and thank you. I love the way mama will usually say thank you, and she will hug you and hail you as if you gave her that gift from your own pocket. She has such a grateful heart and the sweetest smile!

The living room is packed with mama's sons, married, and not married, her two young unmarried daughters, daughter in law, mama herself and now mummy and I, joining that crowd. It's Christmas holiday, and almost everyone is in the village. I love mama's 'oha soup' and 'akpu.' The robust aroma of 'ogili' will make you overeat.

Why is brother standing up and why is he calling me down the hallway, I am asking myself right now? I do not like darkness, and the entrance is dark, and everyone else is still chatting here, so ...? But I do not dare. Ada, 'do you still have a painful period? Yes, brother, as I am walking down to answer his call. Oh, I will give you an injection to stop it, brother yells out to me he stands by the door of the bedroom, so I know which of the rooms he is in.

Mama's house is a small unpainted bungalow, of four bedrooms, a living room, with a shallow ceiling, a separate kitchen, and toilet house, attached at the back of the main living bungalow.

Brother pulls me into the room, and he locks the wooden door with the bolts below the keyhole. He pins me to the wall, shifts his wrapper that he's tying around his waist, and puts his penis inside of me, with his left palm on my mouth. I want to scream, I want to punch, I want to escape, I am praying that someone should accidentally open the connecting door. But I am not sure anyone in his household would dare, because brother is the wealthiest member of the family and so he dictates for everyone else, what happens. Why is he telling me to lift up your dress, 'is the injection painful'? 'the painful period will stop... but there is no injection! I am wearing back my beautiful white 'pant,' which is one of my Christmas gifts from mummy.

I do not want to rejoin the conversation. I am crying, but I am not sure my cry are tears of pain, I think they are tears of disgust, shame, and confusion. Where are you, Ada? Brother calls out from the living room. I reluctantly walk towards everyone, and they are all saying sorry to me.

I am really very upset at my mother for not perceiving the stench from brother's body or from my own body. He is sitting right there with them all, and they cannot recognize any smell, or is this me feeling dirty, smelly and disgusted? Mummy, how can you not suspect what just happened? I am sitting down in one corner, still crying. Mummy let's go home, please. I'm feeling unwell. I am perplexed and too shocked that I cannot talk on this journey back home. I want to crawl into bed without being noticed by anyone. I want to cry. I want to yell at mummy and to blame her for bringing this upon me. Why did you bring me? Must I be the one to escort you to 'Mama Ije Uwa's house? Can you not perceive the smell coming out from my body? Mummy, have you ever asked me if my period is on right now? Why are you a mother? Why? My tears are rolling down my cheeks, and they can't be controlled. My heart is so heavy, and I have so many questions, and I am building up strong hatred for my mother that I don't seem to have control over, but I am also wishing I could stop.

My worst nightmare! It's the end of January, and I haven't seen my period yet! Didn't brother tell me it will come, this is February now and still no sign of my period? Why is daddy surprised that brother is in Enugu to visit us? But we were all together in the village for Christmas, so hope all is well. "Yes, all is well," according to brother. "I just have a few things to do in Enugu, and I will be on my way back to Lagos in 2 days". I seem to be the only one in the family who knows why the impromptu visit by brother. His baby is growing inside of me, and he needs to take care of it. At this point, I am not even sure what he wants to do. But I am sleeping on the same bed with brother, my own blood relative, who is in his 30s or maybe 40s. I am always sharing my bed with anyone who visits the family, whether male or female, old or young! Why is this? Does this mean that mummy and daddy are ignorant?

In the morning, you'll be escorting me to my friend's clinic in Agbani. I'll do a D&C to clean out the 'blocked blood' in your stomach before it becomes a baby. It looks like you're pregnant. As brother is talking, his fingers are inside of my vagina, and he's almost putting his entire hand as he literarily stirs the inside of me. I am screaming in pain, but he's enjoying it, from the look on his face and the size of his penis as he immediately gets on top of me and he's pleading with me to stop screaming.

~~~ *** ~~~

What is the point in screaming anyway? My parents' room is very far from mine, and there is a connecting door, that is always locked at night. Here I am, in this boys' quarter bedroom, alone to be devoured by this 'tiger'!

Brother, what is the meaning of a D&C? Am I pregnant? Is this an abortion? Will I die if I do an abortion? Isn't it a sin to do an abortion? I am bombarding brother with all these questions, but brother seems to be prepared with his answers. He diffuses all my fears, and I am looking forward to seeing what happens with the 'lump of blood inside of me,' according to him.

I am all dressed up in my Christmas outfit. It is well-tailored red silk, skirt, and blouse, with gather on the blouse. It makes me look 6 ft tall, so I am wearing my black and white dotted snickers to be my real height. And we are walking down to get a taxi to Agbani road. We are the only ones in the taxi, it's a chartered taxi.

I am lying down on that stretcher in the doctor's clinic, and I am screaming, terrified. I am dying brother, and there is blood everywhere. Brother, this so painful, please give me an injection to stop the pain, please. Someone, please help me, please! This is so painful! I am screaming loud on top of my lungs! God, where are you? Why are you letting me go through this?

Why is his friend holding my legs and pulling them apart? I want them to stop. Someone, please stop them!

Why isn't mummy noticing that there is something about my looks? She has seven babies that survived and three that did not survive, all in all, she had 10 pregnancies, that I know of. Why would she not sense that I am pregnant, and now that I am no longer pregnant? I thought mothers have a way of detecting these things without being told? I am in the shower, but I am not just crying, I am cursing my mother, and I am wishing her more pains and maybe death. I do not think she deserved to be my mother or anyone's mother for that matter.

I just want to run away. I want to leave home. I want to go elsewhere where I will never see her, or them or anyone again. I want to go away where no one will ever put me through this kind of torture, trauma, and misery again. I want to die! I am praying for death! I am thinking of it. I am contemplating lots of suicide options! But I do not just want to take my life in such a way that they will not know. I want to cause my mother so much pain, just like she is causing me right now. I blame her for everything. She should know better. Or is she using the excuse that she does not have a proper education blind her sense of judgment? Does she really need to go to University or college to know that her little girl should not share a bed with her adult relatives? And what about my father? I am angry with him because he has told us the story of how his own mother, my grandmother, 'Nne,' would separate the boys from the girls whenever they had sleepovers during 'tales by moonlight.' 'Nne' was not formally educated but she knew the right thing to do. Daddy, why don't you do the same?

AN OUTCAST IN MY FATHER'S HOUSE: WHY?

It's Christmas season, and all the relatives are in the village from the large cities as the family tradition is, to spend Christmas, and special occasions with my grandmother. The house is all warmed up with everyone's presence. My father's house is the biggest one, so everyone is there, including all my cousins and aunties. The harmattan makes Christmas in the East very desirable. Because the air is chilly and dry, and there are no flies and mosquitoes. In fact, we get to wear cardigans and sweaters! And everyone is relaxing at my uncle's house, while the adults are chatting and drinking, of course, it's Christmas, we all get to see ourselves, once a year, we, the children are playing in the sand, with stones, and we are searching and scanning the surrounding bushes for 'snails', popularly called, 'congo meat'. Brother beckons on me to come, and he's standing while I pack my precious stones so that no one else takes them before I come out. Brother said he has an extraordinary gift for me, and I am so excited to have it! This relative is my favorite, and in fact, he is everyone's favorite. So, I quickly follow brother behind, and we cross to my daddy's house, so I can get my gift and show everyone. As I follow brother, I am not actually minding that my beautiful purple and white flowered ready-made dress mummy bought me before we left Enugu is full of sand, and I am lifting the front to hold my 'precious stones.' Just as we arrive at the door to the main house, brother asks me to throw away my stones, but I am not interested in the gift if that is the condition to get the gift. My precious stones! But I do want the gift, so I am standing by the door, with my dress lifted and my stones in there, and looking at brother, and then Ngozika, mummy's maid is calling out to me to turn back. Ngozika muttered something in Ibo, and I heard her, but I am not thinking of what she is whispering, because I want to get my gift and quickly run back to the sand and search for snails.

Ngozika yelled out at me in 'Ibo,' " I sokwana ya, chighaa azu, maka ochi gi ja agho akwa." And this translates to mean, "don't follow him, turn back, as this laughter of yours shall soon turn to cry."

Brother says it's ok and that I can pick my stones when I come out. I am about to put my stones down and arrange them by the door when brother quickly got me by the hand, and all my rocks are on the floor by the entrance to the main house, and he leads me to the bedroom, saying to me, "don't listen to Ngozika. I have a gift for you." Brother asks me to sit down on the bed, which, of course, is the only piece of furniture in this bedroom. He is by his traveling bag, opening it and bringing out some nylon bags and putting some back, while I watch in so much excitement, imagining how big my gift must be, for it to be inside brother's big travel bag. And brother sits beside me with a bag beside him, and he keeps the bag down and asks me to remove my dress that he would like to check my size to see if it fits. I am all so excited because this means that my gift is another ready-made dress! I get so fast at removing my dress and brother wants me to lie down on the bed, and I am doing whatever brother says so I can get my gift! And brother pulls down my beautiful red puffy like pant (as we call it, which is my underwear). And he puts his finger in between my legs and spreads it wide, and his fingers are inside of my vagina, and I am so tickled. I am enjoying the tickles. I am not thinking of anything now but the tickling while brother removed his wrapper and laid beside me. He whispers to my ears, "it won't hurt. It will just be like the tickles". And he forces his 'big penis' inside of me, and I cry out, and he covers my mouth, and he's saying sorry. I am in pain and I think I need to go to the loo. Brother walks me to the loo just by the room. And he cleans the blood. I am crying, and I am scared, but he re-assures me that I will be fine if I do not tell anyone about it. He gives me his word that he will take me to vacations to Lagos and he would buy me lots of gifts and take me on the plane. He said it's our little secret just because I am very special to him.

As I leave the room and walking through the hallway to the main door, I am picking up my stones, and as I walk, I am trying to hold back tears that want to drop, due to the pain, and at the same time, I am trying to avoid Ngozika's sharp eyes, piercing through me. I bend my head as I walk to the pavement and this time, I am not raising my dress up, I am carrying as many stones as my tiny palms can hold. I am back to play with the others, and everyone is curious to know what my gift looks like. But I lied to them that it is a dress but that it did not size me and so brother will take it back to Lagos and exchange it. I am trying to avoid eye contact with my siblings and cousins that I am playing with or contact with anyone at all. I am now very conscious of my sitting position, and my standing position and I am feeling afraid to play hide and seek or even to go into the bush for our little snail hunting. I am just feeling afraid also, though I am not sure why. I do want to tell someone what has just happened to me, but I am not sure who to tell. Brother is still here for some more days, and he ensures that he laps me at every opportunity. While I sit on his laps, I feel something hard on my bottom, and most times, he asks me to spread my legs apart and then he asks me to close my legs tight. Brother's stay home clothing is wrapper tied around his waist, the traditional way.

Brother is my best friend. He makes himself readily available to talk to, and I love him because he has solutions for everything. Our relationship is growing stronger and deeper, and the sex has become very rampant. He sends for me to come on holiday to his house. And in his house, once the wife leaves for work, he returns home from his nearby office, and he will eat lunch, and he must have sex with me before returning to work. Sometimes, he gets home before the wife in the evening, and he asks for another round of sex before having supper. When he visits my parents' house also, it was the same routine. Worse still, I share my bedroom with him and with any other visitor, male and female.

I love what I have with brother that I miss not being with him or around him. I feel jealous when he gives attention to another female or even to his wife. In fact, at his wedding, I am secretly wishing that I should be the wife and not a maid of honor. I have now come to the point where I yearn for sex like I cannot survive without it. I want to have it with everyone, male or female. I want to talk to someone, but I don't know who. I should talk to my favorite aunty, but I am not quite sure I can. She might not understand me, or maybe she might report me to daddy. But then, hmmmmmm, I'm thinking of this fateful day, a long time ago, I saw her and brother crawling out of her bed, both tying wrappers. Her bed had four wooden poles at the end, with thick bedsheets and wrappers building it like a tent and my dad had sent me to fetch her. This was also one of those Christmas seasons, and this was in her father's house. And this was after brother had already started our little secret. So, I quickly imagined what they had done or would have done, crawling out of the covered bed, she is tying wrapper around her chest and brother tying wrapper around his waist. While I sat down on the chair, waiting for her, I heard them giggling inside the bed, before they finally crawled out. So, I am not sure I want to tell her. I am in search of a friend, but at the same time, I am afraid, or should I say, confused, or what? I want to have friends, but at the same time, I want to be on my own.

Or maybe finally this other big male relative of mine, who now lives in my father's house might just be the friend I yearn for. Oh no, he is just like brother! I am here again sharing my bed with another big, very much older, male relative! He wants the exact same thing, sex! The only unfortunate thing is that because he lives with us, and he will be with us for a long, long time, to finish his university at least, he will have sex with me daily. And true to my prediction, it is happening; morning, afternoon and night, he kisses me before my siblings, who are all younger than me, plays with my boobs before them and has sex with me whenever he wants! He keeps the diary of my menstrual cycle! Whenever my period delayed or did not show up, he gives me pills. I do not know what they are, and I do not know who to ask, but I am glad that my period always shows up. We share our bedroom like he is my boyfriend. We dress up naked, in the same room and we walk out together, and at the junction, he gets a cab/bus while I walk down to my school. And while we walk down to the intersection, we talk about the previous night.

But the first night he had sex with me is what I want to talk about quickly. I was fast asleep, clinging to the wall, I made sure there is more than enough space between us, and then he wakes me up. As I am awake, I realize my pyjama pant is not on. And he is over me with a full erection. He opens my legs wide apart, and he goes in. And then as I lay down just gazing at his face, with tears in my eyes, not sure why, he asks me,' who dis-virgined you'? I am still gazing at him, and then he answers his question, 'I know it's brother…'. Him referring to that other relative. I am not sure I am paying attention to what he is saying or even doing, all I want is for him to please hurry up and get down, so I can go back to sleep, which I do hope will be possible after this. However, I don't see why not. It may well be that all men are like that and maybe, the world is supposed to be this way. Now, I don't have to travel all the way to Lagos to see big brother, I have another big brother living with me. Our sexual relationship continues, and now brother must have to leave for Lagos, where he's just been offered a better position by the same company he just started working for here in Enugu.

I remember this beautiful evening, my parents are in the village, and we are left with brother and two maids. My friend visits and I saw her off, but instead of coming home, I had gone to visit a very good male friend who has been asking me out for a long while now, but I've been turning him down. While I was at his place, we had an amazing time, watched movies and did everything we were meant to do as new-found lovers. And then I got home with brother waiting for me by the gate, and as soon as I open our giant-sized gate, he pounces on me. He beats me 'blue-black,' and I began bleeding on my right eye. While beating me, he was shouting at me that I cannot be a 'harlot' in this house. He was asking me, which boy did you go to visit? Where have you been? Why are you following boys? And I lied and told him that I was at my girlfriend's house, down the road. But he wouldn't stop. And then my immediate younger sister noticed the blood as it comes out of my eye, she started screaming, that I was going to get blind, and she began to hit him, and all my little ones started crying, and they pleaded with him to stop beating me and to take me to the hospital. He did drive me to the hospital, and that eye was bandaged and thank God there was no internal damage. But what shocked me was that my parents reprimanded me for coming home late, and this late was 7pm. They thanked him for disciplining me! No one asked why I ran away from home because that was truly what it was for me. I am continually looking to visit, so I can go away from him and not come back. That night, I hated myself more, and I wished for death to take me so my parents could feel my loss and pain. I went to the kitchen to look around for something to use to end my life. I thought of a knife. I thought of running away and maybe just going to hide inside a bush and never showing up. I truly wanted to end my life, but I wasn't sure how.

I am sitting here asking myself, where are his morals? Why in the world does he think he can stop me or even correct me while he does what he does to me? WHY??? And here are my parents, who are so mean and dumb, as to let me share my bed and my bedroom with a big male relative, while they sleep and snore in their own bedroom. Here they are giving him 'thumbs' up for nearly damaging my eye! WHY???

So, my ordeal is not about to end for as long as I shared my bed and my bedroom with every single visitor that walks through my parents' doors. There are about seven in number as they all come and go, whether for short visits or for extended holidays, I attend to all their sexual needs!

My commitment to church should be my act of service to God and should be a good thing, but I am not sure whether it is or not. I am here starving to serve God, and these men of God are plotting iniquities in their hearts. They are planning how to have sex and not be caught by humans, with my little me. And they take turns in accomplishing their evil and wicked desires! And again, I ask, WHY??????

What did I do to deserve this kind of humiliation from Dr. E? But I am thinking to myself that this man is a highly respected doctor and a Preacher of God's Word. Your wife is my teacher for crying out loud! And I do have a lot of respect for her! I can't even move any part of my body except for my toes that I wiggle. I feel so sick, lying down on this tiny bed in your office, and you have just assisted the nurse in putting the IV line on my two hands. Tears roll down my cheeks as he pulls down his black trousers, and spreads my legs apart, and pulls down his white 'Hanes' underwear, and pulls up my 'khaki calico' skirt. I watch him pull me down the bed a little bit, and he puts his penis inside of me. What is he doing?

Oh God, he's having sex with me! Tears are rolling down my eyes, and he is still doing it. I am praying that God will answer me and just do something, even though I am not sure what. Why won't someone open the door of his office? Where is my dad that brought me? Where is everyone? God, why me? WHY???? God, I want to die, please take my life! So many thoughts are going on inside of me as the tears roll down and he comes out, pulls out tissue from his drawer and cleans me. He quickly pulls up his underwear and his trousers and walks to the door. And then a nurse comes in to check my temperature or something, not sure what he asked her to check, I know he told her something. And then, the nurse returns with some injections and my eyes are heavy, I am feeling sleepy.

It is tough being surrounded by people you should ordinarily trust but who end up betraying the trust you have for them. How does one function in this kind of an environment and be expected to be normal? I only must exist, and in doing so, I must flow with the crowd. I must pretend to be perfect just like our family looked like. I must be happy. I must study to get good grades in school or else I face the consequences of my father's wrath, which often ends up in you being severely whipped with your own 'whip or stick'. We all have our names inscribed on the very smooth 'sugarcane like,' but skinny sticks called 'aña' in my dialect, nicely tied together and tucked away behind my mother's purple plastic basket, on top of our parent's concrete wardrobe in their bedroom.

This is my life until I leave my father's house. But I did, and I am so happy because my university is so far away from home - I was not able to restrain myself from being so promiscuous. I am dating the young, the middle class, the old, white, black, men old enough to be my grandfather and women also!

Finally, I am married, and I feel fulfilled. But then I realize I must deal with some of my past as I continuously see a reflection of my past, in my present life, and it terrifies me! I approach my parents, and that is the crime I committed! This is my crime! And now, I have become an OUTCAST! I am being treated like some contagious disease, I am facing the kind of threats and humiliation, no one should ever face in the hands of loved ones, especially having been through what I went through!

BUT FOR HIS LOVE: MY HEALING JOURNEY

I just got a call from my younger sister in England, and it's in October of 2010. She sounds so excited, and I am curious to know why all the excitement! I am hoping she is not pregnant as she has a tiny baby! But she has just informed me that daddy and mummy's UK visa has only been approved. I am now really dancing to go see my parents whom I haven't seen in a while. And to spend the New Year with them!

We are finally in my sister's house in England. Everyone is happy. -so many merriments. And the days are going very fast, and it's the eve to our flying back home. We are all chilling out and having some adult chats in the downstairs lounge, while the children are fast asleep. And did I just hear daddy say again for the third time to me, and now in a commanding voice, that "you have to look for your brothers, and start relating with them." At this time, he has just mentioned the name of the two who are the main culprits! I just cannot keep quiet any longer at this 'false' love daddy is forcing me into, and so I flared up, and I am so bitterly crying, shaking and screaming on top of my lungs, narrating my horrible ordeal! I am really very angry with daddy for not even doing or saying anything years ago when I hinted him about what is going on. He waved it aside, and now, he is trying to blackmail me into relating with the people I am trying so hard to 'bury' in my mind! People that have caused me nothing but so much pain and hurt!!!

Daddy, what in the world did I ever do to you and mummy to deserve this inhumane treatment?

Now my sister and her husband, who have never heard of my ordeal, burst into tears. My sister hugs me, and I fell in her warm embrace, weeping and sobbing with so much physical pain, while her husband confronts my dad. My parents are not looking shocked or surprised especially my dad, and I am wondering…

And he says to my brother in law," I will do something about it when we return home." I am still waiting for him to do something about it because he has since returned!

But I am not sure that daddy would do anything about it, because he has isolated me from the extended and nuclear families. He has spread so much lies and rumors about me, just so that everyone thinks I am lying. They almost want to spit at me when I walk by. They run away from me. He, alongside my molesters, his relatives, are openly issuing me threats! He has caused me so much pain, in fact, I think the pain and the humiliation from my parents and the rest of my siblings feel worse than the pain I suffered in the hands of my molesters! And I am forced to ask the question, "WHY," as I constantly sob amidst such great pain, anger and bitterness.

And I am asking the question, "are you guys sure you are my biological parents"?

I am reaching out to everyone who should convince daddy to confront the men that molested and violated his daughter, but no one seems to be making headway. It's either daddy isn't listening, or he is listening, but he is hiding something, himself or maybe he's in denial! Not sure which one but not even sure if he will be willing to answer that question.

Why wait for daddy or for anyone else to answer the numerous questions I have? Who really can clarify the confusion deep down inside of me? Who can I hand this heaviness to? Who can I trust or confide in? My heart is so unbearably heavy, and I am in such great pain, emotional, physical and spiritual, but I have to keep keeping on! I desperately need to heal! I need total healing from inside, out.

I have come to the point where I am saying to myself, I must move on. I need to go past where I am. I need to look past my past pain and hurt and look into a glorious future which God has promised me. I must look beyond what I have been through! I chose to be grateful to God for sparing my life through it all! I have become genuinely thankful for surviving it all! And then I am thinking of how to move on. As I am sitting down with my therapist, narrating my ordeal, sobbing, shaking, screaming, she let me be, and afterward, as she hands me the tissue, I realize one thing…I feel so light! Much lighter than I was when I sat down in her small back office! This is the lightest I have ever felt since after my visit to see my parents in England, which was where this whole incident got triggered. And I am saying to myself, 'I will share my story, and I will not keep quiet or keep it a secret any longer.'

But then just the thought of this sends chills all above my entire being! How can I tell people that I was molested? How can I start talking about my rape? How in the world will I expose myself and my immediate family to the truth of my teen pregnancy? Where do I even begin? How will people look at me or also treat me when they hear my story? I am terrified of the rejection that might come with this new move, but I need to understand right. I want to be sure this is what I am divinely ordained to do. I am feeling so hopeless, broken, exhausted and lonely! I am praying and fasting for divine direction. And I did get that direction I am trusting Him for! It was precise and clear: "…as you tell your story, lives will be changed, it will bring liberation, deliverance, and healing." It's not as easy as it sounds. I have not fully accepted this calling because I am afraid of the unknown! And so true to my fears, the treatment, a.k.a the stigma from my family, my associations/groups, society at large is overwhelming!

The culture of secrecy and societal stigma are terrifying! They are the reasons child sexual abuse and may be an abuse of any kind is still very prevalent in our society.

After putting up a fight against all my fears, and anxieties, I finally come to terms with my 'Calling' and so the Vision is birthed… 'The Cedar Education Foundation,' previously 'The Cedar Foundation. I am thankful to God for calling me, and for strengthening me. I have been speaking as He has instructed me to, sharing my story, my struggles, my fears, and my Victories, and encouraging victims to share theirs and be free, as well as educating caregivers on the prevention. Today, I am an Advocate on the Prevention of Child Sexual Abuse, speaking boldly through my own stories, nationally and internationally.

I am sharing my story, and people are listening, and they are becoming bold, and they too are sharing their own stories. Hold on a second… I have just become aware that the more I share my story, the more I let out 'our little' secret, the lighter I become, and woohooooooo, the freer I feel!

I am not even worried any longer about who stigmatizes me or not. I am not afraid or intimidated any longer about who rejects or accepts me. Neither am I bothered about who relates to me or not! If I am doing what God has called me to do, I am happy, I am healing, and I am feeling fulfilled. I am touching one life at a time. I cannot just share my story, as I share my story, people are hearing, and they too are getting their liberation as they boldly share theirs. Parents and guardians are listening, and they are learning from the mistakes of our own parents. I realize that I can do something better with what I have been through! I can help others! I can save just one child per year/month/week by educating his/her mom on the prevention of Child Sexual Abuse.

I am saying to myself daily, "Onyinye you cannot do anything about your past, but you can definitely do something about your future." I mean it so much so that it has become like my daily pill. I am developing the mindset of a victor and no longer that of a victim. I chose to live life as a victor, and no longer as a victim, and in thinking about it alone, I ask myself, what better way can I help others who have been through this route, and are struggling as adults? And, how can I contribute to preventing the molestation and abuse of children and young people?

This indeed is the beginning of my Healing journey!

MY TRUTH: IT CAN BE YOURS TOO!

I am not sure the level of your own molestation or rape. I don't care how many people violated you. The last time I counted the number of blood relatives, family physicians, and members of the clergy, that violated me, I counted 12, until I decided to stop counting! It saddens me more to keep counting, so why count? Maybe you are still very angry with your siblings and parents for denying you, and for betraying you! Perhaps they alongside your molesters, threatened you? Are you having some crisis, not even sure of who you are anymore? Are you facing turbulence in your marriage or in your relationships and not know how to handle things? Or maybe the doctors have told you that you cannot have any babies because your fallopian tubes are blocked from an untreated STD, and you know you got this from the molestation or rape from your brother, dad, uncle or cousin! And now, you are so angry because you are paying the heavy price for what was not your fault! Have you become an outcast in your own father's household; or your birthright snatched away from you and given to your little one or worse still, you are treated like you are dead? It is ok to feel pain, but **IT IS NOT OK TO CONTINUE TO HURT!!!**

Yes, it is very painful, and I am not denying that fact. Neither am I telling you to deny the fact that it happened, and that it is very… very painful. Instead, what I want you to do is just to take a minute, close your eyes, admit that it happened but then, ask yourself, what next? Yes, you survived it, what next? Yes, you didn't die from pain and trauma of the whole incidence, then there must be a reason your life has been spared.

Then ask yourself, 'why did I not die, after all, I did try to take my life? What really am I living for? You are alive for a reason!

These and many more are my daily meditation, and so in constantly pondering over them, I have come to discover my purpose for living, that I am called to bring healing and liberation to others by sharing my own story'. **THAT I AM A WORLD CHANGER! I AM AN AGENT FOR CHANGE!**

I won't tell you that the road will be easy. Never, it is going to be rough, and it is going to be very tough. You will wake up in the middle of the night wanting to die or crying yourself to sleep. You will be afraid of your own shadow sometimes or maybe always. You will find it very difficult to trust anyone, and anything, including God Almighty Himself! You will be so angry and bitter, and it will be hard to forgive. You will be angry with yourself, with everyone in your sphere of contact and even those not in your sphere of contact. In fact, you will be mad at yourself, always blaming yourself for everything.

It will be almost impossible to relate with people, even when you do, you will be seen as being weird because you are outspoken, never bothering about pleasing anyone, always speaking your mind and saying it just as it is. You will discover that unlike your old you, your new you are no longer interested in wanting to please people. You just want to be you, and you love this your new 'weird' you. Even though no one will understand you. And it's ok because they probably haven't been there. Except they have 'walked a mile in your shoes,' sweetheart, they will never understand what you are talking about or what you are doing. And they will blame you for the 'disunity' in the family. They will blame you for 'mismanaging' the crisis. They will blame you for blowing things out of proportion, and they will call you horrific names. They may even threaten your life, and they will lie and blackmail you, YOU ARE NOT ALONE! Worse things have been done to me and many more that you do not know about. If I can pull through, I think you too can!

You will have to stop being in denial. It happened, and it wasn't your fault. They blame you, and so quit blaming yourself! Stop hitting yourself. Think of the many lives you can touch if only you can get yourself together and walk away from pain and from anything and anyone that causes you that pain. It doesn't really matter who they are, 'JUST WALK AWAY'!

But you will need to forgive them. Yes, I said it, 'forgive them' - your family members who betrayed your trust and who are not there for you at a time you desperately needed them. Instead of standing with you, they threaten and disown you; forgive your molesters/rapists, frenemies and the society at large, who thinks you should just 'shut up,' because 'our culture' does not permit us to speak openly about these things!

Forgiveness is a gift you need to give yourself at this stage. Not forgiving them is letting them rent a space free of charge in your head/life and it can cause you more pain. By constantly reliving the pain of what happened, you are giving your power away to the person who caused you the pain. This is giving them your house to live in, rent-free. They are not worth your time, and not worth your life! The world we live in has become a place where the victim is blamed, and more attention is given to the offender. Do not let the society put you down! You may have to make a conscious effort every day to forgive, to say, "I'm letting this go. I'm not going to invest in hatred, bitterness, anger, and resentment anymore. I will stop blaming myself. I will stop re-victimizing myself." Yes, the pain of what happened is, of course, inevitable, but continuing to suffer is optional. It's a choice. You are the only person who can control you. Remember that un-forgiveness has everything to do with you and not with the other person. It blocks you from taking the risk of love. You end up in a state of isolation. They have robbed you of not just the moment that they violated you, but of your future as well, when you chose to live in un-forgiveness. But when you chose to forgive, you are saying to them, "You robbed me of my past, but I am not going to give you my future."

Stop feeling ashamed. Stop letting your past dictate your future. Get past your past. Do not let your past leave you hopeless about your future. We all have a past, good or not so good. Your future has no vacancies in it for the mistakes or mishaps of the past. Let God embolden you, heal and restore you as you relieve your story.

Surround yourself with positive vibes, and positive people. My own positive vibes come from God's Word and from my relationship with Him! I also try to keep positive friends, that once I sense that a person is trying to be funny or trying to take advantage of my openness or /and niceness, **I CUT** the strings and I take a walk! I do not compromise that!

One thing I can promise you is that for sure, it is going to be quite a journey but trust me, we shall all get there! We need to hold onto the plough and not look back!

I am still walking my own journey, as the family outcast, having been shunned by the people I love so much, people who should have been there for me through it all, people I would always stand up for and defend, people I sacrificed so much for! But I am strengthened daily to hold onto God and to keep being strong, knowing that I am doing it for you, and for generations born and unborn.

I lay aside my past, and I call you to let it pass as you *'walk a mile with me in my shoes.'*

Join me as I bear this torch. Hold my hands so that together we can illuminate the dark places of the earth with our voices and liberate those whose mouths have been shut by the oaths of secrecy that they were forced to swear to!

Hold my hand as I continue to give VOICE to the VOICELESS! I couldn't have come this far, but for His LOVE....

Ms. Onyinye Chukwunyerenwa, a Canadian resident, received her legal education in Nigeria where she was called to the Bar, in 2001. Her legal experience includes but is not limited to serving as a Legal Officer in the office of The Presidency on Boundary Adjustments, appearances in several Federal High Courts as well as Nigeria Supreme Court. She later joined a private law firm in Abuja where she practiced criminal and corporate law. In 2010, Ms. Chukwunyerenwa, obtained a Master of Arts degree in Human Resource Management from Liverpool John Moores University, United Kingdom. Her passion for investigations and criminology led to training in Criminology and Forensic Psychology. Currently, she is a Commissioner for Oaths in Alberta, Canada and a Regulated Canadian Immigration Consultant in good standing. With more than 12yrs experience in training, administration, mentoring/coaching, consulting, and motivational speaking, Ms. Chukwunyerenwa is a strong Advocate for Prevention of Child Sexual Abuse, through education and awareness Campaigns. She has spoken on such cases as well as authored/initiated policies to combat such acts in Africa, Ireland and Canada. Community service experience includes volunteering and helping new immigrants to Canada settle into their new country. She is CEO of Cedar Immigration & Consultancy Services Inc., Canada. A member in good standing of Nigerian Bar Association (NBA), International Bar Association (IBA); Society for Human Resource Management (SHRM); Chartered Professionals in Human Resources of Alberta Association (CPHR); Immigration Consultants of Canada Regulatory Council (ICCRC); Canadian Association of Professional Immigration Consultants (CAPIC), etc. Ms. Chukwunyerenwa is married with children. Her husband is a renowned Orthopaedic surgeon who travels worldwide performing complex and delicate services in deserving and impoverished countries, in addition to working in reputed Canadian hospitals.

CHAPTER 5

THE LOVING ARMS OF ABUSE
by
Chichi Edna Njoku

The noise was so loud that all I could hear was my heartbeat drumming so loud. I can still hear my best friend screaming on the phone. Telling me that she is on her way. The children are crying in the living room, and all I want to do is to make sure that they are okay.

The moment seems far away now, but it also looks just like yesterday. Let's back up to a few weeks before and describe what may have led to this event. My husband and I are fighting all the time about the little things. For instance, he complains about not having free time to take care of himself and his needs. I worked all sorts of hours to pay the bills, and he complained about not having free time to work out.

I am usually exhausted after I get home from work. I walk in on this particular day, and he is ready to go to the gym to work out. I express to him that I am exhausted and that I wanted to get some rest. He starts arguing with me about his day, and that he wants to get out and not babysit any longer. I decide to go into the room and shut out the noise. I take the children with me and try to calm them down in the room. Next, I hear glass shattering in the kitchen area. After a few minutes, he walks into the room panting and asks me to come to see 'something.' I refuse. He insists and drags me by the arm into the living room area.

Upon getting to the living room, I see the kitchen floor filled with shattered plates. He is describing his life as the plates, saying that its all broken into pieces and that he doesn't know how to get the pieces together. I walk away and go back into the room. Not knowing how to help him or myself. My daughter is clinging on to me the whole time as her way of always trying to protect me from the fights.

A few days later I call him during my lunch break to check on him and my son but don't get an answer. So I went home during my lunch break. He wasn't at home. I then tried my mother-in-law's, and as I approached the door, I heard whispering. I had a key, so I tried it, and the door didn't open. I started knocking, and I heard movement inside. No one answered, so I kept knocking. A few moments later, the door is answered by a lady. I go over to check on my son, who is in his playpen. I stomp over towards the back of the one bedroom apartment and see the bathroom door slightly open. He is sitting on the toilet and begins to explain that nothing was going on. I storm out yelling at him. I pick my son from the playpen and ask the young lady how she met my husband.

She says that they met at the gym and that he never told her that he was married. The pain struck my chest so hard. I hear him coming from the hallway into the living room, putting on his belt. I take my son's diaper bag and start raining insults on both of them. He is begging for me to be understanding and to give him a chance to explain. All I am thinking at this point is how often he has been seeing this woman. What he saw in her that he did not see in me. She must have weighed over 250 pounds. He claims, he is trying to help her lose weight and make her a consistent client, since he does not have a job. I did not care to know any of it. She had a shirt on from the gym, and he always got angry about not going to the gym after I got home from work.

I put my son in the car, and ask my husband to have her stop by the house and put all his clothes in her trunk. I asked him to move in with her while she paid his rent and bills. I cried as I rained insults on him, and sped off.

We come back to the beginning of this story, the present day of the 'other woman event.' It's about 7p.m., and I have both my children settled in watching TV. My daughter is on the couch, and my son is in his playpen. I am on the phone with my then best friend who is in the studio recording music. We are discussing the details about the other woman, and I hear a knock at my door. I walk over to the door and look through the peephole. It is him. I am more infuriated that he has the nerve to show up after all that has happened that day. I am telling him to go away. To go and get the lady to come to help him pack his things.

He tells me that he just wants to talk. I start running my mouth on the phone with my friend. Telling her that he is at the door and that he will never see his kids. I am mocking him saying that I will take the children and run off to Africa, and he would never see them again. Just after I say that, I hear a loud bang on the front door, and what happens next is all in slow motion. The front door was kicked down, and I hear both my children screaming at the top of their voices.

To be more explicit, the apartment design was a bit weird. When you walk into the home, the bedroom door was on the first right, and the other bedroom was on the left after a bathroom. There is a small walkway to head into the living room. If not for the sake of the sidewalk, my children may not have survived the kick in. What if I was in that walkway at that time or if any of my children were there.

Back to the story. I am in my bedroom which is to the right of the front door. When he kicks the door in, I am screaming and asking my friend for help. She uses her producer's phone to call 911 and screams that she is on her way. She and her producer get into their vehicle and head towards my home.

He lunges towards me and grabs the phone and throws it away. He is screaming that I have ruined his life, and I will never take away his children. I prayed in my heart that no nails or splinters had hit my children as the door was falling in. We heard sirens as he struggled to take the other phone from me. I was crying at this time asking him, what I had done to deserve being cheated on, and being lied to. He screamed that he was not cheating, and that was the reason why he wanted to talk. He walks over to the kids and kisses them, then he heads out of the door, and tells me its all my fault. He says all I had to do was to let him in so we could talk.

The cops showed up a few moments later, and I am still in shock. There are nails right by my son's playpen, inches away from him. I am being questioned by the police when my friend shows up with her producer, who drove her while she called 911 and kept me on the line the whole time. I can see it all now. How easily I could have avoided the confrontation and just being a wife. Letting him in and allowing him to explain himself, and asking for time. Time to heal from the hurt. All this time, I blamed myself.

He was picked up from his mother's home and taken to jail. In the 10 years of being married to him, I called the cops a few more times and experienced abuse at so many levels. Even though he never hit me, we had so many incidences where we behaved violently to mask our pain. In the wake of it all, we would find ourselves in love with each other again, hoping we would never have to go back into that phase. However, it was ongoing untill I left Texas in 2008 to join my sister with my kids. But let's go way back to how I ended up in the loving arms of abuse.

I was born in Lagos, Nigeria around the early eighties. I was over 10 pounds, and my parents were expecting a boy. But they got me. My father was away and my mom's best friend at the time was by her side. Hence the name Edna. Oh my Gosh! Edna was the least popular name in the 1800s and it still is today. However, it will fit me when I am a grandma, as the kids chant, 'we are going to Grandma Edna's House,' LOL!.

Growing up I was shy but loved to dance. I would be on the dance floor for hours at my mom's parties and would be the center of praise. My mom would often say she wished I did as good in school as I danced. I was the creative kid and back in the eighties in Africa, it was NOT a cool gift. It was frowned upon. I was not as smart as my straight A's student sister, who I always thought thrived in making me look bad, by being first in her class. She barely studied. She played all day with me and then would end up with perfect grades. I would be like how, why? I would get a whooping when I failed, and one time I got an F in math. So my parents curbed that very early, by allowing my sister and mom to travel to the UK for summer vacations and leave me at home that particular summer. I never failed math again, because I loved our summer trips.

My mother worked for British Airways as a revenue Accountant and had to travel quite frequently to the UK. I would pick up accents where ever we went and began at the age of six to speak a British accent when we landed in Heathrow or Gatwick Airport. By the time I went into middle school and high school, I was surprised at how much bolder I became. I was proudly a part of the literature club, the girl scout, the band, the track team, and the dance team. I became the dance leader of the 3 cultural dance groups and loved every bit of my experience at my 6-year boarding school.

Fast forward to coming to America in the late nineties, I was still just a kid, but wanted to be an adult, so fast. I aimed for the industry I loved so well, performing. However, my parents did not see nor accept the arts as well as I did. They insisted on me becoming a lawyer and soon after my first few years in college, I dropped out and got married to my husband.

He had grown up in Beyonce's city. In fact, one of his neighbors were, a Larry Beyonce and he spoke of how the family wanted to keep the tradition of the name by naming their child the mother's maiden name plus Knowles. He told me of growing up in a painful situation where his dad left his mom, and mom worked two jobs to pay the bills and take care of his brother in college. Being left at home alone a lot, he got into things he probably shouldn't have. Wrong friends, the wrong place and the wrong time. He also grew very angry, quickly. He would start fights and beat up anyone who got in his way. He also picked up small bad habits such as stealing and robbing convenient stores. All this eventually lead to juvenile time and even bigger trouble. By the age of 16, he was sentenced to 10 years for almost beating someone to death.

There was so much wrong with this picture, as I was always protected and sheltered growing up. I didn't quite understand how someone could have been through all that pain and survived it. He masked it well and got out on good behavior after 6 years. I met him soon after he got out, and we started dating. I felt sorry for him and all the pain he had been dealt, and the pain he dealt to others. He fell in love with me right away, and we got married on March 2003 without parental consent.

The abuse started because of lack of money. While I didn't know the consequences of his bad behaviors, I knew he could not get a job, and could not provide for us the way he wanted to. This frustrated me and put our family in an awkward position. We argued over money and bills all the time, and all that would help was if he got a job. He kept trying and was a good father to our children. We would take some time to go fishing in his home state Galveston, TX. We would visit family, and my kids would play along the shore while we enjoyed being in love.

He would get the kids up for school and take them on the days I worked early and pick them up. He made breakfast, lunch and dinner too. The house was cleaned, and it frustrated him that it could not be the other way around. I saw no problem with it, as I grew up in a home where mom worked so hard to provide the extra things while dad paid all the bills. Yet we were reaching a boiling point, and soon it would be too late to turn back time.

After that first 'kick the door down' incident, we had several other times where I had to call the police. I became very unstable with jobs, and by taking care of my home. He would leave for days and not come back. I would cry for hours and spent so much time calling friends and family to see if they had seen him.

As a non-U.S citizen, I found myself working without the right documentation. I could not be without a job myself, and could not afford to lose my children in any way. Throughout my marriage, he was unable to file for my status change because he did not make enough money. So after 10 years of being married to him, I was still an illegal immigrant.

Growing up in African culture, it was not the norm to divorce or leave your husband even if he cheated or abused you. It was hard for me to walk away knowing all the good traits he had and that could be and would be developed over time with age and maturity. But the last incident shook me, and I could no longer stay.

I had left the kids with his mom to go out with friends. It was a Sunday night, and I wanted to have a few drinks and party with my friends. Upon arrival at the home, he was out with his friends, and I left the kids uniforms for school the next day with my mother-in-law. The next day I woke up with a throbbing headache and could not move as quickly as I should have been. I had to head over to his place to pick the kids up. I arrived late, and he had already called me over 5 times. Upon walking into the home, he was so furious, that he started cussing at me. I apologized and told him I had a headache. He reminded me that he had a job interview that he was late for it because of my irresponsibilities. He is saying that it is my fault that he will be late and won't be able to use his children as an excuse. I was hurrying to put the kids' jackets on and wondered if I should offer him a ride. He told me we were separated and that he didn't want anything from me except to get the kids on time. I mumbled something under my voice.

He walked over and asked me what I had said. I told him that he should have made sure he took care of home, and he would then always have a car to get to places instead of the bus. He grabbed me by the neck and dangled my body as he asked me two questions. 'What do you think I am trying to do?' 'Am I not trying to go get a job and take care of you?'. My kids are screaming and crying at this point, asking him to put me down. He was so angry, when he dropped me, that I just grabbed my babies and ran. I ran to the car in shock and its disarray. Even though we were not living together, he would always find ways to abuse me, because I let him.

I headed straight to the police station and filed a PPO(Personal Protective Order). Even though I was afraid of deportation and my illegal stay, I was tired of being abused at his convenience. Whenever it felt okay for him to, he could express his anger towards me and I always just called the cops. Never filed a PPO, nor pressed charges. This time I did. He could have broken my neck in front of my children, and I would not be here today writing to you. I weighed about 125 pounds, and he was a solid 6'2, 220 pounds of pure muscle. I could not change it any longer. That day, after filing the PPO, I took my kids home and cuddled next to them promising them that I would not let my abuser take my life.

A few months after that I left TX on a train to Michigan with nine bags. The abuse left me broken and uncared for. I felt I had to take a bold step in a different direction in life and promised myself to one day share the story to the world. I ended things with him before leaving and hoped I could return to our marriage after we both did a bit more growing up. I wanted to go back to school and get a grip on my life somehow. So I arrived in Michigan in September 2008 and turned myself in, claiming I was not a US citizen and needed to file my papers.

This abusive marriage was dissolved in May 2012. I had to file it myself when I learned that he had gotten another woman pregnant upon my exit. I wanted to return, to try again, to see if things could work for the sake of the children, but, it was too late, and I had to move forward. I gained over 50 pounds after I arrived in Michigan. Constantly having nightmares from my past and reliving the abusive moments over and over again.

We were both so angry with each other, and it had caused some damage to our souls, children, and families. I had to force him to spend time with the children. I had to buy round trip tickets just to make sure, my kids got to spend time with him. My daughter currently does not have a relationship with him because he never calls. He never just picks up the phone and checks on them, with a continuous abusive pattern he had dealt upon us. I often wonder how he has not escaped becoming what he always said he would never be, the father who never cared as his dad was. Yet 'till this day, I have to ask my son to please be the bigger man and check on your family. I make sure he visits every summer, so he can get to see and experience the good parts of his father and grow into an amazing man.

Both my children tell the tale as though it was yesterday. My son used to be such an angry little boy, as he would continuously threaten to beat up his dad when he grows up, for 'touching mum that way.' Their last incident was when I was lifted by my neck, and they have never ever seen me physically abused anymore. I choose these words carefully as I write this book to and for any woman who has ever been abused. Speak up and speak out. Ask for help and be free from it. Change the life of your children forever by helping your spouse get help.

Knowing what I know now, we should have gone for counseling and help, but we kept thinking we would be okay until it was too late. I have raised two wonderful children who show no signs of aggressive disorders or behaviors. In fact, my son is so calm, I sometimes wonder where he gets that from. I am grateful that I made the bold choice to leave.

To help free myself, I told my story in a film called 'red flags' the movie. I produced this film in 2012-2016. It as 3 part film, that engages every viewer, with the power of and about the signs we refuse to recognize as men an women. Sometimes we notice abusive behaviors, and we walk right into it, thinking that it is okay. We shot this film to cater to our young families who need to help their husbands or wives escape the depths of abuse.

It could be that the root had been damaged and if a spouse does not get down to the root of things, there could be a terrible loss all around. Let us, therefore, be our brother's keeper like the friend who stayed on the phone with me during that first abusive incident. Let us watch out for friends, families and loved ones, not to separate and destroy the family ties, but to get counseling help and build a better foundation of love, hope, and peace.

Today I am a better woman for leaving my abuser. I came into Lansing MI, with 9 bags and no car and no house. Ten years later, I have two Mercedes Benz vehicles, a home and my daughter is in her first year of college. I have produced seven films to date and just signed a distribution deal with Sony/The Orchard, through Invest Black records. I encourage every reader to turn their pain into purpose and live to tell the story. Keep an eye out for my next book, 'Single mothers can dream too.' There I give the full gist of some of my most intimate secrets and moments that brought success to my doorstep.

Remember to live like there is no tomorrow, thrive like the world depends on you and empower others because you must- Chichi.

Edna Chichi Njoku is a driven, passionate and charismatic entertainer, producer and entrepreneur. She started to venture into the world of stand up comedy, winning over her audience with her remarkable stage presence as well as her unique 8 voice over accents and impersonations! Her work on the stage is not just about stand up comedy: she is a driven singer- songwriter and rapper with an album out, "radio plays", a mix of music and theatricality, where She {Stage name Chichi Stylxz} brilliantly interprets different radio hosts and call- in guests with different accents. She has produced 7 films and several TV shows to date.

CHAPTER 6

NOTHING SHALL BE WASTED
by
Dr. Eveangel Hines Savage

There in the well-lit office, facing the computer with my back to the door, the door opens with a force and hits the wall. A familiar voice, belts out, "Who do you think you are?" Gathering my thoughts, I turn slowly. The fear rises as I turn to match the voice with a face. She is standing there with her hands on her hips and eyes as red as fire spewing foul language and communicating threats. Firmly, I ask, leave my office now! I am calling the police. She slams the door harder against the wall as I sit shaking with the phone in my hand. It is taking them forever to pick up the phone. There on the other end of the phone, an officer answers, "corporate police." She turns and walks away. My hands are trembling out of control as I hold tightly to the phone with fear in my voice as it cracks to report this act of workplace violence. Can you give us a formal statement? Yes. With tears streaming and panic rising I speak with the representative. I couldn't help thinking, I can't go back there. The report states, "she is not permitted within 100 feet of my workspace." How are they going to assure my safety--thinking to myself? Her office is two doors away from me. Within minutes, my phone rings. "We're moving you." One item after the other I start packing my things in the box with tears meeting at my chin. Kneeling to unplug the surge protector I am embarrassed and ashamed of these acts. They never protect me. In walks my manager offering his passive-aggressive position of empathy as I think to myself, "I can't live like this anymore." My only protection from the wrath of her violence was a stowaway in this 6x6 space where the walls hold the vibrations of my thoughts that I cannot speak. My resilience is in the pictures that stare back at me and the yellow stickies of prayers and affirmations I pray for my sanity, but there on the computer is the flashing alert… oh my GOD, my friend is dead.

CRASH

I can't believe he is dead. Staring at the story, I can see them firing the taser as he lays there on the ground helpless. I can hear the eulogy of my grandson playing over and over. I smell the stench of the prison and see the pain of his eyes released as the tears roll down his face. I feel the pain of washing and swaddling his brother and entering that dark hollow space where his brother lay to rest after being killed by the police. The pit of my belly as it drops to the cry of "your sister is dead. " The day my dad, my defender shut his eyes for the last time. The beatings. The sexual assault. The feeling of failing my nephews and sons. My heart is beating out of my chest. Gazing at the pictures of my loved ones there on the wall, I cry. "Why me?", "Why, Lord, why me?" I feel trouble on every side. Maybe a drink can help me lose this pain. I shudder at the thought of time clean. I can hear the sirens as my heart beats faster. Over the intercom, I hear, trauma to the emergency. Terror is rising as I routinely call those I know every time I hear those words-- my heart beats faster.

Unexpectedly someone knocks at the door. I feel my heart pounding like it is coming out of my chest as I gasp for air to pull myself together. Ring, ring (telephone rings). Reaching for the phone, I pause, and decide not to answer--I cannot respond now. I lift the coffee cup to my mouth and place it back on the desk, and my stomach is bubbling. I run for the door. She steps back as I rush past her to get to the bathroom. If I don't hurry, there will be a mess right here. There are others there watching as I rush into the stall. In the moment of recovery, I still feel the onset of anxiety as my thoughts are racing, palms sweating, rocking back and forth in my chair. Feeling like I am hyperventilating. There across the desk was a paper bag from lunch in plain sight. Breathing is getting more difficult. I cannot breathe. Grabbing the bag, I inhale, exhale and begin to regain control of my breath. I sit again, there in front of the wall.

Looking up at the picture wall again of my family, one photo at a time, I scan as the tears stream thinking of the fear I have for their fathers. I shake, wipe, the tears of my anxiety and reach for the phone to make a call as my hands tremble, again. Something strange is happening. I feel the fear rising again it's getting difficult to breathe. My hand begins to shake violently. Beads of sweat form on my head. I stand up and take off my jacket, pacing around the small space. Sitting down, I lay my head in my lap to regain my composure and calm down. It's not working--the fear is worsening. My palm starts to sweat, and my mouth is dry. I must get out of here. If I don't get out of here now, no one will find me-- I'm dying here. I run and stand there in the middle of the office. Feeling vulnerable, I cry aloud to them as they stare up at me. "I don't know what is happening to me." Please help me. One picks up the phone as the other grabs the afib from the wall. Confused and upset I could hear the wheels of the chair rolling across the floor touching the backs of my knees as they help to guide me to take a seat. My pulse is rapid. My heart continues to pound. I could feel my body spirit rise above me as I watched. From all directions there is staff. The nurse watching her watch took a pulse and another as I felt the coldness of a towel against my forehead.

"Her pulse is rapid." In runs a nurse and other staff. "Do you feel pain?" Sweating profusely. "Are you on any medications?" "Are you a smoker?" "Get the wheelchair; we need to get her to the ED." Holding tight to the paper bag, inhale, exhale, inhale, exhale. My airways were opening; however, my pulse was still rapid. She whispered, "stay calm, stay calm." Her pulse is coming down. In walks the hospital escort whirling a wheelchair. "O.K. let's get you in this chair. We are transporting you to the E.D. for evaluation."

Rolling through the hospital, hall after hall I can see nurses and doctors everywhere. Off comes the blanket. Lift help on each side of me; they transfer me from the wheelchair to a bed. Nursing and CNA support start monitors. I lay there. There was so much going on, and I couldn't hear anything. I lay staring into the abyss as a nurse place the monitors to monitor my vitals and an IV for fluids. There was a team outside of my room. The doctor came in. We have ruled out the possibility of a heart attack.

What else is going on? He says. Tragedies of life, I replied. The more they question me, the more I cry, holding on to the bars of the gurney wondering, "what has come over me?" All your tests are inconclusive. I am ordering rest for a few days. Follow up with your family doctor before returning to work. All kinds of threatening thoughts were flowing through my head. I am afraid. It's late, and everyone is asleep. I grab the sharpest of the cutlery trembling and shaking to cut and end it all. The dog barks. I drop the knife. Night after night, the terror continues.

FOLLOW UP

In walks my doctor. Hi, how are you? I hear you are having a tough time. So, what's going on? I replied, "What's going right?" Aloof, my friend is dead. I am afraid of losing my family to violence. Please, take a seat here on the table. Let's take a look. Your heart sounds good. Have you ever taken any antidepressants? Yes, Xanax for a short period for restless nights. I am going to prescribe a small dose of Effexor to help ease the symptoms. The night terrors you are experiencing are consistent with depression and anxiety. This medication will help though it will take some time to regulate your symptoms. The medicine is time released and should stabilize you through the day. I am also recommending you to therapeutic counseling for support. Our office will call you with an appointment. Standing here in this checkout, I feel worried as all these people know--they all know. Before dark, everyone in my town will know about my mental health. The depression and anxiety are residing, and I must fight to survive. These next few days will be the longest ever.

NIGHT TERROR

Standing there taking my medication, I relived the terror in my head. I sat straight up in the bed, screaming, sweating profusely and my night clothing soaking wet as my husband consoles, "wife, are you o.k.?". Curling up next to him, I grip his arm, piercing his skin with my nails, trembling, screaming, and crying with overwhelming fear. What's wrong? He says. I can hardly breathe--they are trying to kill me. Who is trying to kill you? I can see people everywhere. Holding me tightly, he affirms, " I'm right here, and no one is going to hurt you. I lay shaking as the feelings of terror overwhelm me and life flashes before me. I could feel the heat of my breath against his chest, as I pant for control with my eyes blared opened, the tears roll across his chest. He pulls me closer as I lay thinking about life and death--the panic was real. Calmly, he whispers, shhh. I'm here. The hands on the clock go around and round. He would be leaving soon. I will be all alone.

Awakening in the grey fogginess of the morning, my head was spinning out of control, as I turn, feeling for him. I can usually feel the moisture of his lips, with a kiss and proper morning greeting. Not today. Looking up at the ceiling as I lay there in his oversized shirt that gives me security when he is away, I sighed. I reach for my medication on the bedside table. Curl up into a fetal position. I am alone in my head thinking about the immediate threat of my new norm with Post Traumatic Stress Disorder (PTSD), its effect on my life and the moments that led to ending it all. Drowsy, I can feel the release of the medication as I hear a still small voice--"trust the process. you shall live and not die."

THERAPY BEGINS

The day has come. Maybe my therapist can help me make sense of all this. There were few people in the waiting area. I checked in and took my clipboard and paperwork to a comfortable non-traffic area. I picked up a magazine to read. A few minutes later, a young woman emerged in her late 30's or early 40's.

Therapist: Dr. Savage? Come on back. How are you? She says.

Me: It has been a day. Immediately, I clench. My eyes roam the room with its ambiance of white brick wall complete with an aquarium inset. Fish of all different colors swim under spotlight illuminating their beauty to the melody of the soft music. Across the room is a comfy couch separated by a coffee table and a chair for the counselor — a few magazines atop the table. The lighting is low and comfortable. Peaceful.

Therapist: Who are you bringing into the space today?

Me: I am not sure who is here today, this recent onset of panic attacks has me feeling like death. I am taking this medication to put the feelings at bay, but something is out of the ordinary. Something is wrong.

Therapist: What is going well for you today?

Me: I am trying to figure out what is right about life right now. Someone killed my friend.

Therapist: Murder?

Me: Yes, murder. Hearing the word murder, I quiet to the feeling of fear of the unknown all over again. There in my head, I repeat. I will not lose my sons and nephews to the violence of these streets. Church, family, community, extracurricular activities--what was the purpose of it all to lose them to the streets. I sigh. Doc, I am exhausted pouring into everyone and feeling like a failure. Crying, I continue. I am heartbroken. Nearly 15-years of sadness and a lifetime of masking the pain. Why do we have to show up and be present in everyone's life with punctured pain covered by a mere blood patch? The conversations are exhausting as I try to motivate others to thrive. Putting my hand over my face, I exhaled and lay back on the couch feeling perplexed. I'm tired, sad, angry, and some days, I want to die.

Therapist: How old are they?

Me: They are all grown.

Therapist: Have you considered the toll that this is taking on you and the potential outcomes if you continue to carry the burden of others?

Me: Yes. Detaching from it all is difficult. I want the best for my sons and daughters. The emotional pain never ends, and the pain of others triggers me. When he hurts, I hurt. Holding my head, I turned to the paper to doodle. I remember losing my son.

Therapist: Tell me about that

BABY NUMBER FOUR

Me: You are pregnant! Baby number four. The excitement was exhilarating. When is the stork bringing the baby, mommy? Bombarding me with questions, I said Come, come, it's time to learn where babies come from. Let's talk about how the baby grows. Drawing on white paper, here is a mommy with a small belly, on their tummies in a circle, with faces propped on their hands and feet swaging in the air, they giggle. It's 24-weeks--I am safe now. Healthy mommy, healthy baby at least I thought. Staring at my sweet spot there beyond the therapist I begin to feel solemn stalling to say anymore. I think about that day.

I hurry to exercise. If I don't get it in now, I won't. It is hot, and the gym feels a litter warmer today. These two steps should work. Slowing down, I removed a step to avoid overheating. Ouch, that was painful--I grabbed my side. There in the left side of my pelvic area was a pain. Are you o.k., asked my instructor. "I think so, I said--everything seems ok--the pain subsided.

Taking it easy, I managed to get the children a few items together to go to grandmas. Riding down 95, my husband and I were getting away. I enjoy Washington, D.C. I look forward to the annual conference every year. This trip was a bit different with a baby in tow. For some reason, I couldn't quite get it together. The more I walk, the more tired I became. Ouch, my tummy is tightening. This pain is familiar. The pain feels like Braxton Hicks. Honey, I'm not feeling so well. I think I better sit this one out in the hotel and rest. The luxurious suite of Embassy at D.C. was comfortable, but I miss my babies. I want to go home. Thank GOD this is the last day of the conference. Finally, five hours to Greenville, but it seems like forever. We arrive. I could not get out of my clothes fast enough to share some time with my children. I miss them when I am away.

I felt something warm in my underpants. Hmmm. I rush to check. There is a clear watery liquid spotting-this is not normal. Feeling a little nervous, I asked mom, "should I have a clear watery discharge of any kind?" She said, "Sometimes there is a slight discharge during pregnancy; however, I am not sure of what you are describing." Call the doctor. I went in the next morning.

My worst fear was leaking amniotic fluid. Nervous, I looked at the doctor, this cannot be good for the baby. I am only 24 weeks pregnant. What does this all mean? More testing is needed, and the doctor ordered an ultrasound. I have a ruptured sac. Oh, my GOD--my baby! Next step--admissions. The doctor ordered all sorts of test. Viability is slim, and early delivery is inevitable. The doctor was empathetic, leaving the room. I look at my husband and him at me. I could see the disappointment as he tried to be strong for me. I still had to deliver our little boy. Lord, your will I pray. Feeling scared, I closed my eyes. A peace came over me as I slept. There he was, my baby in the center of this white flower. What could this all mean? I labored. Kwame Turre was born 14.6 ounces. He lived for only a few minutes--he was too small to survive. I looked down at this little tiny vessel which was the size of my palm. His eyes were still sealed as he blew his last breath. They called the time of death. They rolled me back to the room. In walks the nurse with my baby for me to say goodbye. The grief begins. As we prepare to receive guests in our home to memorialize our son, my husband cornered me on the staircase and embraced me. I started to cry. This time, he cried, too. What was I thinking, he has lost a son, as well. In my grief, he kept going, and it hit me. I reciprocate his embrace. Our lives will never be the same.

HIS HELP

Feeling defeated and slumped there on the couch, my eyes welling with tears. I can remember it like it was yesterday...

Me: There were some challenges during the pregnancy, but they made it to nine months. It is dusk, foggy, and the visibility difficult. There on the phone, I could hear his somber voice, "Mom, the baby is coming. The doctors say his chance of survival is slim." "Whose report will you believe, son? Here I was, hanging on to every word, the phone went silent. I sped, fast with nearly two hours to Durham, NC, affirming my hope is built on nothing less than GOD. I stood there in the open closet area, she was pushing, and I turned my face to the wall and began to cry--I couldn't let him see me cry. I must be strong. I must get him through this. One final push. A quietness came over the room as the doctor examines the baby. "Mommy, why isn't he crying." His hope never wavered. With tears flowing, I said, "he's gone, baby, he's gone. Take off your shirt, put his skin to yours and remember the warmth of his body." There in the room were familiar sounds of tears and pain from a mother and father grieving. My lost became his help. Hand in hand, I strolled with him in the dark of the night crying together. Life is not fair. First, daddy, his brother, my sister, and now my grandson. Life was spiraling out of control. As if this pain wasn't enough, there was nothing that could have prepared either of us for what came next--police brutality.

Therapist: Police Brutality? Was someone hurt?

Me: Yes, my son. The flowers smell like spring in the air. I was so happy to see him. Even though he mourned the loss of my grandson, Mother's Day was still special. We were all standing clowning with each other. The police were called to the area for noise. Standing there, he was sharing a video with a nephew and the police rushing from the rear of the building, plunged toward him. Put your hands up. Confused, with young adolescents all around, he lifts then lowered his hands. Put your hands up now, in confusion he dropped everything. A taser was fired. He hit the ground. There on the ground in the dark by the dumpster, he lay screaming, "Mommy, help me." Feeling helpless I reach for him. I could feel the officer as he pulls me back from him. Tased, scarred, wounded, he lay there. Swiftly they passed by me and rush him to the hospital.

Speeding, I followed the emergency wagon to the hospital. I must get to him. He has a stress-induced heart condition. All I can think about is his brother, who died from being tased at the hands of the police. He must receive proper medical care. With no probable cause or criminal evidence to detain, they took him to jail for resisting arrest and his son would be buried in a couple of hours.

It's 6:00 a.m. I stood at the jail, numb. There beyond the brick walls and barbed wire, they took him. Pleading with the magistrate--I said, "his son's funeral is in three hours." I paced the floor. I can see him beyond the glass in the distance. They were finally releasing him. He came through the doors with tears streaming, wounded, dirty, bleeding, scars--there were no words. Embracing him tightly, I could feel his sorrow. His son, my grandson, would be buried in two hours. At those most vulnerable time in his life, he suffered police abuse. Experience has been one tragedy after another, and it never seems to end. I am tired of carrying this cross. I am dying.

TIRED OF CARRYING THE CROSS

Therapist: What is your feeling at the moment?

Me: I am feeling intense fear; intrusive memories and nightmares; difficulty sleeping; impaired concentration and living experiences to repeat. I feel afraid of sirens, ringing phones, blue lights, gunshots. Here in the house, it feels safe. I don't want to live with this fear anymore.

Therapist: Have you tried to harm yourself?

Me: On occasion.

Therapist: Do you desire to harm others?

Me: Well, let us pray.

Therapist: Tell me about your childhood. Me: the memories I have are of my mother. There in the hospital, I resembled a fetus in utero. My hands were the size of her fingernail and my feet the size of a penny's diameter, weighing 2.6 oz. born with anomalies--prematurity is complicated. There were few pictures of me around before the age of four in the album. However, I came across a picture of me. I stood wearing the same blue corduroy dress with a white-collar shirt, the same day he touched me in the way my parents never touched me. His eyes were like a bullfrog. I was whining. I stood to the floor and stared back at him and walked to the top of the stairs, looking for her--when would my mommy be home. There in the dimly-lit hallway, I stood, taking refuge behind the old-fashioned washer with the washboard. Snapping away from that moment in time I rejoined

I am the eldest girl of six--four girls and two boys. My father owned a masonry company. My mother was a homemaker for many years until all the children were in school. My father was intentional about ensuring that his children would have the best. Growing up the son of sharecroppers, he led a difficult life. A life he fled for growth in the north to get away from the Jim Crow south. He was authoritative in his parenting style. My mom, on the other hand, was the epitome of grace. She is an only child. We were often referred to as the Hines 6 as my dad loved music. We were a musical family graced with a home full of books to learn "How To." Education was important to my dad. He was protective of his family. However, his protection didn't stop the neighbor from harming me.

THE CANDYMAN

There, six houses away, a family lived — the owners of the candy store. The mother was a school teacher, and the husband ran the corner store. I did not see the son very much as he was always with his mother.

Every day, I sat there on the steps observing my neighbors. The only place I could go was the candy store. Boy, I love candy and every time grandma sends me, I could get candy. Grandma stood on the landing as I went to the candy store to make sure I made it, but she didn't see what happened in the candy store.

He came from behind the closed door when he heard the sound. I rush to the counter. I did not see my favorite candy--tootsie rolls. Where are the tootsie rolls? We just got a shipment of new things today. He summons me with his finger through the open door. He snatched me behind that door and shoved it closed. The candy man was about 350-400 pounds. He held me tight as he pressed his fat, nasty lips against me and groped my private parts snatching my shirts and probing my pants. I was scared and could not escape the heaviness of this big man. I wiggled, kicked, flung my arm to loosen his grip, but he was too big to fight. Suddenly, I heard the store bell ring. His grip loosened. He threatened to kill my mother if I told anyone. He dropped me. I ran beyond the door, the counter and out the door again. I ran and ran and ran. I was frightened. My heart was beating fast. Straight to my room, I ran. Many thoughts were running through my head, but I couldn't tell anyone. He promised to kill my mommy.

Afraid, I didn't want to leave the house. The isolation continues, and no one notices the change in my behavior. I suffered in silence.

Therapist: What about your Relationships?

I LIVED TO WALK AWAY

Me: I am an introvert. I enjoy being alone in my space-I think better. My present relationships centered around my work. I typically wait for others to ask my opinion unless I see the harm. There is something about an injury that triggers my mental status to fight and keep others safe. I wish there were someone there to fight for me.

Looking upon the white-bricked wall, I could see all the accolades and there in plain sight, a trophy that triggered me.

There I stand in front of a streetcar trolley. I make it on the trolley with my back pressed against the door. It's going to be a long ride home. The trolley is full. There at the rear of the trolley, he stood tall with his arms stretched from bar to bar his eyes were locked and the meaning of relationships changed forever. Isolation, possessiveness, stalking, beatings are my new norm. Only 22-years old with little experience in the dating department, I endured for four years. I did not date until I was an adult. One moment I would look up at a school fundraiser to see him standing in the window; or outside of a formal work affair to see him standing there in a white shirt and jeans; or the time I left the movie theatre and had to run back in, because he was outside in the dark waiting for me. I was scared to death. He was dangerous.

The room is dark, cold, and only illuminated by the light from the television. I can smell him. He is near. Who will he confront and accuse today, or will he just beat me? Six-foot-six and bulging eyes he entered the room, shirt wide open, sweating from the heat of the day. He does not have a lot to say, and his expressions suggest that he has not had a good day. I can feel his tension. I say less, listen and watch more. I have come to expect the worse even if he seems happy. He paces back and forth, removing one article of clothing at a time. Soon, the door swings behind him, and in minutes he returns.

Where have you been today? He asked (oh, lord--here we go) "School," I replied.

That is the question he always asks before the accusations begin to fly. What time did you get here? "Right after school," I replied. Mom said you didn't get here until 3:00. "What took you so long? I came here directly. He turns to me with a smirk on his face. I could read that face. My heart begins to beat fast as I braced myself for what would come next. I took a deep breath. Curled up and buried my head to prepare for the blow. Surely, he is going to hit me. At 22, I am trapped in this place with a man who beats me. This room, this house, this dark place, a place he calls home has become a place of entrapment. The friends I use to have, and the places I use to go are a thing of the past.

Therapist: Are you o.k.?

Me: Yes.

Therapist: Are you ok to continue.

Me: Yes. There I am, 22 years old at the Bellevue Stratford with my coworkers from the World Affairs Council to celebrate our guest, the Honorable Anwar Sadat. I stood, in the most elegant evening gown dancing the night away in a place I would have never dreamed. I invited him as my guest. For me, this was work detail. He said, no, you go. I always asked him even if he wasn't still the best company. As I was leaving, I saw him there in the foyer. I was scared to death. Why are you here? I said. Just checking up on you. It was the strangest feeling

Therapist: So, he followed you?

Me: I am not sure. It seemed more like stalking. Once I was having a fundraiser at school--it was a danceathon-a 24-hour danceathon.

I always share where I was going because I never thought anything of it. There beyond a 16-pane window of my school dancehall, he stood in a white t-shirt. I thought I saw a ghost. It was him-- stalking me. I was terrified and afraid to go anywhere outside those walls. I turned and looked to my best friend for help. In my head, I'm screaming, but my lips could not move. I did not want him to hear me. I swallow, and there is a knot in my throat. Anxious. How could I love someone who would hurt me this way? I start to pray. GOD, please let me make it out of here. He sits next to me on the bed, and the rest of my peace leaves the room. There is no escaping him. I am trapped in the corner of this room. I want to go home. I didn't dare to tell my parents that he has been hitting me.

He leans back with his arms above his head, "What's up?", He says. Scared to death, I replied nothing much. I need to get home "Can you take me to check on my mom?" I knew if I invited him, he would be less resistant to my leaving. "Why do you have to leave"? "I've been here for five days. I have to check-in on my mom. I promise I will come right back. "I'll take you home," he said. He quickly changes as I wait.

Maybe I make it out of this room without his insecurities rising to strike me? How many ways can I tell him, that he was the only one? He is so possessive and jealous. I could not go anywhere or do anything without him. As we made our way down the staircase, I prayed that we make it out the door. Suddenly, he kicks me down the stairs. Tumbling, I get to the bottom of the stairs crying, Why? He stands there towering over me. I curl up in a ball to protect myself in case he strikes again because I am pregnant and he doesn't know.

He steps over me and now with beaded sweat and a look that could kill he stood there 6'6. Petrified, I rose slowly to recover. As I timidly moved to the final level of the stairs, I grabbed my coat. Where are you going? I stood still in my tracks. The intimidation was working. The door opens, and I sigh silently. If I could make it out of the house, I would be o.k. He would never hit me in public for fear of what people would say or do. I tried to move around him, and he stepped in the way. With both hands, he crashed into my temples, and all I could see were stars. Terrified, I begin crying. He pulls me close and apologizes repeatedly. I don't know what came over me, he says, and so, I go along with everything because for the first time I felt like I would not make it out of the home alive. Now what felt like seconds, was more like hours later, he finally agrees to take me home.

On our way home, suddenly he makes a quick detour. I start to sweat realizing, this is not the way to my house. He looks at me, and I look at him--he smirks. He turns into a driveway. Oh my GOD, where is he taking me down this alley? I start rubbing my hands together as my palms begin to sweat. I didn't want him to see me sweat or seem unbothered by his detour. He always looked for my reactions to his actions. I learned to be resilient despite his actions.

There in the driveway was one of his colleagues from work. "Why are we here?", I asked. He said, "you wait right here. I will be right back." I was clueless.

The two of them were talking. I couldn't make out the conversation. I could tell from their body language that something was wrong. He seemed, angry. He was yelling and pointing his finger in rage at this man in the driveway. Nervous, I just watched in hopes that a fight would not break out. He comes over to the car and my surprise he begins to accuse me of having an affair with this stranger in the driveway. My eyes were as big as golf balls. There in the middle of nowhere, I panicked. If he strikes again, I cannot get help.

Shaking my head frantically. What are you saying? I know you two have something going and if I find out, I'm going to KILL him. I exhaled and looked straight ahead. He took me home that night and picked me up shortly after that. He never left me alone too long.

There in the room sat his 75-year old mother on the side of her bed in a room surrounded by clutter. She smoked one cigarette after the other as she peered into the television and coughed hard. She was a kind, old lady. Do you have a moment? She invited me in, and I sat down on the side of the bed. It was hard to breathe. I asked her, "Why does he behave this way?" She said, his father was the same way. I couldn't go to work and come home without him smelling my clothing to see if I were with another man. She stared into the television. I left the room. He was doing what he saw his father do to his mother. I know he brings me here, so he doesn't have to worry about where I am. My heart was pounding in fear. I needed space. I needed to be free. He wouldn't be back for hours. I decided on a movie. I'll be back, I said to his mother. The movie was great! However, there he was in the parking lot. I thought to myself, "How did he find me?". I stepped back in the building for my protection. I went to the service desk and called for the police. This is where the rubber meets the road. I cannot live like this. They arrived. I told them I was afraid. He attempted to explain that he meant no harm. I shook my head. Officer, can you take me home? In the car, he recommended a restraining order. I just wanted to go home.

With my head hanging low trying to figure out what I had ever done to deserve this. I hear a little whisper, "love doesn't hurt," I look down at the ring on my finger, slide it off, throw it to the ground and walk away from it all. I can never forget the physical, mental, and emotional pain of him. I had to decide. It was the most difficult decision I have ever had to make. I aborted my ties with him forever.

Therapist: A baby? Me: Yes. I close my eyes at the therapist' cue.

Therapist: You mentioned the panic attacks. Themes are emerging from your conversation that is equivalent to my diagnosis of post-traumatic stress disorder.

Me: I thought that was something soldiers suffered?

Therapist: No. That has been a misperception by many. PTSD develops from disasters, accidents, life-threatening illness, physical abuse, and sexual assault. PTSD can be experienced directly or indirectly. Trauma threatens a person's sense of self, world, and future, causing substantial emotional distress.

Me: Wow! I have taken more losses than I have achieved wins.

Therapist: Let's stop here, we'll see you next week. (To be continued)

A MESSAGE OF HOPE

The vivid description of traumatic events in my life shared in therapy are intended to connect with you, the reader, who might be going through something right now. No matter what you endure in life, there is a purpose in your life over death.

PTSD is a mental illness often perceived as an illness suffered by soldiers. Mental health illness affects millions of people, and only half will receive treatment according to NAMI (2018). PTSD develops from disasters, accidents, life-threatening illness, physical abuse, and sexual assault. PTSD can be experienced directly or indirectly. Trauma threatens a person's sense of self, world, and future, causing substantial emotional distress (NIH, 2005). Untreated, PTSD can lead to suicide.

According to the World Health Organization (2018), there are more than 100,000 deaths every 40 seconds equal to 16 per 1000 people in a population of more than 7 billion. It is the third leading cause of death among those age 15-44 and even higher among elderly males. It is predicted that by 2020 the rate of death by suicide will increase to one every 20 seconds.

Ten% of women to 5% of men develop PTSD due to sexual assault and child sexual abuse. These are not the only events that influence PTSD. Life-threatening events also cause PTSD. How do you define life-threatening events? The thresholds are different for everyone. Another mental health issue can also influence PTSD; a family cycle of mental health problems; a lack of support from family and friends; grief and stressful life changes.

We live in a world where physical, emotional, and psychological abuse are the norm. We have the POWER to change was, into what it should be. Life is fight or flight. I had to choose to live. As the gatekeeper of my home, I hurt when they hurt. Therapy was a bonus to help me address the trauma that influences the level of emotion I feel when others hurt. Week after week I continue active therapy Most will not suffer for a prolonged period if treatment is sought and plans for wellness are developed. The medication allowed me to lose the emotional connection to every problem in the world. There were even some days I could not speak. Therapy helps me to find my voice. Alongside therapy, I have learned to tell my story. Nothing in my life shall be wasted.

I am responsible for more happiness, and I can choose not to feel the pain. I prefer to LOVE. Love is not loving until you give it away. Like the mythical creature, I once settled for the tragedies of life and my life was reduced to ashes. GOD said he would give me beauty for those ashes--being open to receive the assignment that GOD has over my life the Phoenix rose in me. No matter what you are going through today, stop internalizing the pain and pivot for a solution one baby step at a time. People may publicly maim you--they will be exposed. It's in your valley experience where your weakness will be made strong. The credential could never sufficiently prepare me for the journey. I had to tear the veil, layer by layer-one tragedy after another.

A special thank you to Dr. Princess Fumi Hancock, Fearless Visionary leader. Many people have been removed from my life, and that is okay. I continue to recognize my triggers, and when I do, I find peace in community with other fearless visionary leaders who chose to tear their veil. These are our stories. We speak truth to power on a mission to help you tear your veil. Join us on the journey. Today, my life feels like that of the long-lived bird that was regenerated and reborn to obtain new life by arising from the ashes of my predecessors. In the rising, I have found clarity for a purpose-driven life. In the rebirth, GOD ordained Fearless Visionaries as a catalyst to my fulfillment. Join today! (fearlessvisionaries.com)

I am a conscious doctorate prepared Consultant and Master Facilitator. My life's work centers on deep and intentional organizing, and program development that removes barriers and improves the culture of access to sustainable programming for individuals, communities, and organizations to thrive. I began my career in corporate partnership at the Wharton School of Business and continue to use lessons learned today to build strong collaborative initiatives. My career, is strengthened by life as a wife, and mother of four who persevered through a life of poverty and years of social, racial, and economic inequities to own my authority and help others to do the same. My story is influenced by service in academia, corporate, and healthcare where I sharpened the tools I owned and used to build the dreams of corporate America. These meaningful skills coupled with my love for humanity and community propelled me to walk tall in my truth to achieve maximal results in today's climate and push back on the inequities that affect so many. I strategically help individuals, organizations, and communities with the development of culturally responsive programming. When we teach others to organize collectively with the peripheral lens of developing programs that are niche specific, we build strong infrastructures. Strong program infrastructures influence great performance outcomes. I improve the culture of access to innovative programs and measures for collective wins.

CHAPTER 7

I ABORTED AN UNFAITHFUL MARRIAGE.
I'm Not A Quitter – I Just Choose To Rescue Me
by
Ramona E. Jones

Double doors swish open as I follow the male orderly pushing my husband's hospital bed from recovery along the long serpentine halls to the room that he will call home for at least the next several days. The heart monitor is silent now after monitoring his emergency surgery to open his airways ... after an allergic reaction to a new medication that nearly closed off his throat and had swollen his hands like the Pillsbury Dough Boy or the Michelin Tire Man.

Instead of beeps, the cord of the heart monitor knocks a rhythm to match the jerky clicking of the wheels lurching forward to take turns through a maze of hallways. The clear IV bag and tubing sway and bang against the pole making their own rhythm as the bed rolls pass the skeleton crew of two people at the nurses station. One lady wearing a heart-filled scrub top sits behind the desk whispering on the phone that she holds in the crook of her neck while staring at her monitor. A male doctor stands slightly bent forward at the high counter writing notes as his stethoscope dangles midair from around his neck.

Hand sanitizer, soaps, perfume, and some weird sterile scent all mingle with different evening meal aromas wafting out of each hospital room we pass. The recessed fluorescent lights seem dim and barely reflect off the gleaming white tiled floor, separated from the white walls by beige baseboards. A chair in front of a large picture window overlooking the hospital grounds and the highway in the distance marks the end of the hall, and finally the orderly guides the bed into the last room. I look around the room. It's only big enough for one bed to fit comfortably. Overhead cabinets line a section of the wall on the right with a countertop and drawers beneath and a long narrow closet on the right. A male nurse in navy scrubs walks in and introduces himself. After making sure that I'm the wife of the patient, he hands me a clear bag containing my husband's clothes, wallet, shoes and cell phone.

"You can keep his clothes in that closet," he points, "but I suggest you take his personal items home." He then turns and introduces himself to my husband while helping the orderly adjust the bed and connect the equipment. I pull the drawstring and reach inside the bag beneath his jeans and tennis shoes to extract and secure his wallet and phone in my oversized Coach purse. Walking over to the closet to put his clothes away, I hear him call my name in a hoarse voice. I hang the bag from a hook, close the closet door and walk over to his bed.

"Where's my phone," he asks?

"In my purse," I respond.

"I need to call my job to let them know what happened."

I pull the phone out of my purse and hand it to him. He fumbles with it and finally gets it unlocked, but can't dial well or speak too clearly. So, I finish the call and let his boss know that he's in the hospital and will probably be there for a day or two. The nurse and orderly are now gone, and it's just the two of us.

"Call my children and tell them that I'm sorry," he stresses a little choked up.

"I can call them, but they need to hear the apology from you," I respond. So, I call his daughter and son and hold the phone to let him speak with them. A tear rolls down his face. I fill in the gap where he struggles and let them know that I will keep them updated.

NO APOLOGY FOR THE WIFE HE MADE INVISIBLE

I stand patiently waiting for my apology, but he is done. He puts his head back on the pillow and closes his eyes. I give him a few minutes, then ask, "What about me?"

He opens his eyes and looks right through me as if I'm not there. "Since you're passing out apologies, don't I deserve one as well?" I feel the waves of anger mix with disappointment and swell. My vision goes a little blurry as tears try to pool. I squeeze his cellphone in my right hand and command my composure. "You've got me calling your children, so you can apologize," I continue with an unsteady voice. "That's great and noble, but I'm standing right here at your call—left my job to be here to see about you, and you don't feel like you owe me an apology for all that you've put me through?" I stare at him for several minutes that seem like an eternity, waiting for a response, an acknowledgment, a validation, but his eyes are empty, face expressionless, and he is silent. He finally turns away and asks, "What did they do with my stuff?"

It is as if I do not exist. "So, I guess I don't get an answer. Well, your answer is that your clothes are over there in the closet, and I have your wallet in my purse."

"Yeah, you can take that home." He says, as a matter of fact, dismissing me and my needs.

My right-hand twitches. I hold it tighter to my side to keep from punching him dead in his swollen face with his cell phone. I push down the rising, sad reality that I will never get a faithful, loving, and caring husband out of this man. It seems that nothing I have done or given over all these years to heal this toxic relationship matters. I stand in limbo, hit by the fact that as far as he is concerned, my tasks are done for the moment; he has no further use for me until he needs something else. I'm lost and don't know my place, or if I even have a place left in his heart and mind; I wonder if I ever really did. I feel myself going missing with the marriage. A million thoughts race, collide, raise evidence and give an argument. So many conversations waiting to be had, unmet needs, and questions to be answered for my mind to conclude a solution. My stomach tightens as a flash of heat covers me, and my breathing becomes shallower. I look to the one person who should have my back, that I should be able to turn to with my problems and know that he is not available and has never been. I hate him for stealing my dream of wifehood and a happy home and for trampling it under his feet. Although crushed, I am not ready to let my dream die. I keep looking for someplace in him where I am valued and treasured without understanding why it matters so much to me.

Before I could sort out these fixating thoughts and feelings to form questions to interrogate the man who poses a threat to my wellbeing and dream of one day reaping a happy, un-adulterous marriage, we are no longer alone. The doctor, the male nurse from earlier and another female nurse, announce themselves. They are here to do a final check on him and give a prognosis and next steps. I put on my dutiful wife smile and ask all the right concerning questions.

I ABORTED AN UNFAITHFUL MARRIAGE.

THE INVISIBLE WIFE SAVES THE DAY

As the doctor shines a light into his eyes, his arms suddenly flail, and he points to me and shouts, "Save John instead of me. I've got to go back for my men. I can't leave them behind."

He is agitated and trying to get out of bed, but the swelling makes it hard to move. The heart monitor is beeping like crazy. The doctor quickly stumbles back from his bed, bumping into the assisting nurses, knocking them back to the right of the bed against the counter where they all lineup. For a moment, we are in shock and silence against beeping and outbursts, not knowing what to make of the situation. I look to the medical staff, expecting them to do something, but they stand back useless—looking from him to me, and at each other with distress and bewilderment etched on their faces. The female nurse, eyes wide, holds her right hand over her mouth. The male nurse stands with his mouth gaped. The doctor stands statuesque. I alone stand at the foot of his bed, the closes to him.

More agitated and looking around the room in frustration, because no one is responding, he directs his attention to me. Shaking his index finger at me, he says, "Haji, Haji, get me out of here. I've got to go save my men.

His eyes are open and wild, but he is not in the hospital room with us. I realize that he is living a flashback rather than having one of his rare nightmares. I sense this situation requires more than a nudge to wake him. As usual, I assume the role of fixer and jump in to save him from himself despite my feelings of rejection, abandonment, anger, dejection, and heartache from his lack of apology to me or recognition that he has deeply wounded me. I step closer to the bed and enter the medic tent of his forward operating base (FOB) in Iraq. It is night and bombs are exploding in the distance. The sounds of sirens and Blackhawk choppers dropping off wounded soldiers drown out the beeping of the heart monitor. The walls of the tent billow in and out, and the heat makes me sweat. "All your men are safe," I reassure him.

"Haji, save John and not me. I should die, not him. I can't leave my men. I've got to go back. Haji, let me go."

"John is safe," I reassure again, but it isn't working. He gets belligerent and pulls rank on me.

"You don't tell me. I tell you, Haji. I run this base," he barks.

I stand up straighter and counter as a Captain. I bark back in my best drill sergeant voice, "Stand down Sergeant. I'm not Haji. This is Captain Jones. I outrank you. You will stand down."

He stares at me through narrowed eyes sizing me up. I stare back without blinking. The wildness in his eyes slowly turns into a calmer blank stare, but he is still not with us. I praise him. "The base is secure, and all your men are safe thanks to you. Well done soldier. Now let the doctor help you," I continue.

He finally lays back releasing a long sigh.

I turn to the doctor who is instructing one of the nurses to give him a sedative and say, "He's a veteran, and I think the light in his eyes triggered a flashback. I've never seen him like this before."

"Really," she looks puzzled. "You handled that quite well. We are glad you were here, because we didn't know what was going on or what to do. Thank you for that."

She looks to the female nurse, "Note that in his chart," she instructs.

Turning back to me, she says, "We are giving him something to help him sleep. Hopefully, he won't have another episode. You can stay in the room if you like or wait outside the door," she finishes.

I step back out of the way, and for a moment watch the empty eyes of this stranger of a man propped up in a bed nearly too short for his reclining frame. The medical team fusses in the background with beeping equipment, administer a sedative into his IV, and go about finishing their checks. I try to peer deeper into these same empty eyes that made me as invisible as the silence that met my request for an apology. Such a great soldier with such kindred care for his men. A man with a near-death experience able to finally give an apology to his grown children, so wonderful. Yet, I see nothing for me, my time, my life of honor that supported both of those roles, including his education and careers. I wonder, "Where is my place in your life beyond using me?" As the sedative begins to take its effect, his eyes close on whatever world he is in now. Feeling tired myself and dejected, I turn and leave the room.

DANGLING SIDE CHICKS AND SERIAL INFIDELITY, OH MY!

I glance down when the phone vibrates in my hand. I remember I'm holding his 11th appendage when a text message flashes on the screen from a lady whose name I recognize as one of his co-workers. I switch the phone to my left hand and read.

"Still thinking about last night. Can't wait to see you when you get off tonight. The kids are with Dee, so we don't have sneak in the car. LOL. Feeling like a school girl," It reads.

Mouth half open. Eyes narrow. I stand, staring at the blaring words and tap them as they begin to fade. He is always silent, but his phone is full of cheaters chatter on this cold October night. With no barrier between the answers to my questions and suspicions, I can't resist the deep need to scroll up. I glance over my shoulder into the room; he is laying back with his eyes closed. The doctor and nurses are still working; I have a few minutes. I quickly step to the left out of view with my back to the window. With nervous hands and bated breath, I touch the screen again to enter deeper into the world where I've only been through my tormented imagination. This time it is real. Although I do not want to go back to that tiring place of depressing thoughts about his cheating, much less the reality of the details now before me, I must know why I am not worthy, why I am not enough, why I am invisible.

I scan the mounting evidence—that afternoon, that morning, last night, the day before. The threading conversation slits my heart in all the glued together places. I hiss through the grit of my teeth, "You lying sack of sh…!"

I purse my lips even tighter and feel my nostrils flare as I push down against the rising heat of tumultuous thoughts. Without blinking, I shift into investigation mode—cross-referencing dates and times against our missing date nights, late work nights, extra shifts, gifts, and new phrases that he would utter and then give a dumb look in response to my question, "where did that come from?"

Intuition becomes a reality, and my brain goes into overdrive rapidly flashing every lie and past impropriety against the details now revealing themselves. Each scroll steals more of my time, mutes my voice, and diverts my husband's affection to another woman. In intimate "textsations" at 1:00 a.m., he is horney thinking about her lips. He coaxes her to let him come by for a little kiss. He leaves me alone and unfulfilled in our bed to prowl and rouse forbidden passion somewhere in the dark city. Rage swells up from the deep running river of anger and too many disappointments. The waves threaten the beautiful white walls I so carefully erect. I lean against the cold white hospital wall and tell myself to breathe. It's too late. I'm in all the hurt places at once. The pounding of my heart echoes the urgency of every bleeping instrument in the hospital. My thoughts intersect with the muffled voices from inside the room and several feet down the hall at the nurses' station. My goodness goes out of me on the clicking of visitors' heels leaving hard tiles for the evening. All is black and silent in the tunnel of quiet rage. My body can no longer support the mounting weight of his lies.

My legs begin to buckle beneath me. I'm hot and faint with everything spinning. Gripping the phone, I stumble back towards the chair sitting a few steps away. The legs screech an inch to a halt against the wall beneath the window. The years of serial infidelity and emotional abuse reaches its toll on my hope. I am no longer the patient wife. I want him to suffer and die! Then, the phone vibrates again. Another woman wants to see him. She's apologetic for last week and wants to try again. I shake my head in disbelief. I peer more in-depth into the dark abyss of his serial adultery and ask, "Who is this man?"

FLIGHT, FIGHT, SURRENDER TO GOOD, OR SUCCUMB TO THE DARKNESS

The sham of my marriage is unhinged in this moment of truth. The funny thing is, I'm still looking for me—my place as wife, a last shred of some decency that honors the more than 24 years of my life devoted to him that I can never get back, the 19 years of raising his son and healing from that, and all the hurts between and after. No. I must hold on and fight for my place. Sit on the nest as my aunt would say.

I pray, "God help me to do the right thing. Help me to see the real enemy and wage the right warfare. Let the prince of this world come but find no evil in me. Keep my feet from faltering and give me the courage to stand. God, lift me up to where I belong and give me peace."

I vacillate between being numb and doing nothing, to fighting for my marriage, to vivid thoughts of his death and funeral. He came close; I wish I were walking away a widow tonight. I like the sound of widow more than the shame and defeat attached to divorcée. How beautiful it would be to tell the world, "My husband is dead." No messy divorce. No fight over property. Just move on from here. Death is a period at the end of a relationship with no questions asked because the covenant is not broken. But with divorce, there is always the question of what happened in the relationship—who failed who—that people want to know. Even if they don't ask, you can see the inquiry in their eyes and read it in their half smile. Besides, there is no love or hatred in the grave—just cold nothingness. But two divorced, living bodies can collide in the physical world, wonder what the other is up to, or see progress or regress in the severed mate. Divorce seems too hard to handle—too much to untangle—Too much entrusted and invested, to give up.

I jump up from the chair to shake off the melancholy and start my fight by speaking out loud. I forcefully say the opposite of my destructive thoughts under my breath, "No, devil you are a liar. I speak life and not death over him and our marriage."

"God, let him live to be a faithful husband and a better father."

I look back and catch my reflection in the window—a dutiful wife, now a woman more scorned by a man who cares only for himself. I stand ghostly against the city's nightscape and watch the lights of passing cars, changing stoplights, illuminated houses and businesses all pushing back against the darkness. I too look for a light to push back this growing darkness that seeps into my soul to squeeze out my last drop of hope. I need more time to search for his secrets. More time to find me in his conversations.

"He's resting now, and the swelling is going down but may take a day or so to return to normal," the doctor says.

I turn wearing my concerned wife's face and nod at her.

"There doesn't seem to be any swelling to the brain, and his throat is open enough for him to breath on his own. We will keep monitoring him. No lights, of course," she concludes with a nervous laugh.

They all laugh and shake their heads in agreement.

"Yeah, I know right?" I join the laughter. "Thank you all."

"Thank you," they say in unison with a knowing look as they turn and head down the hall towards the nurses station.

I watch them until they turn and are out of sight. I sigh, dreading what's next. He calls my name in a weak voice that grates against my soul. The wife in me wants to hurry to his side, while the woman scorned wants him dead, and the detective wants to go home to finish the investigation. I slip the phone into the side pocket of my brown and beige Coach purse and decide that I will probably be up all night. It's a good thing it's Friday. I drag my feet forward and stand in the doorway before moving a few steps into the room.

"Do you have my stuff?" he slurs.

"Yes," I reply.

"Where's my phone? I need it," he slobbers and tries to keep his eyes open.

I feel sorry for him and angry with him all at the same time. "I have it; I'll bring it back when I come tomorrow," I firmly state. "Besides, your hands are so swollen, you can barely hold it, and you are in no shape to be talking. Good night." I abruptly turn and walk out of the room followed by his reluctant agreement.

THE EXHAUSTING BATTLE OF TROUBLED THOUGHTS
AND THE DISCIPLINE OF SELF CONTROL

The wide heels of my brown leather ankle boots click briskly against the hard, white tiles. I pass the nurses station and see that it's 9:00 p.m. I catch the eyes of the male nurse as I look down from the clock on the wall behind him; I nod. He seems a little concerned, nods, and looks back down at the computer screen. Slowing my gate, I walk more upon my toes to quiet my hurried exit through the empty meandering halls until I reach the elevator. A little annoyed, I push the down button several times. I can barely wait to get home. The elevator seems to take forever. The doors finally open on the 9th floor. I step on and nod at the three other late visitors. I reach and press the button for the Lobby again as if the elevator will move any faster. I'm the first one out and nearly run past the gift shop before I remember that I need to pay for parking. I turn and head to the ticket machines on the wall, fishing in my purse for my parking ticket. I put the ticket in the machine, and it reads $12. Now, I'm even more annoyed to have to pay so much for parking on top of wasting nine hours of my day on someone who does not deserve me. I feed a $10 bill into the machine, but it refuses to take the last of my two single dollar bills or give me back the money that I put in so I can try the $20. I look around for assistance, but it's a ghost town. I dig in the bottom of my purse and pull out a handful of change. My lotion and Chapstick fall to the floor with some scattered coins. "GRRRR!" At least, I have four quarters in the mess. I take a deep breath and gather myself as I gather my things. Finally, with a paid ticket in hand, I quickly make my way across the overhead tunnel to the escalator leading to the garage. My journey is not over. My car is all the way in the back of the garage. I look around me. A few men are walking in the garage, but no security. I nod and walk fast and purposely until I'm safely inside my car. My heart pounds with anticipation as I drive out of the garage and along the half-empty streets. My stomach growls, and I realize I have not eaten. I left work before lunch when I got the call from the emergency room. I recall all the times I drop what I'm doing to make time for him, and I feel foolish and cheated. Another wave of anger sweeps over me at the thought of him giving his time to other women in all the ways that I longed for, and that rightfully belonged to me exclusively. I angrily shut off the radio's added noise. Nothing is making sense. There are too many different thoughts flying into my mind space unregulated, unwelcomed and overwhelming. I want silence for now during this short drive—a break from the noisiness of racing thoughts ruminating and playing back the last several hours with interjected snippets of all the bad experiences from the last 20 plus years and speculations that fill in the missing gaps where details are lacking. These silent, colliding scenes in my vivid imagination become deafening and tiring, contending for access to my tongue to be released into the atmosphere—given life outside my thoughts. A few of these negative thoughts escape, and I hear myself repeat, "He played me like a fiddle after all I've done for him. I've been good to him, and he's going to do me like this. I've got him." I realize that negative thoughts are hijacking my tongue, and I switch my thinking to focusing on the road. I count the stop lights and think about driving until I pull into my driveway.

The garage door seems to open slower than usual. I pull in and push the remote's button to close the door, shut out the night. I fumble in my purse for my keys and then put my purse strap on my right shoulder, that sags under the weight of his infidelity. My hands shake as I unlock the garage door leading into the house. I drop the keys and stand looking down at them for a moment. I take several deep breaths and remember that I have all night and the morning. I calmly pick up my keys, find the right one and let myself into the house. I move purposefully locking both locks on the basement door and restrain myself from running up the stairs to the first floor. I stop to check the messages on the landline phone—just telemarketers. At the front door, I collect the mail from the floor and open the door to look outside for any packages—nothing. I lock the door and slowly turn to walk upstairs to the second-floor master bedroom. My legs suddenly feel heavy, and the climb seems arduous. I hear my mother's voice fill my thoughts.

BEFORE I BECAME THE INVISIBLE WIFE

"I don't think you should marry him. He's much older than you and has been married before."

I say, "I've known him a year... He's a hard worker, and I think he'll be a good provider. He says he's been hurt before and wants someone he can trust and raise a family with."

"I just think you should wait before jumping into marriage. You've got your whole life ahead of you," she counters.

She tries every way possible to deter me from marrying him, but I had seen the callousness of men and very few examples of good marriages. I am not in love; I don't see stars and rainbows or hear music playing. But I choose to love him, because I think he loves me more. So, I convince myself that I'm playing it safe with him. Even though I see a few warning signs of his moodiness and impatience, he makes me think that he really loves me.

He says, "I love the hell out of you. I want a good woman that I can trust, because I never want to get divorced again."

I feel both sad for him and safe in his words. I know that I can be all that he is asking for in a faithful, good wife, and in turn believe he will be faithful to me forever. I think his declaration of love is enough. I know that my choice to love him can be enough because I am willing to swear to my own hurt without changing my vows.

I feel a deep sadness sweep over me as I lay my purse on my side of the bed. I look at the purse and want to pull his phone and wallet out to search for what went wrong, but I resist. Instead, I take off my jewelry, undress, and hang up my brown plaid pantsuit and burnt-orange turtleneck. I retreat to the comfort of a hot shower. I run the water in the tub before turning on the shower. I brace myself for the initial blast of cold water, much like I brace myself against the coldness of the marriage and what else I will find out about the man I call husband. As the water warms, I close my eyes and stand still under the pelting spray, feeling the sting of the heat neutralize the fire of hell scorching my soul. I try not to think about the other times I've caught him cheating, the time I filed for a divorce and his then six-year-old son begged me not to leave, the time in 2006 when he sent me an email from overseas saying he met someone and wanted a divorce. An email, really. Then wanted to go to counseling when he came home empty-handed and out of a job. The hot water now running cold reminded me of how unwelcomed the thought of him was to me at that moment and how things between us had grown so frigid to the point of numbing prickly pain.

I put on my lotion and perfume, and brush my teeth with rote precision, while my mind fills in the gaps left by the text messages. I am numb and no longer as hungry for food as I am for answers. I look at my bed, and it's too crowded with all these other women between us. The sacredness spoiled and tainted by infidelity. I take my purse, my pillow and the throw blanket from the foot of the bed and head downstairs for the sectional couch.

THE INVISIBLE WIFE, INVESTIGATION AND SIDE CHICK WHOOPEE TOYS

I turn on the TV out of habit but know that I'll need a dose of humor or a good Hallmark romance to get me through the night and the rest of my investigation. I pop some popcorn, get a bottle of water, and settle in for a long silent text movie. He overwhelmingly introduces me to woman after woman who takes my place. With each scroll through multiple messages, I find conversations with different women—my sweet banters of desire, my date nights, my quality time all given to strangers and some familiar names of his co-workers. My temples throb as my mind race to connect more dates and at least six women all the way back for a year. I'm flabbergasted. He's currently seeing three women at the same time. One poor girl pours out her heart. She's finally kicked out her no-good man and wants my man back, only she doesn't know that he's mine. He looks like a knight in shining armor, telling her that she doesn't have to put up with the other dude's mess and that she deserves better. Imagine that. I like his advice. I think I'll use it myself.

I keep reading. I'm speechless at this debauchery. "Who does this?" I exclaim, throwing my hands up. I find it hard to wrap my brain around what I'm seeing unfold.

At his request, she sends several pictures of herself wearing the sexy panties and bra that he bought her. He dangles her on a string of courting lines and well-strung lies. Got her begging to be back with him. She thinks she's getting a good man in exchange for her other one, but my husband, the serial adulterer, is full of self-serving evil.

I was glad that we had not been intimate over the last few months. He always had an excuse for his illness or oldness. Now I see. The thought of those missed moments denied me to save his virility for the others ticks me off even more. I make a mental note to call and schedule a special well-woman visit. I think about all these other women who crowd my bed, especially the one he casts aside for a while who is missing him and making room for him. She doesn't know that the whole while he is seeing two other women besides her. I want to hate her, but I hate him more for the lives he is endangering and the heartache he is causing. Instead, I feel sorry for her. I must call her to give her closure and a heads up. If she takes the warning, good for her. If not, then at least she can pursue the cheater with more knowledge than I had. The old cliché, "If I knew then what I know now," pushes its way into my thoughts. I shake my head and purse my lips. That joker. I rock back and forth judging my decision to call this woman.

A SISTERLY CONVERSATION WITH A SIDE CHICK

What will I say to a side chick? Although she has not hung out with my husband for a month, she has stolen my quality time, worn my gifts, enjoyed my dates and experienced my pleasure at my deficit. I should hate her, but I know she is in the dark. A prey, like me, left mangled by his lies and missing his hands. I decide that we are in the same boat, and she deserves to know the real deal. She sounds desperate in her pleas to see him again. He leads her on with a maybe. But I see what she can't see—the other women who replace her. Replace me. I sense that she too is trying to figure out what she did wrong, why she isn't enough. I wonder if her guy that she puts out is a cheater too, or if he has less detestable flaws than my husband who she is willing to trade him in for. I feel her loneliness and know that sad place of rejection and abandonment. Rationally, I know that she is not the problem. Yet, I still want her out of the picture. I want her out of my bed and out of my man's face along with all the other women on the list. But what good is moving them out of the way when he is the collector? I vacillate between feeling jealous and feeling a sisterhood with the betrayed ones—those who genuinely don't know they are caught in the net of his diabolical workings. I feel a need to give them a level playing field to make an informed decision about their continuing relationship with my husband. I check my heart against the plan to uncover the truth and decided she should know. Without even thinking about what I would say, I click the phone icon in her text, and she answers before I can hang up.

The first words out of my mouth seem so ridiculously juvenile but sincere, "Are you still messing with my husband?" I ask as a matter of fact.

She pauses and answers, "No mam. I haven't talked to him for about a month. I didn't know he was married, or I would never have dealt with him."

She is truthful about the time; I believe her, and I'm glad it turns out to be a dignified conversation. "I'm sure he didn't tell you. Well, he is and has been for over 20 years. The papers are on file for anyone to check out," I say.

"Well, I'm sorry. I really didn't know… and we haven't talked lately," she apologizes.

"Yeah, I know that, but you're trying to get back with him, and I want to let you know don't feel bad about him; you are not the only one he's messing with right now; there are currently two other women at the top of the long list that I need to call. He's not the person you think he is—playing a knight in shining armor when he's lying and cheating himself. If I were you, I would go get checked out and go on with my life. Okay. Have a good night," I end.

"You too," she replies. "Thanks for letting me know." We hang up.

I can't believe that I've just done that. I forgo calling the rest of the women. I pray for them, for myself, and especially for her. She's younger and hurting too. I can hear it in her voice. I'm not angry with her or the other women who don't know what they don't know about him. We are all prey caught in his web of lies. We believe that he is our answer to a better relationship than we've witnessed or experienced. I see me particularly in her—hopeful; hearing all the right words that slowly opens my heart to trust enough to finally let him in, because I believe that he cares enough, and loves enough to enter my close circle. In my quest to look for my place in his heart on this web of side chicks, I make it my mission to free all the other victimized women that I encounter along the way. While I want to take my man back from these other women, I also have compassion for them and want to hurt him for not only hurting me but for all the cumulative hurts. I keep challenging my motives, not wanting anyone to experience any additional pain. I am overwhelmed with jealousy, envy, hatred, disgust, disappointment, anger, helplessness, hopelessness, defeat, fear of starting over and a whole slew of other emotions that I have no words for. However, my greatest passion is to expose the darkness and draw back the curtain for the light to shine through. In doing so, I know this is a delicate operation because everyone is not ready to face the light of truth; not even me. I just want my eyes to be open and to stay open. It can be a painful and blinding experience when the brightness of light shines on the awakening sleeper all at once. All I know is that I cannot go back down to the depths of sadness and wounding from which I've been healing since the first time I found out that he cheated and brought a son into our family. I hear my mother's words, "It's a long, long, long lane with no end and a bad wind that never changes."

YOU CAN'T GET BLOOD OUT OF A TURNIP, SO QUIT WHILE YOU'RE AHEAD

I recall that journey of forgiveness and acceptance of his son as my own as a hard road that he keeps lengthening with every indiscretion ripping huge holes in my trust in him and even in myself. The gap is now a gulf widening with each of his unfolding deceitful deeds. Bombarding negative thoughts dredge up bad, undesirable feelings that I know that I don't want to go back to. I do not want to live in the place of guessing what he's up to when he leaves my presence. I want to find some evidence that weighs against the substantial proof, but I find none. I hear another of my mother's sayings on my own tongue, "The cat is out of the bag," I say out loud. At that moment, I know that the bag of our marriage is too small, too confining, and too ripped to shreds to put his serial infidelity back in, but I seek to try for my vow's sake. There are too many holes in this relationship to ignore the light of truth, or to keep it from shining through; yet, I squint against the light, because I know it means vast change that I am not quite ready for. I want to change on my own terms. This jarring awakening is not from denial, because I have already told him that I do not want what we've had. I want what marriage should be—A partnership of respect, honor, truthfulness, love, and collaboration. This discovery of the diabolical depths of his choices brings our whole relationship—past, present, and future—into question. Each segment of the long road of matrimony floods into my thoughts all at once, bringing their own images, memories, and projections of hurts. Scars from each of these phases seek retribution for labor, life, and love given in the pursuit of the simple things that he so costly gives to these other women at my expense. Freedom from the dysfunction beckons and offers to provide me with asylum—a new place of existence on my own outside of this relationship that has finally taken its toll on my wellbeing. I move from diminishing returns to negative returns, and my energy and self-worth take hard hits. I need a chance to recover me—my identity. Yet, fear of the unknown and my desire to play it safe become wardens to deny my release from this self-imprisonment. But my will to move on unlocks the cell. I know that all I need do is step out. Nevertheless, I keep looking for my place with him inside this prison of unavailable love, disrespect, and dishonor. Why? Because I believe in miracles, turnarounds, and breakthroughs, and I hate losing and giving up. But everywhere I look in my marriage, I am slowly being erased and silenced trying to fix a man and a relationship that every text message and email confirms does not value marriage, honor me as a wife, nor celebrate women in general—we are only prey to his serial sexual addiction. No, I don't blame most of these women who are crowding my bed. He is good looking, and they think they are getting someone special, but he is unavailable love. We bite the hook, thinking that we are the ones fishing to catch a good man, but find our hearts snatched out of the safety of our own waters, dangling midair with our secrets spilling, to be eaten.

I follow their texted lives. Hear them talk about the no-good men they deal with while leaving their children in bed to go make out with him, a married man who dangles several side chicks like sex toys. His words are like an elixir to their relational hurts, but a slow poison that withers unsuspecting hearts. It is all unfolding. The trips he did not want to take me on are romantic getaways for his lovers. I am glad to see that one of these women figures it out.

"No. You just want to have sex," she replies.

"Good for you," I say out loud. I applaud her astuteness.

A few text messages later, he prowls on to the next victim without even giving me a rebound. How far down on his stick am I? That sinking feeling of being replaced makes me want to fight for my place as the wife even more. Everywhere I look, I am either non-existent or "don't matter" in his own words. I am not just cheated on but cheated out of my place as a wife—robbed of honor, respect, appreciation and a whole lot of other things. For some insane reason, I want to fight for my marriage—not for what it is, but for my dream of what it could be with the man that I chose to love. I want to make him want me, pick me again, see me, hear me, and give me what is rightfully mine as his wife. The role of wife that I have toiled to nurture for nearly twenty-four years is never given a chance to grow to full bloom; I am here with the pain of being stuck in the matrimonial bed. I feel too much is invested for someone else just to sashay in and take. I keep putting in the time and energy and demanding a return that I now realize I will never get. As my mother would say, "You can't get blood out of a turnip." So, I might as well cut my losses, but a quitter never wins.

I'M NOT A QUITTER; I JUST CHOOSE TO RESCUE ME

It's hard to walk away from a relationship that I put so much energy into. Like a gambler playing with all her savings, I keep feeling like I may hit the jackpot if I keep the faith and keep pouring life and love into him. I don't want to give up too soon, because, after all these years of working this marriage, I don't know if the change in him is right around the corner, or if I will hit a vein of gold in another five feet of digging. I don't want it to be said that I didn't try. But, when I count the cost to my wellbeing, look at the emotional scars from the difficulties I face, mark the dangers that his infidelity continues to put me in, and weigh the emotional fortitude and grit that it takes to survive, I have overstayed the mission that I willingly fight to recover the man I thought I married. Now, I realize that by not choosing me, I am quitting on myself. Therefore, I proudly declare that I am not a quitter, but a winner in this game of life called "Me."

You know the story—you see a few warning signs. Your family never takes to him. Your mother tells you not to marry him, and a quick prayer down on one knee and up on the other doesn't give you a "yes," but neither does it reveal a "no" other than the one deep in your soul. If you are anything like me, the gentle no in your knower gets silenced by your natural inclination to fix and nurture. You go to work on life, relationships, careers, and problems that people bring to you for your wise wisdom, but sometimes the fixer wears rose-colored glasses that become her shaded eyes in the dark places long after the sun stops shining. Like me, you choose to see the good in every situation and can't imagine the evil of the people who you embrace in your inner circle, much less the man sharing your bed. That's me, standing here between two defining moments in one night that forever changes my life. I must accept the truth about who he really is and embrace the truth that I am playing small and have been since the beginning. He is happy with his lifestyle and wants to keep things as they are—two strangers coexisting. But I am awake now from my dream of what marriage with him could be if he had truly wanted it as much as he declared when he proposed. I can no longer settle for less than I deserve. I see that he has no intentions to change, so, although I hate it, I can't help it. I mourn the loss of the potential and all the time, love, energy and care that I gave. My demands for a return fall on deaf ears, and I see our roads veering further off in different directions. Soon, we will inevitably lose sight of each other completely. After all, to him, I am already invisible.

For six whole months, I fight the intense tormenting thoughts and emotions that come with the knowledge of his blatant, serial infidelity uncovered—rejection, abandonment, anger, rage, murder, violence, low self-esteem, doubt, fear, unbelief, heaviness, grief, jealousy, envy, and self-pity, to name a few. Breaking free from him with my sanity ensues an intense battle of wit, courage, and strength to let go of the damming familiar to move forward into the unknown of the rest of my life. Little do I know that the journey out will take over a year and not end as I had hoped with a testimony of a serial cheater redeemed to the status of a faithful husband who values the sanctity of marriage as a loving, monogamous, mutually beneficial relationship. Throughout the journey through the pending divorce and the actual decree, I find myself living in the upper echelons of mediocrity where my tenacity and goodwill partners with pride, complacency, and fear of failure for my demise. I slip into a silent, neutral stupor—that place just before the death of me as a person that negatively affects every area of my life. But

God favors me, divorce finds me, and life asks me a question that I cannot escape answering, "What will you do with this?"

My answer is, "I will let the truth set me free to heal so that my experience can provide hope and help to free others."

Thanks be unto God who always causes us to triumph in every trouble as a testimony to the world that we can overcome our mistakes, heal from our wounds, and be the difference for someone else to see a way out of distress. I'm now recoloring my life, so vitality is seen in all the dry, withered places. I'm flexing my voice to be heard over the naysayers. I am looking in the right places with the right perspective to recover the woman I was always meant to be. After 26 years of denial, emotional abuse, and sabotage, I am now visibly living my best life forward. I am unerasable and rescued from not only an ex who was never for me, but also from my old self. The former me sat in limbo with a dream of a good marriage, because it was easier to do so until the reality of the matrimonial bud became too painfully small to hold my worth. Now, I'm out the bud and learning to bloom full open without apology.

What I know for sure is that when you sincerely desire to see behind the curtains of your life and are ready to face the dysfunctional marriage that is wasting you, be prepared to rescue the you that went missing after you said, "I do." After doing all that I knew to do from taking classes, going to counseling, compromising where I could within my own conscience, and trying to reason with him to make our marriage right, I can bless him away. The way I see it, we chose different paths, and the relationship finished its course. I put in a lot of time and energy, but in the end, it wasn't wasted, because the real mission of that journey was always about who I am, and who I can be. So, yes, I'm not a quitter, I just choose to rescue me.

Ramona Jones helps organizations develop strategic end user communications and user support training. She is a poet, speaker and bestselling author using creative language and technology to tell stories that inspire, instruct, and inform to transform. She also coaches, mentors and encourages women to bloom in faith and live in hope to provoke their change that leads to freedom.
Other Books By This Author:
The Prelude To Your Breakthrough
From Tongue To Ear, To Heart: So Says The Wise

CHAPTER 8

FROM PAIN TO POWER
by
Chanelle Washington

Here I am in the room with my suit on, formal makeup, and a ponytail, trying to look as polished and sophisticated as I can. I sit at the table with my attorney on my left side, facing the judge. Over to the far-right corner are the jury. And, the prosecutor is also present in the courtroom. One of the jury members rises slowly to give the verdict: 'Guilty for aggravated assault!' — aggravated assault, guilty. (These words are still floating in my head. Constantly) She shared the decision of the jury. And as soon as those words reach my ears and consciousness, I get still. I feel assured that God will help me through anything, any circumstance, no matter the outcome. Because I have already been continuously praying to have a positive experience and to be able to cope with whatever the outcome was going to be. Well, 'guilty' was the word that aches.

My lovely mother behind me is gasping when she hears 'guilty.' My attorney next to me keeps her professional composure, and I, understanding that I still am to be sentenced, sit quietly and keep my composure. Now that the verdict is read, we take a break and wait for the judge to make her sentence. It is only for 30 minutes, but it feels like hours. I, again, keep my trust and my faith in God and know that no matter what the outcome is going to be, I will get through this.

It has been more than 30 minutes, and here they call us in. We return to our seats. The judge has her papers in front of her. She constantly shifts in her chair. Her body is tense and uncertain, unsure of something. Maybe she is going to give her toughest decision this week perhaps this month, and probably in her life.

The prosecutor and my attorney are there to have their final words. The prosecutor said to the judge: "Whatever you do, please, make sure to give her some time. No matter what you do, those are the two things I ask from you that you make sure to give her some time and that she is not a first offender!". The judge, the look of her face, her body language, seem to feel the pressure of the court. Before making a sentence, she sits there for minutes, and minutes, and minutes, being conflicted about what decision to make. And ultimately, she starts by warning me never to see her and courtroom again. She says that I should be on probation for three years meaning that I cannot leave the state of Georgia without permission and must meet with a probation officer regularly, that I should serve community service for a certain number of hours. I look at her face as she says those terms and think that abiding by those terms are going to be tough, but I feel overwhelming gratitude that I am not going to serve one more day of the 17 years that the prosecutor recommended. Although I feel frustrated or disappointed, one thing that I am well aware of is that my nursing career will never be the same, and I don't know what to expect, I walked out those court doors baldly. I am still grateful that I don't have to return to a correctional facility, after spending 11 days waiting to be bailed out of jail.

~~~ *** ~~~

I walk out boldly, yet frustrated thinking about how all this started. So, I walk… I walk down a street downtown in Philadelphia. I am a student at Temple University, in my nursing program. Since this is my last year at college, I walk around. There are various shops, and I am in a certain area in Philadelphia. I come across this African shop. It just looks very eclectic and nice. They have some mosaic glass tiles outside. It's a little step-down, but very inviting.

I decide to walk into the store, in his business. I look at authentic African jewelry, sculptures, and various handcrafted things. While listening to local music, it smells like a frankincense & myrrh incense burning. Senses are stimulated at every turn. I notice a tall, dark, handsome young man working behind the counter. He introduces himself to me and starts explaining different items in the store. I linger in the store, decide on a few things, and prepare to be on my way. Finally, before I go, he asks for my phone number. After a couple of days, he calls me to invite me out for a date. We end up at Penn's Landing to go ice-skating, how different and exciting is that! We go there enjoy each other's company. It was my first-time skating on ice, so after slipping and sliding one too many times, I fell to the ground. OMG, how embarrassing! The worse part was I got light headed and fainted. This happened to me before, so I knew to call out quick for some 'orange juice.' Thank God I got myself together and he escorted me home.

It is my senior year at Temple. While a nursing student, I have my apartment in University City. I loved living independently with plenty of time to focus on my academics. My internship at Children's Hospital of Philadelphia turned out to be a real challenge and so rewarding. This year I had worked there over the summer on the weekends. Everything is great. Life is great. I would not have much trouble finding a date, because I know that there are others who are interested in me. But him … He seemed so different from the rest that I feel like getting attracted to him day by day. Every time we meet, I fancy him more. We meet at diners to have our meals, sometimes just for a cup of coffee. Then he takes me out to wander. He holds my hand in a way that he doesn't want me to leave him. But gently, softly, yet passionately. This should be love, this should be happiness, and I am living my life. I don't worry much, for I am about to graduate and have already started to build my career, as they say, it: from scratch. I earned what I have, and I deserve it.

Nevertheless, life is not flat. After seeing each other very often, we fall apart for a long time. A long enough time to realize that I am pregnant. There is nothing to do other than telling him. So, I go to his apartment. I sit there. His apartment was not as fancy as mine. I am not going to be distracted. Here I go, I tell him that it should be his baby.

I tell him that I am pregnant. I start telling how and when it happened. The more persuasive I try to be, the more positively he reacts to what I say. He listens to me with profound attention, having a smile in his eyes. He hushes me for a moment, and says: 'Babe, you are going to be my wife.' Just that. I didn't know what to think when I was coming here, but now, am I going to be his 'wife'?

A Senegalese guy asks for my hand, not that I judge, but it is a whole different culture. They have their food, their language, his family doesn't even live in the States and believes in the Islamic God. Am I open to an intercultural marriage? Have I thought this well? Have I been dating with this handsome African guy, am I ready for more?

When he says those words, I stand still. I did not expect that, for sure. I have never wanted to have a kid with a guy like him. I know how it is to ask for an acknowledgment from one's father. I know how much it hurts when you do something meaningful for you, and he is not there. I remember well that it has nothing to do with his monetary problems because he was making enough money. Enough for himself, enough for my mother and me. He chose not to provide me anything besides what he was forced to do. I never wanted to have a kid with such a guy who is not going to be in the lives of his children. I guess, having a lot of daddy issues and issues around acceptance and belonging in a family, makes people more sensitive and precautions. And this guy opens his arms and puts them around me, saying: 'You are going to be my wife because you are pregnant, and I cannot let you go anywhere.' What am I going to do? I don't know what to say. But those words comfort me. Is this dream plausible? This all may be true. Maybe, I will be your wife.

Next step is to tell about it to introduce him to my mother. Maybe I can take him to my mom's job since she works at my university. This way I can show him the activities of African Student Union which I am a member. Maybe this way, I can show him how an Afro-centric young girl I am. Here we are in college. He wears a white shirt, and I have a white African wrap on top of my head. He meets with my mother has a friendly chit-chat with her. Where are you from, what do you do for a living, how old are you, and similar questions floating around. I feel a little bit embarrassed but try not to show it. Finally, all three of us will do something more fun. We take some pictures. In one of them, my mom poses right between us, as if she approves the relationship between him and me. I feel like it is the time to reveal the secret. There, I go and tell my mother that her little 21-year-old girl is going to have the cutest baby on earth — no wonder that she gets surprised, yet very excited.

We begin to tell some of my family members. But he has no family here, only a few fellows from his small community. I meet with them from time to time. But, of course, his family remains the biggest mystery for me. He arranges a phone call with them since his parents, brothers, and sisters are all overseas. We talk with them, but it is strange because he must translate everything from French to English for me to understand and the vice- versa. As he explains, I realize that the same kind of questions is now being asked me. How old are you, what do you study, can you cook, and so on? They seem to be excited to have me as part of his life and for our wedding, though. These all had a good influence on our relationship, that is for sure. We start to see each other more often, again. I go to his place, and he comes to mine. Sometimes we eat together with my mother and other times with his close friends. It seems like we are bonding tighter, and everything is more severe than ever. We even find a place to get married.

After some time, we decide to go further and live together. We are going to get married anyway! He moves into my place which should be a reasonable choice since my apartment is bigger and fancier than his. Therefore, mine suits better for a family. However, it is not about apartment, furniture, or kitchen. Living with him is like a challenging life. It feels like I am more responsible than ever. Or, does it? It is possible that I am just playing house. Nonsense! I am a grown-up, I am having a baby, and if this is not real, then what is?

He is there for me all the time, including my graduation in spring. We are moving closer to the wedding. But something extraordinary happens before then. I end up having a miscarriage. None of my friends have any idea what I am going through. Mothers could not understand me, either. Losing a baby, without having the chance to say 'Hi!' to it with loving eyes, without letting him grab my finger… This is something that even my mother has not experienced. I need a recovery, don't want to see anybody. I need to rest from everything. It aches. It aches a lot, and I cannot scream! I don't have the strength to get over it and have got nothing other than my faith in God. Mercy!

~~~ *** ~~~

But I must face my future husband, too. Someone must tell him, yet I am afraid. After all, he accepted to marry me, because I am giving birth, a baby to him. No matter how much you know a person, you cannot tell how they are going to react in such extraordinary cases. This is stressful. What am I going to say?

There, he comes in. I cannot make my lips move, yet he understands everything. He approaches me with a smile of compassion. Despite the sad fact, he tells me that he still wants to move on, that he still loves me and wants to get old with me under one ceiling. What a romance, and a big heart. A true man!

I have not been living a normal life - I had so many changes in a short time. I get pregnant, and he moves into my place, I graduate and bring a miscarriage. Now, I see that him belonging to a different culture do not affect much on our relationship. On the other hand, I find many things that I like about him. He is an alpha male, very protective, very attentive. I don't feel in need of anything when I am with him. He has already made it clear to me that he is going to make a good father. Being raised in a family with many siblings, unlike many, he seems to understand what it takes to be a family guy.

Days pass one by one. I go to the Children's Hospital, for I still have my internship, and he has his job at the store downtown. It's not like I was at the college anymore since we both spend most of our times at work. But after a long tiring day, it is worth to sit together on the couch and have dinner staring at each other. Sometimes not even bothering to talk. Our love makes us communicate through our eyes. I cannot believe what I have been getting through for all this time. And no matter what my loving man stands by me. I don't want anything to be spoiled.

One day, I come home as exhausted as always. I love caring for the children. This is one of the sacred things on earth because children are innocent and sweet. Besides, I was too close to becoming a mother. Just a few could understand what I feel when I see a kid, let alone seeing a sick baby. So, I am in the kitchen, reaching for a glass of water. I hear him come in and say: "Hi, babe! I'm home, where are you?"

And, I am all happy again. — "Stay where you are, I'm coming!" He hugs me; we kiss like still, it is our first kiss.

—"I'm hungry, babe, I haven't eaten since the morning."

It annoys me that he keeps doing it. As if he doesn't need the energy to remain healthy with his busy schedule. He gets up and leaves the house almost before the sunset and comes back after me. He works 6-7 days a week at the store. I know he is frustrated because he is not back in college. He goes to change and start setting the dinner table. He finally joins me.

—"Honey, what took you so long? Are you OK?"

—"Yes, I am. I'm just a bit preoccupied these days. I overthink."

—"Why? Is it us? Is it your job?"

—"No, none of those. I have not been attending my classes for a while. And, I think my dreams of being a successful civil engineer may be slipping away. It is complicated, and we have never really discussed it, Chanelle.'

— "I think, what could be so complicated?" "Sweetheart why don't you just order your transcripts and register for the next semester."

—"Thank you, babe. I knew that you were going to say that. I love you, too. But our love is not enough for this. My situation is more complicated than it seems. You have never had these kinds of problems to worry about, and I don't expect you to understand it right now. But you have to help me out with this. I am in the States on a "Student Visa," meaning that I am not allowed to stay here if I am not enrolled in college. If I am going to stay. I will need a green card. My boss won't sponsor me. Meaning that soon, I will be deported back to Senegal. But if we get married, like we have been planning. We are going to be together for the rest of our lives. Share our lives and have a bunch of kids tumbling all over the place. But it requires a long procedure that we should go through together. There are papers to sign, people to meet, interviews, etc. We don't even have to lie to them, since we are in love with each other; aren't we? And, everything is going to be just like in our dreams afterward. So, what do you say?"

—"Sure, honey, of course."

What? What did I say? What is this immigration thing? What is this procedure that 'we' will go through? This is all new to me. But this is my love, significant other who speaks. I should trust his words. I should trust him in anything for the rest of my life. Yes, I should stand behind what I said.

—"I didn't know that you had such a problem. You should have told me before. What have you been thinking? We will just have to do what we have to do."

~~~ *** ~~~

He is again all these; dedicating, adoring me, protective, attentive, hard working. He provides everything to me. Any money that he earns, he brings it to our house, he pays the bills, shops for groceries, mainly deals with any financial issue. He tells me that he has to provide his family as a part of his West African culture. He takes a lot of pride in providing for everything. That is strange to me because as a matter of fact, he never earned near what I made as an intern. And I will get a huge promotion after becoming a registered nurse. On the other hand, he doesn't have a chance to make a financial leap shortly. Despite the gap in our incomes, I kind of like that he is so obsessive about overseeing monetary problems. I guess, it is not about how much he puts in. No, of course, not. I am not and have never been interested in his pocket. It is his attitude towards me and our situation. I did not see this kind of reaction from any other man, not even from my father, nor my stepfather. I like him when he says such things: "I want you to take care of you." He is sweet and so caring, so I am thinking that I have found my soul mate, and it feels good to be loved.

Although now I am an independent individual, capable of coming through anything, I still need to talk to my mother and grandmother about this immigration process. I do not want to admit to myself, but this issue is big enough. I meet them one day at my mother's house. I find them having been cooking for my fiancé and me. After having small talk, I would like to hear their opinions about the strange offer that he made me. I am not sure if I can describe their reactions. They say nothing other than some warnings. I have not come here to… Anyway, I tend not to listen to them. But they don't have a proper view on the issue, that is why they cannot respond to my decision with a solid, well-based argument. I doubt that they know what they are talking about.

—"OK, pumpkin, I see that you have made your decision. But make sure that you're going to be careful. I don't want you to get hurt in any way. You have made me proud at any stage of your life since I gave birth to you. Promise me, please, that you don't believe everything he says, that you will think twice at every step, and be careful all the time."

—"What's the worst that could happen? If it doesn't work, I will get a divorce. Don't act as if I am a naive young girl. I have been on my own for years. I know what's going on, and I believe that I can handle it. Please, mom, don't worry. You will be proud again. Besides, we were going to get married, anyway."

~~~ *** ~~~

OK, the big day is closer. We are going to unite our lives in a few days now. And, man, I am excited! My emotions were supercharged. It is hard to describe these days with all these preparations, invitations, instructions, etc. The most exciting thing should be the man who is going to marry us is an Imam. Growing up in Philly, I knew that an Imam is the spiritual leader of Muslims. Only he can bless the couples before Allah.

I have a meeting with the Imam in a few minutes. Since I don't know if he is licensed to perform the ceremony in the States, I have some questions for him. I believe that this is him who approaches me wearing a white dress.

—'Hello, this is Chanelle. You must be the Imam.'

—"Yes, I am. I have heard about you, Chanelle. Surely, all good things. I should explain to you about our wedding ceremonials. It doesn't take that much, but there are strict things that you should know."

—"Thank you Sir, but before we begin, I would like to ask you a question. Is there a legal obstacle before us to get married? I don't know if you are aware of my fiancé's immigration status. Are you sure that you can legally marry us?"

—"Yes, yes, yes. I am confident that I have the right credentials to marry you."

~~~ *** ~~~

We have an intimate day ceremony in the park, just as I wanted. He is ready in his suit, which is the most important. I am a little bit nervous, but my mother is with me as always. We have invited only family friends and the close ones. A small, simple summer wedding for a young couple like us... And, of course, a weekend honeymoon in New Jersey.

The Imam asks us sacred questions we also have our own vows. We both say, 'I do.' He says that the groom can take my hand, now. But wait, we have not signed for anything. There has not been anyone recording this event, other than me writing only my invitations. The head of their community says that we are married before God. What does that mean? I ask my 'husband' about it. *And, he tells me that the Imam has no authority in the States. It is so because the governmental bodies do not recognize him and there is no such an organization in Islam such as the Church in Christianity. So, in their community could become an imam, not needing the approval of authorities of the country. And, I find out that it takes only two witnesses to get married in his religion which makes the wedding not necessary at all.*

So, we are married, but only according to his religion. Therefore, we must get married again, this time properly and legally. After one month, in August, we are heading to a small chapel called Yerkes Wedding Salon, just outside Philadelphia. No invitations, no guests, not a single relative. The witness was provided by the wedding salon. ***

I am a registered nurse since September 1999. I have passed my boards, all my exams at once. I have been working as a licensed registered nurse at the Children's Hospital in Philadelphia. I want to stay in the Cardiac Intensive Care Unit, since I was there as an intern. So, I have been working on the surgical trauma floor for children since then. For the first time in my life, I feel good not to worry about money. It was a struggle growing up. Being raised by a single mom gives you pride on one side but can be very stressful on the other. Finally, I am making my nursing money. And, God, this feels right! I am so excited to spend it on something I deserve.

I am happy and should be able to share this with my beloved ones. No! No, no! He doesn't like it. He just doesn't get it that it is okay that I make more money than he does. There is an income gap, which is expected, since I have been waiting for this, studying for many years and worked hard. I deserved it. Now, he comes to me saying that he cannot stand for it and that he should be the superior in the house, that he should earn more not to feel less of a man than he is, that this is not acceptable in his culture, etc. Whenever we start talking about it, he gets frustrated and gives an annoying vibe due to his growing anger inside.

I don't want to deal with ego issues, I work hard, and deserve to rest when I come home. I get one of those Gateway computers I ordered on credit, and it arrived in the mail. I set it up and start playing. As I enjoy my new toy, he comes home and sees the bill on the table. After seeing the sum at the bottom, he goes crazy and acts unreasonably. Eventually, he forbids me to buy anything else for the house. The reason for which is that according to his culture, he is not only responsible for utilities, but anything that gets into the house. As I realize that the list of things with which he is to provide for the house, I know that my money is to be spent on getting my hair done, lunch or some costume jewelry. Why do I work so hard, then? Just for fun? Or, maybe for self-esteem? This is not a utopia where we do not have to pay for anything. If I work decently, I should be paid accordingly and be able to enjoy leisure time and my existence on earth! No matter who it is before me, they should understand this. I feel complete when working.

He makes some progress on the Green Card process but still has to wait for more to get it and find a legal job. He has never worked on a legal one because his student visa would allow him to work only at the campus, and now that he is no longer a student, he could find just low-profile jobs which makes him only more frustrated. I may understand how he feels, but he must be patient. As soon as he obtains the Green Card, he should be able to find jobs with a salary over the average. I believe in him, he is not dumb, for sure. He is a smart man. He graduated back in Senegal as a civil engineer, plus he speaks perfect French. If nothing, he could work as a translator at an international company. But these plans do not matter. Nevertheless, he should earn more than me, and cannot stand the opposite even for six months. And, he takes it out on me. Why does he take it out on me?

~~~ *** ~~~

I reach for my photo album to have a glance at my favorite moments. I remember this one! I had fun that night with my friends. Who doesn't recognize their prom nights, anyway? I look quite proud of my prom in the photo and seem to enjoy it, too. We posed in our house, my prom mate and me. He came to my house, asked for the permission from my mother. I remember going to another one the next day. I had back-to-back two proms: mine and my boyfriend's. I still have those boots that I wore at the galas. Suddenly, my husband comes to engage with what I have been doing. He sees the prom pictures and starts saying nonsense: "Who is this guy? … Where is he now, are you still in touch with him? … I don't want them and these pictures in here. I don't want to come across to them. I don't want our children to find them and ask questions about them. Because you wore them with your ex-boyfriend, but now you live with me, we are married. You should get used to it and behave accordingly."

What did he say? I cannot even find a word to answer him. What is it that annoys him? I mean, it is normal phenomena in our country that our girls take a picture with their prom partners, enjoy the night and don't even think if they still have some stuff in their houses remaining from those years. And which children? We don't have any yet. I cannot recognize him sometimes.

—"Hey, hey, you know what? These are my prom pictures. I don't know where you come from, but this is very normal and very healthy, and I am keeping my prom pictures."

Now he keeps saying the same things repeatedly, torturing me mentally… I lose control and reach for the scissors and cut my prom partner out of all of those pictures. Now, the moment is spoiled. I keep cutting, no matter what! I release my muscles to get relief. Eventually, I calm down and start breathing with a somewhat slower rhythm. I realize that I will have no proper memory from those beautiful moments of my youth. And, I feel like I have been cutting my arm instead of cutting those pictures into pieces. What could substitute them now?

Why would someone do this? I just don't get it! No-one can put constraints in my life and tell me what to do. This was not an innocent outburst of his. He keeps asking for such things, then forbidding me to go to some places by myself; he insists on oppressing me with his strange customs and worldview that does not coincide with the norms of an American man. Now, I realize that that time when he forced me to take those pictures apart was a clear sign that things had already started changing.

Our love is not like before. I see the passion in his eyes, moves, lips… However, he gets his outbursts more often.

~~~ *** ~~~

I am making my money in my dream career, still in Philadelphia. And he gets his Green Card and Social Security, meaning that he is now eligible for higher-profile jobs, the jobs that would pay him way more money than he used to make for the past years. Nevertheless, he doesn't seem to calm down much. He is still frustrated that I make my money. I cannot be sure, of course, but maybe the reason for his primitive attitude towards my career is the fact that I have already obtained my financial independence. This may annoy only an old-fashion guy like my husband. Yes, maybe this is the word to describe him. Old-fashion…

I believe that no one wants to live a miserable life. We should be, technically, doing just fine regarding our financial status. But I cannot find any other word to put it other than 'misery.' I've never wanted to admit it, yet for the last couple of weeks, what I experience is **misery** in bold. It gets even worse each day. For the previous days, it is continuously tense in the house. But I don't let this affect my dreams.

I have always dreamt of being an extraordinary person. A person who could achieve many more things than others expect them to do. A nursing school is an excellent start; I don't regret it. After all, it's my dream profession. I should be adding some more qualifications to myself. For instance, even when I was a student at the college, I was dreaming of moving to somewhere else and going on with my education. I have heard of this school in Atlanta. Maybe there. I can save some money for my education in MSN, MBA or MPH at one of those schools for the sake of a successful career. In that case, what is it going to be? Admittedly, I haven't thought this through, and we never had a word about this: me moving to another city, another state actually, to study more. What is his answer to this going be?

Maybe, " Yes, honey, I would like to come with you, I can find another job there. Maybe, changing our residence could change our situation. You know, ease things up.", Or "What? No! Why would you do that? You have a job here already. You don't want to leave sick children, do you? Your mother, your grandmother? They are all here, which means that you belong here. Besides, what are you going to become after MBA?

What is this about? Do you want to become a manager or something?? Just, let it go!" These thoughts occupy a lot of my time and make me extra nervous about what things could be, rather than what the words are.

I build up the nerve, decide to talk to him. If he is going to say something negative, that will be it! He comes home, again later than me. He says nothing, goes straight to change. I wait for him in the living room and sitting on the couch all relaxed and cold. Here, he comes in the place and gets closer to me.

—"How was your day?"

—"It was fine."

—"How does your job search go?"

—"You know how. It's the same each day. I need some time. Working and searching for a job at the same time is not the easiest."

—"I hear you. Listen! I was thinking. Maybe we should get away from this place for some time. I have been thinking of continuing my education, only not here, but in Atlanta. They have the second-best school in the field. Other colleges are also above the average. I feel that I should take a shot and apply for them."

—"Wait, that's new. How long have you been thinking about this?"

—"To be honest, for quite a long time."

—"And, do you think that you can get an approval from any of them?"

—"I believe that I can. No. I'm pretty sure that I will."

—"I don't know what to say. I didn't see that coming. You understand that it is huge, right?"

Did he belittle me?

—"Yes, I do. But it shouldn't be you who says that it is huge. Isn't it you who abandoned his family and homeland to live a better life in a new country? Does it matter to you where you reside as long as you remain in the States?"

—"First, I never abandoned them, and they know about it. Who are you to judge me and my deeds? You could never understand it! You were raised here. You hold a US citizenship since your birth. Second, it matters where I live in the States. It matters big time, because not every city is full of opportunities. A man… Especially, a man in my situation should always aim for the best he can do and the best place he can benefit. Oh, would you know about it? You have always had your opportunities before you."

—"Don't start talking about the opportunities I had. You know nothing about it!"

I go out, crying. I don't remember how I took my coat and ran along. It is not that cold outside, but it is dark, and the season is autumn. I don't want to get sick. I walk down the street to the Columbus Boulevard on the coast of Delaware River. Watching the river flow always make me regain my temper. This is what I do after fights lately.

I find him asleep when I finally come back home at around 11:00 pm. He gets tired, so I give him credit for his efforts. But does it give him the right to make my life miserable? My mom used to work hard, too. She is the most hard-working person I have ever known. I never expect her to act like this not just to me because I am her little princess but to anyone. This should be about attitudes and one's character, then, not about the situation. I guess I overthink. I shouldn't spend my youth overthinking things like this. I shouldn't harm anybody, in any way, physically or mentally. And, it seems only fair to me if I should require the same from others. "Better, if I sleep on it."

~~~ *** ~~~

—"Good morning, honey! Did you sleep well?"
—"Good morning. Yes, I guess."
—"When did you come back last night?"
—"Around 11:00 pm."
—"Look, I was thinking of, maybe, taking a road trip to Atlanta for the moment. I have some friends down there. They could show us around for the weekend. What do you say?"
—"Yeah? It sounds great. Let's do it."

We take his old car. It is not the best for the job, but it is our best choice now. It is going to be like a break to me since I want to get distracted from all this just for a while. I am tired of handling our relationship problems, and on top of that, I am tired of taking care of housework. Cleaning, making the bed, setting the table, and man, cooking… I cook a lot. Every day another dish for him in significant portions. Only to tranquilize and make him love me more. If we don't fight in the evening, mostly rent a movie, cook delicious food, sometimes even international authentic food, we sit on the couch and watch the film of the day and try to bond. I do that for the sake of our relationship, but I realize that I have been eating a lot to get rid of this oppressing atmosphere. As a natural consequence, I have gained a lot of weight. As a result I have lower self-esteem now. Why does everything go in the wrong way?

We take our road trip to Atlanta. His friends take us to the most exciting places and to campuses of the universities that I have been willing to apply for. Other times, as if I am a gourmet who came to taste local cuisine of Atlanta, I keep eating a lot. Long, in short, we decide to move to the city. Atlanta is going to be our new home, at least for a while. And I hope that everything is going to evolve in a positive direction.

Everybody comes in to help us pack all of our stuff. We empty my beautiful apartment. Now, it looks ugly, and as if I have never lived here. I am the one who wants to move on, I know. But it is not that easy to leave a place which you have been emotionally attached. Of course, the most difficult was to say goodbye to my mother.

We move to Atlanta. The first thing we do, of course, is to rent a room for the moment. Then we apply for jobs. I ask for a nursing license to state authorities, and he applies for a civil engineering job. This job requires outside working. He measures the geographical status of public areas, like streets, parks, etc. collecting data for a construction company. I can understand how he is not satisfied with his job. He hates it, to be accurate. On the other side, he finally makes decent money. However, I temporarily work at Macy's. I plan to work there until I get my nursing license. As an upside of this temporary job is that it seems like our conflicts are ended.

Our days pass in harmony and peace comparing to those in Philadelphia lately. He wakes up later than he used to. At last, we do have our breakfasts together; that too helps us move forward, I believe. We spend a bit more time both in quantity and quality than before. Nevertheless, I feel the dissatisfaction on him. Something is missing, but what? Maybe, he doesn't like the room we rent. It is possible that he regrets the move. No, it is impossible. There should be something else. Maybe, it is all about his background.

One of those cultural differences between him and me has nothing to do with his religion, his customs or beliefs. By the way, one's native language adds up a lot to their character, to the form of perception of the world around. Since people learn things from childhood by naming them in their mother tongue, those innocent words, give people the way they look at the world, people and life. Theoretically, for instance, an apple can be recognized by two people from different countries with different mother tongues, if we show them an apple.

Surely, they would name apple differently because of their people's approach to it throughout history, that gives those two people different perceptions of an apple which they share only with their peoples. In my case, his official language is Wolof and mine is English. And, people say that French and English have many words in common. That may be true. But there are times that he does not understand me even when I speak some of the common words. It is all about the change in the meaning of those words back in time. Some have preserved their spelling and meaning, though, such as the word 'relation.' But there are some like the word 'present.' One day he introduces me to his friend saying, "I present you Chanelle." I'm not a presentation, and people cannot present me to anyone. I may be 'introduced,' but not presented. In the French language, though, apparently one can present people. Or if I demand something from him, I mean that I require him to do it. But he assumes that I only ask him to do because the word 'demand' means only to ask in French. I guess it was not a bad idea to attend speech classes in college after all. Thanks to them, I can try to analyze people and their perceptions by the words they use. Though, it is something else that conflicts behind the scenes.

He comes from a well to do family, especially in comparison to his people. He grew up with a maid, with a housekeeper. His father is wealthy enough to provide his seven kids with life over average. I, on the other hand, was raised by a single mom and so on. We come from different social classes. We both recognize apple but perceive it in different ways not only because of our mother tongues but also because of our backgrounds. I remember he moved to my house, for it was better and more beautiful than his. But I can live in this small room. The only thing that I am looking for is his love — nothing more, nothing less. Our poor temporary residence makes him even sad because he used to have everything in Senegal. And, the reason he came to the States is to have more, unlike our current situation.

~~~ *** ~~~

—"Honey, I'm home!"
—"Hi, babe! How was your day?"
—"It was alright. I feel better. I quit today."
—"You, what?"
—"You heard me, I quit. I never liked the job, babe. You see? They made me do things that have nothing to contribute to my career."

—"Which career you mean? That job was your career. Honey don't get me wrong. But have you applied for another job already?"

—"Not yet. Why the rush? I was not happy with that job. The salary was also not satisfying at all. I have felt that everything will be good."

—"I don't get it. You don't want me to make more money than you, maybe I can empathize with that, I cannot understand, but I can empathize. Though, you quit your job before you get another one. I'm sorry, but I just don't get it."

—"Babe, babe, you get this all wrong. Think of it this way. Do you want me to be tortured at work by letting them degrade me? Or, do you want me to be happy at a new job?"

—"Of course, I want you to be happy. Don't you see by far how much I love you?"

We are broke though we still have fun. One of our most favorite things to do together is to wander around the city since we have met. One of the reasons is that it is healthy, as far as they taught us in nursing school, the other is that it is free of charge. Take a step to the street and follow the road, look at people and try to guess what their lives are like. For instance, a woman at around the age of 50 going to her job in a black-white classical suit should tell you enough about her career, her dwelling and its location in the city, even her lunch. We discuss these kind of things and try to guess people's personalities. Besides, walking on the streets is the best way to get to know the city. It takes a lot of time.

In this time, I get my nursing license. But the job requires me to visit adult patients in their houses as a part of the visiting nurse help system. They call me and tell me about the job description. The job is not as smooth and preferable as the one that I had in Philadelphia. Not having a determined workplace, visiting patients' houses, unstable working hours are just a few downsides of the job.

On the other hand, I have no other choice and have been waiting for a job in my field for quite a long time. Apart from that, those are the patients who cannot go to the hospitals because of their medical conditions, and it is better for them to remain at home. It is an excellent opportunity in both financial and moral terms. I should take it: "Yes, I accept your job offer. When can I start?"

He, though, doesn't work at the moment and all of a sudden, he decides to go to an engineering school. What is the point, if he is not going to attend classes? If he is going to be expelled, why to consider taking a loan for the college? He talks about it every day, but he doesn't seem to make any effort to realize it. I motivate him to prepare his documents if he wants to be accepted. But as always, I end up putting all my focus on him instead of myself and ordering his transcript from Senegal to Atlanta, finding an authorized translator online and having his degree and all the classes that he had in Senegal from French to English. I also helped him to get his resume done, to show what he can do in a way so that he could find a job without a degree. Eventually, he finds a proper engineering job with an office, blueprints on desks, 15-minute coffee breaks, etc. No need to mention how his salary went high, and he becomes happy again. Now that we both work at excellent jobs, we move from the sick room to a beautiful apartment.

We have been together for some time in which we have been through many moments that were both disastrous and happy. I don't feel as if I am one year older, but more than ten years. This marriage has made me more mature if nothing. I have never met his parents, his sisters, and brothers in person. Other than what they can manage to tell about themselves over the short phone calls which he arranges from time to time, I know pretty much nothing about them. So, we would like to go to Africa. Admittedly, the flight will cost more expensive than domestic flights. Therefore, we should start stretching a dollar for a while.

One day he sits next to me with a sincere, beautiful smile on his face. The first thing he asked me why don't we have kids? He started talking about how much he likes kids, and about the importance of having kids in early ages because of some possible hardships that older parents go through.

—"Honey, I admire your love for kids very much. You know how hard it was for me to get over the miscarriage." I start crying. "There is no-one in the world who wants a baby more than I do. But I am scared to have another miscarriage. I am not ready for it. Just wait for some time, another year maybe. Let me start with the college and get distracted from everything sad that we have been through. Excuse me, but I need more time."

—"Babe, I understand you. And, I know that you are not going to change your mind. But you have to understand, too. A guy at my age has to start a family, you know, have many kids. He has to prove that he is capable of making his family grow bigger. This is a matter of pride in my culture. I understand that you are not ready for pregnancy, yet. But there are ways to solve this."

—"What are those ways?"

Then he asks me something bizarre in a quiet kind and soft manner also coldblooded as if he were asking for a toothbrush.

—"Well, you know, that it is encouraged to have more than one wife in my culture."

What did he say? Does he ask me if I am okay with him getting married to another woman in his country, Senegal?

—"My mother may need some help in getting housework done. She gets old, and I realize that she cannot do as much as she used to. She may find a girl to get married to me. Thus, she can help my mother without asking for money. If she gives birth to babies, then our problem will be solved, too." Noticing my appalled face, he alters his words: "Well, maybe not right now, but later, when you will be ready to agree. You know, maybe when you grow old and grow old… What would you say, honey?"

Not even answering him, I start crying and run to the phone, dial my mother-in-law to tell her what he said to me. His little sister translates for me, immediately. His mother goes crazy over what she hears and starts cursing him. Hearing those, he goes mad and punches a hole in the wall. Everything happens in about five minutes, charging all of us with an overwhelming negative feeling. I start calling everyone telling the same story, releasing my emotions and asking for their advice. It's like my brain is frozen. No part of my body functions properly. But it is not only me that he hurts. His mom is worried, too. She swears to stop talking to him and feel a great shame before me for what he asked for.

It gets more complicated as other members of the family get involved. This is just too much. I get up and go near the window for some fresh air. I am still in shock. I have never heard of a single example where a husband asks his wife to bring a co-wife. There is no way on earth that I could accept it, and he should have known it! Hasn't he learned anything about me? How dare him to degrade me by proposing this unacceptable thing. I have dignity as a human being, as a woman, as a wife, for God's sake! I don't care if it is accepted by his country, by his fellowmen here in the States. I don't mind people getting along with this folkway. But there are laws in this country against it, and I will not be a part of this sick medieval custom. All that he wants is to cuddle another woman and produce children with her under the disguise of the verses of his holy book and thoughtfulness to her mother. Was it worth to even mention it in the first place? After some time, I relax and turn to him saying:

—"We should better pretend that this conversation has never taken place."

This marriage has been taking so much from me, and I feel exhausted. I should get rid of this and be left alone for some time to rest, to make my mind. I'm still married to him, though. So, I take one step at a time. I look for another apartment. Since I make enough money, now, I am sure that I can manage to live by myself. When he is at work, I call movers to carry my stuff out of our apartment, and I move to the next one. I leave him, not to give him a lesson, but because I need to leave for my sanity. This move of mine breaks him down. Let alone moving on he is not ready to live without me. As weeks go, we lead our own lives separated in our apartments and paying only for ourselves. I am well aware that there is a melancholic atmosphere in his studio and he lives in misery. A still loving heart will eventually soften and forgive. So, he makes his way back to me. He moves to my place, and we start over, only for the worse.

Admittedly, we had fights before like any other married couple. Maybe we had more than usual, but never in physical form. He is a charming, handsome, bodied, very tall and muscular guy. He goes out of his mind from time to time. On one of those days, he goes crazy and starts hitting me in the face, leaving me no choice other than defending myself by answering in the same manner and crying "Are you going to intimidate me?". I am a bit scared of what could happen. Because if he lacks morals and considers physically attacking me with his big hands and muscled arms, inevitably, I stand no chance against him.

But monetary issues are the toughest when it comes to our marriage since they seem to be the real problem hid behind all those excuses to start a fight. Loosely speaking, just a warm bed is not enough for most of the time. If one of the sides buys something and the other one doesn't agree that that something is necessary, then a fight is most probably what is going to happen. We sleep together in peace, but until the time we go to bed, we start having tense discussions, again. We fight and makeup, on and off. In one of those nights, though, he uses this argument that it is not about our finances, but it is preferably the time that I spend with him. He does not like the fact that I work hard, and sometimes come home later than usual, as if it all depends on me. It is not like that I have total control of my work schedule. Besides, I am new to the city, and I don't see a good command for the roads, yet. That's why I drive with a map all the time. But suddenly, I am the problem, again, just because my patient needed extra care for another hour, since he is not a robot that you can switch on and off any time you like, and I got lost while driving back home. Who does he think he is to demand me to quit my job? Doesn't he realize that he is trying to change who I am? It seems like my world is upside down. What I have in my life is a physiological disaster, mental torture. What he has, is clinically called narcissistic manipulation.

I start working PRN (when it is needed), meaning that I spend more time at home dealing with housework and issues regarding his work and life more. Now that I don't deal with my real business actively, I am just bored out of my mind. I am gradually getting depressed, to be accurate, losing myself day by day. I feel lonelier than ever. I have not made as many friends here as I did have in Philadelphia and cannot see my mother and grandmother that often. I have lots of things to tell about as to my marriage, but I have no-one around me ready to share my agony. I may not be raised in a church, in a religious family, yet I believe in God. Sometimes, he is the only thing that I hold on to. My faith gives me a way out and makes me stronger.

Despite the negative views to it and what happened on 9/11, I am interested in Islam recently. I am not sure if I am a proper Muslim, though. I read books, the Koran, and try to discover it because of my curiosity and my mental status lately. I am more depressed than ever and need a way out. He likes this approach of mine to Islam. Maybe he thinks that I want to become Senegalese. He tries to shape me and my behaviors. A Muslim wife should be this and that. She should wear hijab all the time; she should not attract much attention on her and behave well in the society, and all those stereotypical nonsenses. I have a hard time to get it. If I accept something to my life, it is because I like it after I have analyzed and reasoned it out.

On the other hand, this wrong attitude of his comes off that he learned and adopted his religion, Islam, as a part of the tradition of the nation. Some Christians have the same problem. They believe in God only because of their mothers, and their grandmothers before them, the thought in him. Well, I go to the mosque and wear hijab. Just because I am seeking the truth no matter what it takes. Not because someone else, my father, my husband demanded me to wear. It is apparent that I also partly like being a Muslim. Otherwise, it would have been impossible to open my hands in my prayers to another God than the one that is followed by this country's majority.

Apart from that, I find this religion quite beautiful, helping and calming. Besides, the ideas that are demonstrated in it coincide with my point of view regarding African and American histories. Mainly, its revolutionary beginning and the support of African people 1500 years ago to its spread is enough to fascinate me. Then, why would I need someone to inject their traditional way of thinking that is not flexible and not tailored to this culture that we live in? Why cannot I discover my religion by myself? I should be the one who adopts a new religion to my own life, not someone else, no!

Again, I can understand why he acts like that, but I cannot approve such behavior, not only against me but against anyone. I get it that he approaches me in a controlling, dominating manner as to religion because he was raised in the same way. He always had someone to tell what is right and what is wrong to do within the frame of a religion, Islam. He did not even have a choice to question his faith, the dogmas that are repeated for generations. On the other hand, I did not grow up in a strict, religious family. From time to time, I used to go to church with some of my Catholic family members, of course, nothing more. Therefore, I had the chance to approach religion or similar teachings with care. I tend to reason out things as unbiased as I can before accepting them.

I was at high school when Christianity was introduced to me for the first time correctly which was a slightly later date for an ordinary child. Then I had circles at college to discuss not only religious or spiritual matters but also African history and culture. All those intellectual attempts of mine have made me what I am. I have a basic algorithm that is nothing more than learning and discussing with others. Though, I should be able to give question if something does not sound reasonable. I get that I cannot address religious issues with him; it discomforts him. They are, apparently, 'highly sacred' to touch. I have no other choice to read about it myself. Every week or every other, I go to bookstores to find reliable sources. As I find them one by one, I spend most of my time at home by reading about this religion of his. Ironically enough, I speeded up my studies on Islam to get away from him. Naturally, the more I learned, the more I got into it. Even though its 'his' religion, I began to embrace the teachings of Mohammad.

Praying in those sacred days and nights of Muslims with everybody around you, meditating, opening your hands and asking forgiveness out loud from the God, *Allah* (Arabic word for 'the God') for everybody regardless of their languages, countries, skins, wealth, educational levels, etc. feel so right that I start loving this religion and the way of life that comes along. Connecting with Muslims who are from all around the world is very exotic, too. We have a Pakistani imam in the mosque; other fellows are mostly from the Middle East, Balkans, and Africa. Apart from that, I have never felt satisfied spiritually this much. So, I even start wearing hijab and covering myself for inner purification. Besides, I get much positive feedback and good care from Muslims. They are happy that I became a wife of a Muslim and accept Islam voluntarily as if it has something to do with them. Though I don't mind the /over-attention on me, I seem to have like it, as long as I am not overwhelmed by the attention. After-all, I need some attention, considering my depressive marriage. I take advantage that he does not spend much time at home, lately. Since I work less as a PRN nurse and we have decided to fly to Africa, he has to make more money than usual. Therefore, he drives for Domino's after work and on weekends, besides his desk job at an engineering company. I, now, realize that having a trip to his homeland has been a significant burden to both of us. Buying flight tickets for two is one thing, buying presents for every member of his family is another. If you come from abroad, you are almost obliged to bring gifts as a sign of your love and your thoughtfulness. I hope that it is going to be worth it, though.

~~~ *** ~~~

We fly to Africa today. So, I am excited. This is my first time flying over the Atlantic Ocean and visiting another country at the same time. A state where you don't understand a person, where people don't understand you. It is both surprising and a beautiful experience that you grasp the fact that the world is not about your country and people do not have the same worldview as you do. Maybe it wouldn't strike me that much if I flew to Europe, but Africa is a total exotic land where people are more miserable, yet more brave and proud. Everywhere that I look has a detail, which I have not met before. I never knew that a country having financial difficulties would be so thrilling.

Other than every beauty surrounding me, an event makes me excited the most. I have another wedding in Africa! This time inviting all the beloved ones of his, too. Of course, a traditional one has been arranged already by the time we got here. Every detail has been taken into consideration. It is not a high-budget wedding, though, it probably is the most exotic and extraordinary one that I have seen in my life. And, I am the bride! Everything is fascinating; the crowd is unbelievably energetic, everyone looks happy, just like a daydream. Women are cooking outside, and I take photos, people eat and dance almost at the same time. Beautiful, like a cultural festival to me. Though, I feel a little sad, since I could not bring my mother with me. I have no kin from my side. That may be one of the reasons why his family, especially, my mother-in-law and sisters-in-law take excellent care of me.

We do not understand a word we say to each other, yet there is already a connection between us, I can feel it. If my husband is around, he translates everything, which gave me confidence because I could follow everything that is being said in the room. Otherwise, I sit there as they come to me one by one and say something. When I mime that I don't get what they are trying to tell me, they start mimicking, too. We communicate well in that manner, but there is still one problem. Some of our hand and body moves mean way different things, therefore it sometimes takes more than five minutes to end a sentence. Even though before the wedding, we went shopping with my mother-in-law and sisters-in-law both to find me a dress for the wedding and to bond with them. My husband left us alone, meaning that I am useless on the street. The oldest sister-in-law of mine points me a store to go in, I nod, agreeing with her. She talks something with the vendor inside, then turning to me, she makes ahead, and we get out. After several times, I feel like a bag carried here and there. Though, they make it clear all the time that they embrace me as a part of the family already.

Everything is being arranged for a wedding of an already married couple. It is fun and beautiful, though except for one thing that I cannot recognize my husband. He was acting weird. He was bragging over the fact that he is American, that he has a legitimate and desirable job and makes a right amount of money there. Is this the guy that I have gotten married to? Sure, the thing is that I do not approve this kind of behavior. What is he trying to prove to his countrymen? Some of the people here are poor. Occasionally, a slim and probably sick person nears you in a partly torn cloth, then opens his hand while pointing at his stomach as if trying to tell you that he is starving but does not have enough money for nutrition. No matter how many times I see a similar scene, I cannot help my eyes brimming with tears. Naturally, I reach into my pocket for some coins, but my husband hinders me and says: "Don't do that, honey! He didn't deserve it. He should have worked if he wanted to eat something. By giving them money, you do not help them. You encourage them to keep on begging." It is not his words that annoy me. It is his attitude and the tone of his while saying them. He may be right, though. Maybe I encourage them to beg instead of helping them when I give them money out of pity. If that person is very sick, so sick that he cannot even work, then what is he going to do? Write a resume and send it to employers? He may not even spell his name correctly. Besides, I am also on a spiritual journey here in Africa. When seeing an extraordinary thing, I review my behaviors, life, and everything. I don't need anyone to spoil those precious moments of mine since they surely help me discover myself. Everything aside, again the same thing, if I want to give charity, I should be able to give it to anyone I please. It is like the same thing over and over again. The reason on the surface why he manipulates me may differ, yet it is still taking control of me. Maybe the main reason for all these is that, maybe, he tries to with me, and he feels insecure around me. Again, I overthink!

~~~ *** ~~~

I walk on the street in Dakar, the capital of Senegal, where my husband is originally from, only to realize that I am at home in spite of all those cultural differences. I feel a closeness to local people when I get into the crowd. I look around and say to myself: "Hey, this could be Barbara, and this is, maybe, Michelle," It goes on and on until they open their mouth and start speaking utterly tricky words. Not just words, there were other things that I could not get at first.

Everyone, almost every woman has their own business. Entrepreneurial women are very active in Senegal. Women instead have a hustle than only sitting at home, taking care of their 'family.' Whereas every other woman in Senegal sells or produces something, I am fooled with so-called Senegalese customs. He wants to put me in a house-wife status, but things are the opposite where he comes from. Though, I am very inspired by these women, by their auto-creativity, even in Africa. They demonstrate that there is always a piece of positivity which you can pull out of some hardship. I should act as they do. I should not give up my dreams, my hustles only to sit at home.

~~~ *** ~~~

We fly back home. I had the most fun trip, but I am tired. It appears to me that I am always tired during the last year. Anyway, I think there is no better place than your home. I can tell that by looking at my husband's face. He misses Africa already.

183

There is nothing to eat in the house. I try not to get down. I need to rest, but it is too early to go to bed. Instead, I decided to look at our photos that were taken during our trip to Africa. They were made mostly at our wedding. I cannot still believe that I had another one, where I had no kin from the States. I felt many opposite feelings at the same time. I felt alone, and in a comforting company, it was overwhelming and relaxing at the same time, … Here they are, I take them out and start looking at them one by one, only to realize how much depressed I was. They are highly strange. I cannot even recognize myself. Hadn't I also looked at the mirror? I don't know what was happening when we took these pictures, and I don't remember what I was thinking. I am in a depressed mood, almost with a long face all the time.

Some of my pictures, including the one on my passport, look like as if I am being held, hostage. After getting over my first shock, I see what was going on there. I seem to look at the bright sides and concentrate on the things that I appreciate more and more every time I felt trapped and desperate. "Huh, I have created a defense mechanism to ignore my agony." This mechanism had no use when it comes to posing for a camera. I show those pictures to my mom ask for her idea. She gets sad, most probably because she knows that it is not much for her to do.

There seems not much for me to do, either. I am in this marriage. I don't want to fail it because my family has nothing but failed marriages. I always feel this pressure on my shoulders. I don't want to be a statistic. At least, I have my family to support me every time I need. And his mom, she is always so constructive and sweet to me. It was not her fault definitely that we have difficulties in our marriage. Well, partly her fault, because she raised him.

On the other hand, she was following the child-rearing traditions of her society. So, the blame belongs partly to her and slightly to society. Anyway, she may not understand me a hundred percent, which is normal, because our backgrounds and the communities that we live in are not similar at all. But I remember her being sincere to me every time.

Lately, I think about what she said to me once. What were her words? "He is not only a husband to you, but a brother (in a religious sense), too. Please, hold on and don't break up." She was begging me not to leave him. She must have realized that some things in our marriage were not going well, and she must have sensed that I could leave him, again, as I did once before. By looking at her tone of voice, I can even interpret that she knew that it is all about her son's attitude. What a sad situation for a mother! You ask forgiveness for your son, from his wife.

What if I try explaining this concerning cultural difference? In that case, she was not asking forgiveness for her son, but she was instead preparing me for their way of problem-solving as to the wife-husband relationship. If I an American were to decide on the problematic marriage, she might well choose to leave her husband and ask for a divorce. Though, as far as I have seen, this is a rare case in Senegal. They instead hold on to their marriages and wait for the storm to spend itself. They should spend more effort to make their friendships, in other words, the unity of their families, continue than a usual American wife, and a woman acting on the opposite way is very much despised by the society.

His mother was his father's first wife. After some time, his father brought another wife after her. The first wife who bore seven children was not happy with this at all. Supposedly, he was against it, trying to persuade me that he would never do that to me. I am confused, though. Was it someone else who asked for my permission to have a second wife in Senegal?

—"What? Don't make me bring up the things that we went over long before. Did you, or did you not ask for my permission to get married to another woman?"

—"No, babe, you get everything wrong. I asked for it, but all was for a good purpose. You know, how much I love my mom and I cannot…"

—"We both know that it had nothing to do with your innocent mom. She almost died from the disappointment you caused to her. Don't even try to fool me; you wanted to have another girl to cuddle!"

—"Ok, you were jealous. I get you. But, be reasonable, she was going to stay in Senegal. I had no intention to bring her with me at all. My request was different and hundred percent harmless."

—"What! I cannot even believe that you haven't changed your mind. You still stand behind what you asked for. You know what it means to me? It means that we haven't gotten anywhere. Why do I spend my time with you, then?"

—"Wait, are you trying to change me? Is it what you want, babe?"

—"Of course, not. It's you who wants to change the other, not me. You make a big deal out of anything and play against me!"

~~~ *** ~~~

Since we get back from Africa, there is nothing in the house to eat and no money to buy things to eat. We have only a bag of rice and some spices. I make miracles every night. I hold on to my religion, trying to be strong because I know that I am the pillar of this marriage. If I give up, everything related to our 'love' will end. Being aware of that, I cook for Thanksgiving another miracle that is called 'boiled rice with onions and some exotic flavors'! That is so because I am not allowed to borrow money or ingredients from others. His pride is so big that even starving may not excuse us to ask for help. Tragicomic though, that if we hadn't gone to Africa, we wouldn't have been craving, and I could have baked a turkey for the Thanksgiving.

As days pass, I understand that it is not getting any better. I require some freedom. One day I make my mind to move back to Philadelphia. He begs me not to go, but I have decided this time, and nothing can turn me back from my decision. It was hard to, maybe, end this problematic marriage of ours, but I feel like this is the right thing to do. And, I should have done it long before. Yes, that's it, I move to Philly!

First, I move to my mother and start searching for the job. Since I already have a license here, things should proceed faster. In a few months, I seem to get back on my feet, again. But my new job doesn't satisfy me regarding salary and career opportunities. Besides, I live with my mother here in Philadelphia, and it gets tough after a certain age, no matter how much you love your mother. By the time, he moves to a smaller house where he shares the rent with someone else. Although we live in different states, our financial situation was damaged once, and we struggle to make things better. I realize that I was reasonable when I wanted to move to Atlanta in the first place. So, I decide to move to Atlanta once again. Only this time by myself.

The first thing I do is to get in contact with one of my nurse friends to offer her to share her rent. Moving with her is followed by an active and systematic job search. Finally, I get the job at the Children's Hospital that I have craved for a long time. The reason that I did not apply for it before was that he forbids it to me due to its night shifts. Now, I work a night shift, make enough money to live, share my rent with a friend, and try to put my life in order, again. I don't know what to do with my husband, though. We may live separately, but he still is my legal husband. Maybe I will get a divorce, perhaps not. I am not ready to get involved in this. I should get up on my feet again to make healthy decisions. And, the last thing I am looking for is insisting calls from him.

He tells how much he misses me, how desperate he is without me, how cold his bed gets during endless nights. After some sweet attempts of reconciliation and a thousand 'please,' I give up and let him get back to me. I keep telling myself, though, that this is going to be the last time and his last chance.

He comes to my roommate's house, packs my stuff for me and carries everything in the car by himself. He is pleased to have me back. I can even tell it by sitting in the next room. By the time, he parts company with his roommate for me to move back in.

Everything with him seems very promising this time. He allows me to contribute in-house budget. He doesn't even comment on my night shifts. Instead, he adopts his eating order according to my schedule to have a meal with me. He also starts working at another job. He delivers papers in the morning, comes back home to change and goes to work while I sleep. I appreciate his hustle, and I try to make things easier for him, too. Although I work hard, I deal with housework. I cook for him, do cleaning and laundry, etc. Albeit, there is this awkward vibe between us. It seems to fade out day by day, though. After all, we sleep on the same bed.

One day, when he is out for his delivery job, I get a phone call. I get out of my bed and answer it. That is a girl's voice on the other side. I kindly ask whom I am speaking with. She has the guts to tell me that she is his girlfriend. I am frustrated, shocked. I tell her that I am his wife and she needs to cut it off. She goes on:

—"Look, I am not lying, OK? I don't want to make things harder. It is what it is. We used to meet at his house. If you don't believe me, I can say that there is a picture of a clock on the wall in the living room, …"

She starts counting everything in the house, finishing with his work schedule. I am furious by listening to her. I know girls, they may become intriguing. And, if my husband had a clearer history, I might have ignored her and not even mentioned about her. But I have no hesitation in this situation. His bed still gets cold during my night shifts! I hang up the phone and call my mother, as I always do. This time things are a bit different.

—"Mom? Hello, mom?"

—"Chanelle, the babe, are you crying?"

—"Mom, something terrible has happened."

—"Please, calm down honey. Just tell me what happened."

—"The bastard cheated on me, mom! He cheated on me when I was in Philadelphia. He got a girl pregnant. I don't know what to do. I am full of anger. He should get it this time."

—"He should get what, honey? Don't do anything crazy, alright?"

—"I am going to hurt him, mom. He is going to be hurt this time."

—"You are going to hurt no one, did you hear me? No one. They will put you in prison, and I cannot stand it, do you hear me?"

—"But, mom, you don't get it. That girl was in my house. She used my kitchen, sat on my couch, used my towels, slept on my bed. He invites her in when I go to night shifts. How can I live with this shame? Did I deserve this? Tell me! Does he deserve me?"

—"Chanelle, honey, please, come back here. You are going to get divorced, and everything is going to be fine. You are still young, don't do anything crazy. I beg you!"

—"He doesn't let me have my prom pictures, but he has his lover in the house. Some things in should change!"

I simulate every possible scenario in mind and start waiting for him. He must have skipped home for today. I cannot wait to do anything. I cry "Where are your clothes?" I start being creative with them. I work on his stuff while I imagine that what I hold is him and work on it. I constantly think about how he has been oppressing me for years, and in return, he brings a girl to my bed. "Now, I see why you bought that garish jacket! Where is it, huh?" I look for his new jacket that I realize when moved back in. He even made up a story about it! I go here and there in the house and ask the same question over and over, again: what should I do with him?

So, I wait until the evening, until he finally shows up at the threshold. I immediately start asking some questions. He denies each one of my accusations. I did not expect him to confess, anyway. I did not plan it, but I realize a knife within my sight and reach for it.

—"Deny it once again!"

—"OK, OK, but are you going to kill me for it?"

Everything is a game to him. I lose control of myself and make my move on him. He makes his way to the kitchen and grabs a knife. We go back and forth, swinging blades to each other. There comes the moment when somehow, I distract him and while he ducks, I injure him on the back of his neck. Suddenly, there is blood everywhere, and he runs out in no time. Witnessing neighbors call for cops, and he goes directly to ER.

The cops come. I am still in the room. I have nothing to hide. He did all this to me. I am a human being after all. I have limits. Besides, I did not kill him or anything. That was a momentary thing, and it is over. I have nothing to defend, especially to cops. He is my husband, and our marital problems concern only us. I am justified, and he was swinging a knife, too. They get me to the back of a police car and tell me that I am going to jail for what I did. Am I? Jail?

They take my clothes off and put a gown on me and leave me 24 hours for observation, because I may still be 'dangerous' for me or anyone around me. It is cold in the room, and I only have the gown on. What am I going to do now? I have no family in Georgia. Who is going to tell this to my mother? Who can come to bail me out of jail? Not him! I stay in the county jail for eleven days. Finally, they allow me to get the bail finally, and Brenda Eggby brought money to get me out. She put her house up to gather the needed amount. I get out of jail. Brenda picks me up to get me home.

I get a public defender to get on the court. The whole process is new to me. It feels like they have removed my emotions. I spend my day like a zombie, even though I am not in jail anymore. I lost my job already because no-one gave notice about me. But still, I must get back on track somehow. So, Brenda gives me a drive to my house. I will pack my stuff. As soon as I get in, I notice lined up boxes that are full of my stuff. He wants me to leave for the first time. The furniture, TV and some of my other stuff are still in the house that I always pay rent for. Nevertheless, I don't even mind. Let everything be his. When I carry my boxes downstairs, he walks and passes me in traditional African clothes. Why? Oh, yes, I went creative with his clothes that day. He didn't buy anything to wear, instead of borrowed someone's clothes. I don't laugh at it, but it is funny. It could have been a lot worse. At least, he leaves.

I get my boxes to the car and drive off. I have another year to be getting on my trial. During that year they try to make an example out of me for the massive violence. They ask for 17 years in prison. It doesn't even matter to them that I have never been in trouble before. My sad story that justifies me to some extent doesn't matter to them.

~~~ *** ~~~

THE LESSONS THAT I GOT FROM THIS EXPERIENCE:

- Heal your hurts: I had a lot of injuries that made it OK for me to move five thousand miles an hour in a relationship with someone I did not know. I had a lot of hurts from childhood. Not feeling wanted, loved or protected. So, I let myself into the first shiny thing that I came across.

- Don't fill your emptiness with another person: although I was successful academically, I had a void, but I was filling that with my husband. I was offering him everything I got to feel more complete in life. It is fine if you teach people how to treat you, too.

- Pay attention to the signs: now, I realize how many posters I have seen and completely ignore.

- Trust your intuition: my intuition was telling that it is OK to keep your prom pictures, that his jacket has some secrets.

- Get professional help: it was a time where it was very dark, I got depressed, I had anxiety because I felt trapped. It would have been good for me to have some professional help to find the best path in my life. We get physical check-ups, always skip having our mental and emotional check-up.

- Get a spiritual practice and begin to know the truth and what you are: if I was plugged in spiritually, I wouldn't have reacted the way I acted. I have suffered a lot for years due to the outcomes that affected me criminally and professionally.

- Don't allow others to keep replaying the pass: People have been asking me the same question: what happened? If it is my story, then I should have the right to tell it when I want to say to it. Otherwise, when I was not ready to say it, I used to see bad dreams and used to feel an unpleasant pressure on me all the time.

- Focus on the future: What's next? I was able to move on because I focused on my future and what I was going to create. I took accountability for my life.

- Create your happy life: I have the power to create the experience that I want to live in. I can determine my values and build everything on them.

- Create your radiant business: I utilized my talents and gifts in creating my own business. Being an entrepreneur gave me my dignity and freedom. Thanks to my business, I was not dependent on anyone. Besides that, I made money out of it.

-      I love and believe in entrepreneurship so much, and it has such a personal significance to me because it saved my life when I went through specific difficulties.

My life is in divine order. I am grateful to be alive and accept everything as a lesson of wisdom and as opportunities for growth.

Chanelle Washington is the lead Profit Strategist for Radiant Living Biz in Atlanta, Georgia, Serial Entrepreneur, Registered Nurse, Business Consultant and Pumpkin Pie's Mom. A Master Six Figure Sales Trainer, this mompreneur launched her first venture Indigofera Beauty in the year 2000. Turning investment of $500 into $200k in just one revenue stream. Chanelle is responsible for generating $95k in revenue for her clients, multiple business, startups and joint ventures over the span of 7 months in 2018. Today, she teaches Smart Successful Lady Bosses to earn their next six figures. She also helps women to take a single source of income and turn it into recurring revenue streams. Some call her the "Queen of Livestream" masterfully attracting dream clients and delivering compelling content to her Radiant Living Biz Community. Chanelle's first book, Radiant Living: How to Abide in Joy, Confidence and Abundance has helped women transform their lives globally. Most recently, she has created the Mindset and Money Mentorship Program and the Mindset & Money Tour igniting a movement of women who are creating their radiant lives and businesses. Her second book Clients & Cashflow: How to scale your business to 10-20k Monthly is empowering women in business with proven success principles.

CHAPTER 9

JUST WHEN I THOUGHT LIFE WAS GOOD
by
Teri Charles

I am on cloud nine as I head towards the elevator after a client meeting on Michigan Avenue in the Loop, the central business district and downtown area of Chicago, Illinois. "Well," I say to myself, "I think the client meeting went very well." Walking down the brightly lit open and airy office space with high ceilings, I pass two men in blue business suits on the left reading the Chicago Tribune, newspaper, and ladies on the right chatting across their cubicle walls about the latest gossip (none of my persuasion, of course). No one ever once looked up to acknowledge me. I tell you, I like Chicago, but to be such a modern, cosmopolitan city, it remains one of the most segregated cities I have ever seen. At the end of each workday, everyone returns to the familiar comfort of their ethnic community – be it Jewtown, Chinatown, black communities on the Southside or Westside, white communities on the Northside or the green ($$$$) communities on the Goldcoast. If it were not for the workplace, many would never see, let alone interact, with anyone outside of their ethnic group. I distinctly remember having had meetings with attorneys at the firm, then ten minutes later, see them on the street during the lunch hour and they act like they don't know you.

Raised in a military family, this is so foreign to me. I grew up in an integrated community in Maryland, not far from the Washington, DC line. Growing up, I attended integrated churches with white pastors. Although I was the only black in my kindergarten class, I remember it being diverse. I remember having, not only white classmates, but Philipino, Indian, Costa Rican, and Mexican classmates, as well. For some reason, while many flocked with their own, I always developed connections with people of other cultures. It was not until I reached junior high school that I personally witnessed any racial tension. My earliest memory of racial tension is the periodic fighting after school between blacks and a group of whites, called "Grits." Grits were like Rednecks, angry, crass and unsophisticated. They were known to carry chains which they used in their fights. By the time I reached high school, the demographics had changed significantly. Between the relocation of Military families, which tend to be transient, and others that moved to newer housing developments in the outlying suburbs, my high school class, although still integrated, was now predominantly black.

Math was my favorite subject in high school, and my math teacher was my favorite teacher. He was a comedian, a white Richard Pryor. He looked funny - a white, skinny, hippy-looking guy with long untamed dark brown hair and a beard. He saw my potential and helped me stay focused by pulling my coat tail when I contracted senioritis, a decreased motivation towards my studies after acceptance to college as graduation neared. It was his counsel that encouraged me to pursue engineering. He is still teaching math there to this day. I saw him at a class reunion a few years ago. He recognized me and even remembered my name! That meant so much to me. I was so grateful to have the chance to thank him and let him know the impact he had on my life. He was one of many who saw me as special and exceptionally smart and gifted. Teachers, my friends, and their parents, as well as my family, especially, my nieces looked up to me and held me in high esteem. I was never really personally impressed by all of that, but I felt pressured to live up to the successful image that they kept of me. A little of that remains in me to this day.

After picturing myself walking down Michigan Avenue, taking in the famous Chicago Skyline with its skyscrapers, high-rise office buildings, and historic hotels from the gangster era, the outdoor art sculptures, getting a glimpse of the folks biking and jogging along the Lake Michigan beachfront... peeking in the shops and giving in to the temptation of a caramel cheese popcorn mix as I dodge the commuters hustling to flag down cabs, and running to catch the bus or the elevated train, I decide to walk back to the office. If I needed any other incentive, there was guaranteed to be a lively festival with food vendors and music going on across the street in Grant Park. So I step into the elevator, and as I reach to press the button for the ground floor, I start to feel a warm trickle down my leg. "Oh my goodness," I say to myself, "did I just pee on myself? How embarrassing." I look around discreetly to see if anyone noticed, thinking this is one time I pray no one is paying any attention to me. Oh, Lord, I hope that's not what I think it is. It is too soon! It's too soon! What do I do? I don't know what to do. Should I go to the hospital? Where is the closest hospital? Let me call the doctor – where is that number,? I ask while scrolling through the contacts on my flip phone. I finally find it and dial. The phone rings, the receptionist answers and I frantically interject in a soft voice so that no one overhears me, "Hello I'm a patient of Dr. Jones I think my water just broke. My name is Teri Charles I'm five months pregnant. Please help me! I'm not sure what to do. Should I go to the hospital?" "Can you come into the office?" she asks. "You want me to come to your office? Are you sure? I'm nowhere near your office. I'm downtown in the Loop right now." "Try to relax," she says, " the doctor would like to examine you in the office." " Ok, I'll come to the office." As I hang up the phone, I remember, "Shoot, I did not drive today." Should I catch a cab? No - Too far. Oh, Lord. I can't believe this. I cannot believe this! I guess I will have to catch the train. I need to call the office. What do I tell them? This is too intimate. I don't want those guys in my personal business nor do I want their pity. I'll just tell them I had an emergency. It's not like they could relate or empathize with what I am going through anyway. Being a female, and black on top of that, in a white-male-dominated environment is tough. All they care about is the bottom line. "O Lord, I am shaking like a leaf." My heart is racing. My mind is racing. Let me call Anthony. I dread making that call to my husband. He has not given me the support I hoped for during the pregnancy. I feel as though he really doesn't want this child anyway. It has been stressful at home. We are constantly bickering. It's like walking on eggshells at home. I had hopes that perhaps this child could be the glue that holds the family together. If not, at least something good would come out of the marriage. But right now, I must swallow my pride and call him. I need my husband's strength.

The only thing I can honestly say that was weak about my husband was that weak pick-up line he used to draw my attention to him at college. Ah, the memories. Tall, dark and handsome – a dime a dozen at Howard University, the Mecca of historically black colleges and universities. But there is something different about this one. It's the second semester of my junior year at Howard University. I am in the study room on the second floor in the Engineering Building. We called it the Green Room. Why? Because the walls were green, of course! I chuckle. As I pack up my books to head to my next class, I hear a low, but strong voice say, "Excuse me, did Dr. Evans give a homework assignment today?" "Really," I think to myself, "Dr. Evans has never given any homework assignments. What is with this dude? And why is he asking me? Probably just a line." I turn to him and simply say "No. No homework today." I sensed he was a foreigner, although I did not detect his Trinidadian accent. My last boyfriend happened to be from Trinidad, as well. What are the chances? All I see before me is a tall stature, at least six feet, strong presence but not aggressive, in faded jeans and a tee shirt and a thick mustache." Not being into mustaches, I keep walking. Ironically, I had a fit when he shaved it off after we got married! Heading towards the door, I overhear two girls whispering, "Is that Anthony Charles?" one asks. "Yes. Isn't he fine?" the other answers. Hearing that, I stop and turn to take a second look. "He is kind of cute. Maybe I blew him off too quickly." Well, his "mac" may be wack, but he got my attention. Subtle but effective. He was no longer invisible. I started to speak to him when I saw him around campus. Next thing you know, we started studying together. It turns out he was pretty smart! I will never forget that one evening, during one of our study sessions, sitting at the kitchen table in the room he rented out of a row house off campus, Anthony developed an approach that we could use to solve a complex math problem. He named it "The Holt-Charles Theorem." Now that is sexy! He has always been good at breaking down complex matters and finding a practical way to solve them. Well, he certainly figured out a way to break me down and get me to marry him. The rest is history in the making.

Great, Anthony's phone is ringing. "Hun, pick up. I need you. What a nightmare. Please pick up." "Hey, Babe" I hear on the other end. Bursting out in tears, "Hun, I think my water just broke. I just spoke to the doctor, and he told me to come to the office. I guess I'm going to get on the train. I'm wet. I don't have a change of clothes. Thank goodness I have on a dark skirt. I hope no one notices. I don't know if the baby is OK." "Calm down, Hun. Where are you? I'll come to get you", he says. "I'm trying to- I'm trying to stay calm. I don't want to wait here. I will catch the train." "Are you sure?" "Yes, meet me at the train station. I can't believe this. I can't believe this!" Just when I thought life was good.

THE DOCTOR WILL SEE YOU NOW

It feels so cold here in the doctor's office, both literally and figuratively. The dim recessed lighting is not at all comforting. But my husband's embrace reminds me that I am not going through this alone. Nevertheless, as I look around at the mahogany wood desk and bookcase, gray carpet on the floor, degrees, and awards hanging on the wall, I can't help but wonder, "Could this have been prevented? Why couldn't the doctor see this coming? Are there no tests or examinations for this sort of thing? And why the heck does this feel like a regular doctor's visit, with no apparent level of urgency?" I never really felt connected to this doctor. But he came highly recommended by a friend and his office was close to home, so I used him. I've only had a couple of visits with him. I expected closer monitoring, but this was my first pregnancy. So I accepted this was normal.

After what feels like an eternity, in strolls, a short, pudgy, middle-aged Caucasian man with brown hair and a receding hairline. He plops down in the leather chair behind his mahogany desk and places a manila folder on the desk. His face says it all. I squeeze my husband's hand as I brace myself for the news. I'm thinking, "Please don't let me lose this baby. I've fought too hard to get here." He leans forward and says, "Mrs. Charles, as you know, your water has broken. You have started dilating and will likely go into labor within the next several hours. At this stage, we cannot be certain that the baby has developed enough to survive. Even if so, it's likely that infection has set in. It's too early to head to the hospital. They won't admit you until your contractions are further apart and you have dilated further. So at this point, I would say that you can return home. Once your contractions are closer together head to the emergency room. I will meet you there. However, expecting some explanation for why this happened, I say, "Doctor, I don't understand. I thought everything was going fine what could've caused this? My husband and I have been arguing a lot lately. Could that stress have caused this?" "It's hard to say. We can run additional tests later to see if we see anything that can help us to understand what took place. It is possible that your cervix was too weak to sustain the pregnancy. If that is the case, placing a stitch around the third month may help next time. Since this is your first pregnancy, we don't have a history to look at, but we hope to learn from this one." "Learn?" I think to myself, "You hope to learn? You are supposed to be the expert! I am trying to have a baby! I am five months pregnant." Without saying so, it was evident that he did not expect the baby to survive.

SORRY, NOT THAT KIND OF HOSPITAL

The room is stark and cold like most hospital rooms. No frills. No windows or furniture, other than this bed. Not even pictures on the pale green walls. It seems, unusually, quiet to me for a hospital. At least I have some privacy – no roommate. It feels like there is no one else in the world except my husband and me and the attending staff. I am lying here in pain, and I feel as though the staff has no sense of urgency. I'm thinking, "Are you even trying to save my baby? Where is the doctor?"

Moments later, a comely older caucasian nurse in pale beige scrubs appears at my bedside, " Hi Mrs. Charles can you tell me what happened?" Annoyed to have to repeat this story, again, I answer, "I was at a meeting at a client's office downtown, as I was leaving I just felt something dripping down the back of my leg, I thought to myself what in the world is going on. So I called the doctor and told him what happened. He said it sounds like my water broke and told me to come into the office. I told him I caught the train into work and that I am an hour away from his office. He repeated that I should come to his office, so I did. He examined me and told me to go home until the contractions were closer apart, and once they got closer, I should go to the hospital. So I did. I don't know what happened. I didn't feel any pain, no fall or injury or anything like that. All of a sudden I just felt water going down my leg. I don't know. I don't know what happened. I don't know why my water broke. This is my first pregnancy. I'm five months. Actually, this is our second pregnancy - the first was aborted before we were married. After repeating the play by play, something struck me different this time. It occurred to me that the doctor didn't send me home in anticipation of the successful delivery of my baby, he sent me home anticipating the eventual disposal of my baby."

The contractions get more intense, "I am in so much pain. Oh my God is there anything you can give me - anything for the pain?," I ask the nurse. I was not prepared for her response. She said "I'm sorry Mrs. Charles this is a Catholic hospital and we're not allowed to induce – only natural vaginal childbirth. Nor can we give you any medication that may affect the baby or your faculties. Try to relax. The baby is in distress, and unfortunately, we are not equipped to treat a premature baby and would have to transfer the baby to another hospital if viable. Try to relax and let nature take its course." I can't believe my ears. If someone tells me to relax one more time, I am going to lose it. Can it get any worse? Of all the hospitals, how did I end up here? The contractions get more intense. "This is unbearable. I need something for this pain." Seeing my agony, she finally says "Let me see. Sometimes the doctor will authorize an epidural or something to help you to relax."

I did eventually get the shot. I had never experienced anything so painful. Now I feel like I am in a dream-like state, but at least the pain is dull. A few minutes later, I see the doctor and a team of about five or six others parading down the hall. Within moments they are gathered around my bed. Why so many? I wonder. I guess most are here to learn. The doctor pulls up his stool and says "Mrs. Charles, we've come to see how your labor is progressing." So upon request, back in the stirrups, I go. He immediately says, "yes, it is time. He preps for the delivery and then says "I need you to take a deep breath and push." So I pushed. It went pretty quickly – it could not have been more than an hour.

Still, in a daze, I look over and see my husband, towering over me with our son in the palm of his left hand. I couldn't bear the pain of holding him, myself, but I couldn't take my eyes off of him. He's so tiny. So precious. I see he looks just like Anthony, with his round head, high cheekbones, and his eyes but he has my complexion. I see him fighting for his breath. We can't help him. I hear a final gasp. I knew he was gone. When life passed from him, it was as if life passed from me. I died. I was in a daze – a dreamlike state. Please wake me and tell me I had a bad dream. It was like I was outside my body watching a movie. Hearing voices. Activity around me. What is happening? No control. Then I understand, "So sorry for your loss Mrs. Charles. I know how difficult it must be to lose the baby five months into your pregnancy. But you are young. Try again. You have plenty of time. We will need to take him and gather information. "Gee, can we have a moment please?" I ask. "Of course," she says. Everyone leaves the room.

She comes back a while later, "Mrs. and Mr. Charles since this was a live birth we will be preparing a birth certificate. What name would you like us to put on the birth certificate?" I turned to my husband, "Hun?" I was led to give my husband the honor of naming his son. "Anthony," he said. "Are you sure," I said thinking he may want to save Anthony for a future son. "Yes use Anthony," he said, "Anthony Charles." Then she asked, "Would you like for us to take care of your son's remains or would like to make other arrangements?" I quickly responded "No. No, I can't. I don't have the mind to do that. I can't make any decisions around that right now. How do you feel about that Hun?" "Let them handle it," he said. He had said very little since they took Anthony. I could tell he was in shock. "Okay. We will be preparing the birth certificate and the other paperwork. Again our condolences," she said and left the room.

Wow. I gave birth to my baby boy. I was a mother. But only for a moment. I didn't have a chance to bond. I didn't have a chance to say anything to my son. Joy and pain at the same moment; seeing my husband hold our son and take his last breath. It was too painful for me to hold him – to acknowledge his life and death. Hope gone. Joy is gone. Motivation is gone. I felt like I died. In one moment. A shattered dream. A birth certificate and death certificate on the same day.

IF AT FIRST, YOU DON'T SUCCEED, TRY AGAIN

I never really felt complete after the loss of our son. There was a void that could not be filled. I had so many questions yet no answers. So many what-ifs. What if I went to a different hospital that could have saved our son? What if my husband was more supportive? What if we weren't fighting all of the time? Was this punishment for having an abortion before we got married?

Well, I recall the doctor saying, "The best thing you can do is try again as soon as possible." So try we did. A few months after our loss, I conceived again. I should have been happy, right? I was for a while. I was happy that I conceived so quickly. I was happy that my husband was more supportive and protective this time. I believe he may have wanted this baby more than I did. Perhaps, the moment he had to bond with his son gave him a change of heart. I was happy that I experienced less nausea this time around. Most of all, I remember being so excited to reach the third month so I could finally get that stitch! Since that was the only option presented, I was convinced that the stitch would help me hold the baby at least until sufficiently developed this time.

Lying on the bed in the hospital surgery room, I looked around. The room was a huge, cold, open space with white walls and a high ceiling and nothing but my bed, a stool and, of course, those stirrups. "What a waste of space," I thought. It felt super sterile and impersonal. I was given medication to relax me, but I was awake throughout the procedure. Surrounded by white coats, masks, and gloves, I laid there, in such peace, praying with great expectations, until I saw the doctor pull out a needle and a long piece of clear thread. "Is he really going to stitch me up with that needle and thread? Like darning a pair of socks?," I thought. Needless to say, this journey has left me less than impressed with the medical profession. The procedure only lasted a few minutes.

"That's it. The stitch looks great!" the doctor said, proudly and confidently. His confidence made me even more hopeful.

I returned home the same day with no special instructions or restrictions and returned to work a couple of days later. Expecting to be on bed rest at some point, I started picking up items here and there in preparation for the baby. Once I entered the fifth month, the torment began. I remembered that this was around the time that I went into premature labor the last time. I was paranoid. I was so afraid I would miscarry. Well, my worst fear eventually came upon me. I experienced some leaking. Not the volume as before, so I remained hopeful that the pregnancy could be saved.

We went to see the doctor. He confirmed that I had started dilating early again. The stitch did not hold as expected. I was put on bedrest at home with instructions to help reduce the chance of infection in hopes to give the baby as much time as possible to continue to develop. Laying in bed all day, my mind was overactive. I tried to keep my mind on the Word. Praying, listening to healing tapes, reading the Bible, and listening to worship music all day. But the fear of a miscarriage was there. I dreaded going to the bathroom for fear of infecting the baby or putting too much pressure on my cervix. A few days later, I experienced severe cramps. An infection had set in. By the time I reached the emergency room, it was too late. Still-birth this time. We never saw the baby. When asked whether it was a boy or girl, we were told they believe the baby was a girl, this time.

Here again, so many questions and no answers. So many what-ifs. What happened this time? I thought putting the stitch in at three months was the answer. Was it put it too late? What if I had been put on bed rest sooner? Was something else going on? I don't know. I don't know if I can do this again. It's too stressful. It's too painful. Losing two babies in the fifth month? I don't think I can do this again. Why would God allow this? Why would God withhold this from us? He knows this is the desire of our hearts. The Word says he would never withhold any good thing from us. It says that a child is God's reward. It seems so unfair that other women can have babies so easily. Some have thrown them in the trashcan or even worse. Why let me conceive and go so far into the pregnancy, Lord? Not just once, but twice! All I wanted was to go to school, get a good job, get married, have children and live happily ever after. I feel like this dream is shattered. I feel so defeated. So helpless."

IF AT SECOND YOU DON'T SUCCEED, TRY SOMETHING ELSE

I hoped my heart would be comforted in time, but the comfort did not come. I had no explanation for the losses. So I had little hope in trying again. I could see the concern in my husband's face – a concern that I was becoming depressed. At the same time, I recognized that he was working through his own emotions and grief. He was more resilient than I was. I sensed he wanted to keep trying. But here again, I felt as though, he could not appreciate what I went through.

After a while, we finally broke the silence and had the heart to heart needed for us, or me, to move on. Although still disappointed, I had a desire to arise and pursue a new dream. One evening, we were sitting in our living room on our gray velvet couch with the plush pillows facing the large bay window framed by the dimmed recessed lights. The lighting from the huge mauve and gold ceramic table lamps gave off a warm glow and reflected off the glass tables. The atmosphere felt unusually warm and safe that day. I opened up to my husband, "Hun, I feel like the doctors have let me down. I feel as though, for some reason, God has denied us a child. I can't do this again. At least not right away. I certainly do not plan to try to prevent a pregnancy. If it happens, it happens. But I cannot put my heart and soul into pursuing a child again. But now what? How can I get up and move on from here? I feel like I need to pursue something else. Something that I have more control over. With all the changes at work, I am not enjoying that anymore. My options appear to be limited to the management track or becoming a marketing rep. I have no interest in either of those tracks. Maybe this is the time to start to make a fresh start in my career. I've always thought about going to law school. Maybe now is the time." His response gave me strength, "Hun, I fully support you if that's what you want to do. Go for it. Start applying to some schools right away. You have my full support."

So I did. Pouring myself into law school, helped take my mind off the failed pregnancies. I did well on the law school aptitude test. Every day I walked across our front lawn to our curbside opening the mailbox with anticipation of an acceptance letter. I remember the day I received my first acceptance letter. I remember opening the mailbox and pulling out an envelope with purple letters spelling out Northwestern School of Law, Chicago, Illinois, my number one choice. I had butterflies in my stomach as I opened the letter. It said I had been accepted and awarded a grant! I was so happy! My first acceptance letter was from my number one choice, Northwestern School of Law. What are the chances? Every school to which I applied either accepted me or extended an invitation to interview. What are the chances? I felt like I was winning again.

An alumni reception was held on the first day of law school. I was seated at a large round mahogany table next to a female partner at a major Chicago law firm. She was a tall, slender, older, Caucasian woman with short gray hair and a stern demeanor. She was dressed in a fashionable, yet conservative, dark tailored business suit. One of her areas of concentration was computer law. My background was in computers. What are the chances? After sharing my background and interests with her, she offered me a paid summer associate position at her firm right there on the spot. I had not yet attended a single law school class, but I already had a job offer. What are the chances? As a result of grants and law firm summer associate positions, I graduated from a top ten law school debt-free. I never had the need to take out a student loan. Again, what are the chances?

FERTILITY – FALSE HOPE?

It was a sunny, Sunday afternoon. I am reclined in the car with my husband driving home following service at our church located on the Southside of Chicago. We are cruising down Interstate 57, and I am looking out the window at the billboards, and storefront stores as we pass 147th street when, suddenly, I experience the worst cramps I have ever had. I never have menstrual cramps, and I had not eaten anything. "Hun, I am having painful cramps. Take me to the emergency room. I am late, and I suspect I may be miscarrying." Without asking any questions, he picks up speed and races to the closest hospital. As we reach the emergency room, the cramping gets worse.

I remember sitting in the waiting room, waiting to see a doctor. The intake is taking forever. Panning the waiting room, I see the room is not crowded, but the hospital seems to be short-staffed, and the staff is operating without any sense of urgency. All of a sudden, I feel the urgency to go to the bathroom. I look up and see the sign for the restroom. I race to the bathroom down the hall, shut the door, squat and out gushes a bloody flow of liquid with bloody clot-like lumps. With anguish, I wonder "Did the fetus pass? Is there something in there?" I look for something to use to fish for anything of substance. All I find are clumps of blood that dissolved once manipulated. Another miscarriage leaving me with more questions and no answers? "Well, at least this pregnancy ended early," I say to console myself, "I couldn't bear getting far into the pregnancy and losing again." I rush back to the waiting room, hoping that no one flushes the toilet, and tell the attendants what happened, "Miss, I just used the bathroom and I passed a lot of blood and bloody tissue. I fear I may have passed the fetus. Can the discharged tissue be tested?" It was clear, no one shared my urgency. No one even bothered to check the toilet. "We don't do that here. We only treat your symptoms. There is nothing we can do with that," she said.

When I was finally seen by the doctor, he said "We can do a pregnancy blood test. There is a chance we can at least confirm whether or not you are pregnant or perhaps were pregnant." They did the test, and it turned out the pregnancy test was negative. No surprise. But they did say my levels were elevated so I could have been. "If you were pregnant, it was early in the first trimester," he said, "and it is likely something was wrong with the fetus. It is more common than most women realize. Many miscarry without even knowing they are pregnant. It is likely that is what happened in your case. I recommend following up with your doctor." I was fresh out of law school and was not, actively, trying to conceive anyway, given the early stage of my legal career, but in our hearts, we certainly hoped it would happen. But once again, nothing conclusive. Still, I have no answers. Accepting this thing I cannot change is getting easier. Life goes on.

A couple of years went by without conceiving, but not for lack of trying, so we decided to seek a specialist to help us. We were referred to an African American male doctor who came highly recommended. We heard dozens of success stories regarding his patients. If he did it for them, surely he would do it for me. Although he was not accepting new patients, he agreed to take me on. I was happy with him. I sensed he was a Believer. He seemed very thorough and had an excellent bedside manner. When attending to me, he was always present, gave me detailed information and didn't spend the first fifteen minutes reviewing my file as though I was a new patient. I felt like he really cared about his patients.

Our first round of fertility treatments was unsuccessful. I was so sure the fetus was going to attach the second time again. Once again, everything looked good. But, once again, the pregnancy test came back negative. "I don't get it. We're fertile. The doctors can't find anything wrong. All the tests and examinations look good. No one can explain why I haven't been able to conceive. All the injections. All the testing. The waiting. The emotional toll. My hormones are all over the place. The disappointment. The financial strain. I'm tired. Are we wasting our money? Are we wasting our time?"

I GIVE UP

After getting the call from the nurse, advising of the negative test results, I laid on my back across our kingsize bed staring at the black ceiling fan and cried out "Why encourage me, Lord, give me hope, then take it away? I can't comprehend that. I am questioning why I would serve a God that would do that to me. I felt such assurance that this time would be a success. I felt your presence. I felt your peace. Then you allowed my heart to be broken again. I cannot possibly be hearing from you. If I am not hearing from you, how can I accept the invitation to speak at the church on Women's Day? I can't. I won't. There is a world out there that seems to be doing fine without you. Why not go that way? It can't be any worse than this. I certainly don't feel like I have an advantage with you or help from you. Is this all there is to this life? A good paying job. The money is good - but I feel pigeon-holed at work. I am married but have been unable to have children. This isn't abundant life. I am starting to question everything - even you. Why follow if my prayers are not being answered? I can do bad all by myself. I must have no favor with you. So just let me be. I don't want any of this or this life anymore. I want to be happy. I don't need any more disappointment, and I feel you have forsaken me. I'm losing faith. I don't know what to believe at this moment. Maybe you aren't even real. Whatever this is, you can have it. I don't want it. I'm done."

Suddenly the room went totally dark and turned frigid. "What just happened?", I wondered, "I feel hollow. Empty. Alone. Actually, I don't feel anything at all. I am lifeless. Am I dead? Has His Spirit left me? I fell on my knees, praying "Father help me. I am in such agony, but I can't live in this darkness. I have never experienced such darkness. This is hell. If this is what it is like to live without you, I can't bear it. Forgive me. Restore me." The light gradually returned. I felt the warmth. "Thank you for restoring me. You are real. I never want to experience that again. That was worse than any miscarriage, worse than the labor." As frightening as it was, I thank you for this experience. You are real. Thank you for your life." Sometimes you don't know what you have until you lose it.

WOMENS DAY

"Sister Charles! Sister Charles!" I hear calling behind me in a high pitched voice. I turned around to see who was calling me. It was another one of the Minister's Wives. She was more senior and seasoned than I and well respected at the church. As she came near, she extended a white envelope with my name on it and said, "We would like you to be our 11 am speaker for Women's Day. You don't have to answer right now. Pray on it and get back to us." Then she turned and briskly walked back down the long dark hallway.

I was speechless. "Me?" I thought, "Of all the women they could choose, they want *me* to speak? This is sure to ruffle some feathers. I am the new kid on the block. I can hear the murmuring already." This is a big deal. Our church, at the time, had no woman ministers and no woman deacons. We did have one woman Trustee. The only time women spoke at our church was on Women's Day and most of the time, we brought in a speaker from outside for the 11am service. This was new. I could hardly wait to share this news with my husband. He was so proud. "Babe, this is your season," he said. [I open the envelope, and the letter reads "…..The Theme, Women of God, with a Vision of Victory" Prophetic, huh? I think so. God is up to something. I believe God used this to bring spiritual healing to me. Of course, I didn't know it at the time.

Well, this day is finally here. With the Lord's help, I surrendered and pressed through the pain, the anger, and the disappointment. A few months ago I died. His Holy Spirit left me. Today, I am so full of Him, I could burst. Lord, I make myself available to you. I am thankful that you would trust me to deliver your message to the congregation. You've clothed me in your glory, in flowing white linen with the gold trim and the gold sash is perfect. The sanctuary is packed. I am sitting here in the pulpit with my sisters, my intercessors to my left, and to my right, a father in the ministry who afterward nicknamed me "Lil Preacher." This Women's Day Choir is the largest I have seen since being a member here eleven years ago. The Choir, at least 50 voices strong, sounds like a mighty army. But its like we are celebrating a victory, not going to battle. Lord, your glory has filled this place. Fill my mouth as I take this pulpit. Have your way Holy Spirit. Have your way.

TRANSITION

Not long after that act of obedience in delivering that message, I started looking for a new job. I desired to find a position, preferably, with a corporation where I could apply both my legal and technology background. I worked with a couple of headhunters in this pursuit. That July, my prayer was answered. The job was in Maryland, not far from where I grew up. I was headed home for the 4th of July holiday, and was able to schedule interviews with the General Counsel on the 4th, along with a couple of other DC law firms, while in town.

The General Counsel was a Jewish woman, not much older than I was. To my surprise, she showed up in shorts. I thought that was a good sign. A refreshing change from the stuffy law firms, where I had been interviewing. I could tell she valued family – she was a loving mother and wife. We clicked, and she offered me a job on the spot. After some negotiations, I submitted my two-week notice to my then-current firm and left for Maryland.

It all happened so fast, it left my husband bewildered and feeling a little insecure. I think he thought I was leaving him. To put his mind at ease, I assured him I would only commit to two years, although I distinctly heard the Lord say five years, and we agreed to maintain a residence in both states. I remained on that job precisely five years. I remembered my covenant with the Lord, and left rejoicing, yielding to His leading.

What a journey it has been. Traveling the globe has been a highlight. I have visited five different continents, and the Caribbean is like our second home. Little did I know that God would use my love for adventure and travel and my passion for other cultures, to give birth to global ministry. The greatest, I believe, being the ministry of presence, a ministry that I did not appreciate before that dark day when the Holy Spirit left me, but now means everything to me. Before, I traveled strictly for business or vacation for relief from the brutal Chicago winters. Now I travel for what my husband and I call "Birthcation." More on that to come...

Teri Charles, after 22 years practicing law and 7 years as an electrical engineer with IBM, has answered the call to global missions and serves alongside her husband, Dr. Ray Charles, as Special Assistant In Leadership Development for Europe, the Middle East and Liberia with International Ministries. She received her law degree from Northwestern School of Law in Chicago, Illinois, USA and her electrical engineering degree from Howard University in Washington, DC, and has worked in the technology, financial services and insurance industries. She and her husband, Dr. Ray Charles, have founded two leadership development organizations, The KIIP Group, which stands for Keep Investing In People, and a not-for-profit called A Ray of Light Ministries. She and her husband currently reside outside of Baltimore, Maryland, USA and are members of Beit Chesed, a multicultural Messianic Jewish congregation in Reisterstown, Maryland.

CHAPTER 10

STICKS AND STONES
by
Markita D. Collins

"Kita! (That's what my family calls me) Kita, come here. Sing a song and dance for us. Come on and show how to do it, baby."

"Eww you have Jheri curl, you're too black, you have train tracks in your mouth. You're pretty…pretty ugly."

How do I go from being called beautiful, pretty, chocolate kiss, to now being called fat, black, and ugly girl?

That's what I heard a lot growing up. As a child I was loved and nurtured by two amazing parents who did nothing but love my sisters and me. They instilled values, morals, and self-esteem.

Still, I would like the words of relatives and classmates in elementary school that is, they would often remind me that what parents said to us was a lie.

Throughout my life, I have had many encounters with people who said some awful things to me and about me. Some things were said behind my back and then right in my face. I would run to my mother and explain to her how I felt when people would say mean and cruel things to me. She bends down to grab my cheeks, look me in the eyes and say "Markita, sticks, and stones may break your bones, but words will never hurt you. As long as they don't touch you ignore them."

As I grew up, I was taunted, bullied, and the same words would ring in my head "Sticks and stones."

I knew that words couldn't break my bones, but they broke my heart. Yes, repeatedly, the words I would hear tortured me long after they were said. Words also have the power to shape your world. Have you ever heard someone say something negative about themselves only to see that what they spoke begins to manifest right before your eyes? Have you ever wondered what might've happened just if they spoke: "life" instead of "death?"

Low self-esteem and I became friends. We got to hang out. Talk to each other. It was part of my makeup. It was with me all the time until I was sure people who would remind me that I was pretty, talented, funny and one day would be a star. However, the one day wouldn't cover five to six days of the torment.

Like the parable told of the prodigal son, I came to myself. Yes. There was something on the inside of me that begins to fight back. I just didn't know what that was. I start to speak up and say how I felt. The word NO felt good coming out my mouth when my peers would try to bully and humiliate me. Giving that sarcasm right back became easy for me and a part of my nature when cousins and god-family members would come for me.

Enough was enough. But what do you do when you're now having people tell you one thing, and then your mind agrees with them?

My heart was heavy. I didn't realize at the time that I conformed to the world, and I begin to be in my head what others said I was. Can you imagine embracing lies and accepting false realities? Guess what, even to fit in. Let's pause there for a second. Have you ever been in place and you know GOD is shifting and changing you for the better, but you on purpose dim down? You on mission extinguish your own fire because you don't want people to really see you in the fullness? We were all guilty of doing that at some point in our lives. The weird thing we see the good and greatness in everyone else but have limited vision for ourselves.

During high school I took on the hero role. I never called anybody ugly or unattractive and complimented everyone. It was to the point that my peers said that I was just saying it to be nice. That was not the case. I just wasn't having it! Standing up for the bullied and telling them how great that they were, but never standing up fully for myself. It never dawned on me at the time that even though what I gave wasn't given back to me the way I was pouring out, God was using me to help build up. Now I had to learn how to build me up. But how?

In the Bible Proverbs 18:21 teaches us that life and death are in the power of our tongue.

"Death and life are in the power of the tongue: and they that love it shall eat the fruit thereof.

I heard it, I read it, but I didn't know how words could bring forth life and death.

High School was hard for me. I struggled with dyslexia.

Dyslexia is a general term for disorders that involve difficulty in learning to read or interpret words, letters, and other symbols but that do not affect general intelligence.

You see no one knew about this condition for a while. So, by the time my junior year came, some decisions had to be made. I learned again the hard way about how WORDS had power.

It was time to choose my profession. My teacher called me up to his desk and said its time for your appointment with that guidance counselor. Good luck.

I rushed to the guidance office for my career meeting. Nobody could know how excited I was because at this marking period I'm finally a "B" student and I'm passing my regents tests.

Knock knock. "Hey, Markita come in. Have a seat."

My counselor is on the computer and pulling up my records.

So Markita looks like you've gotten your grades up and your test scores are passing.

Have you decided what you wanted to do when you graduate high school?

My heart was pounding, and I'm sitting thinking in my head there are so many things I would love to do, but it would be great if I were a music major and minor in business.

Ok here goes about to say it out loud.

"Yes, I want to go to college and..."

She interrupted me.

"Umm have you ever considered cosmetology school? Your hair is always nice, and you have a great personality! Oh yes, you can sing but do you know how hard it is to make that a paying career?"

She spun around to the computer and was raving about how great I would be at doing hair!

Right then my heart dropped. My eyes welled up with tears.

Not because she suggested that I be a hairstylist or nail tech, but she didn't even mention college to me. It was as if she knew that wasn't an option.

After a while, I didn't hear a word she said, all I heard was "black girl go downtown to tech school and get a trade. You are not smart enough for college! Hahaha"

Remember I was already dealing with dyslexia and somewhere deep inside I was hoping for my "guidance" counselor to say "college, of course! It's going to take hard work but Markita you can do it!"

I left that office hurt and defeated, not before I was registered for cosmetology classes.

The hallway felt at least 5 miles long. How was I going to tell my father college wasn't in the cards for me? Most of my friends and family members were talking about college or going to college.

My classes started about 4 weeks after my appointment with the guidance counselor, to my surprise I enjoyed the course. Oh, my goodness I'm very good at this. Manicures, Pedicures, forms, powder, tips, silk nails and test taking was natural for me. Although being a nail tech was easy for me and fun, but it wasn't my passion. Something on the inside wasn't satisfied with this being my career.

Decision made! I'm registering for college! My father wrote me a check, and I went to the local community college, and for 1.5 years I struggled. I kept hearing "you're not smart enough for higher education." No one said it out loud, but I still listened to the words in my head.

Frustrated and insecure, classes were a joke to me. The mall, my boyfriend and wasting time is what I did. Accepting the words that were spoken over me followed me for so many years.

Accepting that I was only going to be good at making people laugh, making people feel good, and singing was all I had. What could I possibly offer the world?

It never dawned on me that God was going to use the very things that I thought weren't valuable and made it a part of my DNA. The enemy through words and self-doubt had me accepting the following: rejection, fear, low self-esteem, and brokenness.

At the age of 19, I was engaged by the time I was 20 going on 21 I was married & moving to the good ole south. I was living the good life. Oh, so I believed. Only to have anything with a reflection continually reminding me about my imperfections and that I wasn't good enough.

"You're gaining weight."

"Hey, wear your hair like this."

"I don't like that on you."

"You need to sing but not always gospel."

"I've heard better."

"My Mama don't like you."

"I trust you, but I'll have someone else handle my accounts while I'm gone, I think it's best."

Have you ever been surrounded by people but still felt very alone? What's wrong with me he just wants me to be better and do, better right? Why am I being so ungrateful? Why am I sad all the time? I'm in one of the fastest upcoming cities in the nation. Atlanta GA. I should be the happiest woman on earth. I lived in a luxury gated community, beautiful furniture, fabulous clothes and a husband in the military. What else I could want?

I know what to do. Get a job! He won't reject me when I bring some money up in here. I'll work. If that means working minimum wage jobs, call centers, and temp agencies. I was willing to pull my weight. One thing my father and mother taught me was to work no matter what kind of job it is. Have your own money.

So, working was easy for me, I worked 2 jobs to occupy my time while he was overseas fighting in a war. At the time September 11th rocked our worlds, and he was gone on and off for 2years. He would only be back for a month to 3 months and then gone again.

Calling cards and emails were my friends. I ran my phone bills back then. Homesick, lonely, I'm getting no love, no attention. I found comfort in food. I'm in my luxury apartment and depressed.

I was yelled at and regularly chastised about spending "his" money and not holding the fort down. I just notched it off because of the condition he was in being away and fighting for our country. Work and work some more. Church and Church some more. That's all I did. I really didn't have much of a social life. Just phone calls and emails to communicate. My local Christian stations and writing songs.

Still, no matter what I did it was never good enough. I was never good enough. I ended up going through the divorce and being humiliated and ashamed. Interrogated and embarrassed. Only to hear again "Failure, you fail at everything.

Even in the church. I was only "great" when I opened my mouth to sing. I was good enough to exhort but not good enough to preach or speak.

The assistant pastor at a church that I was faithful to and served for years looked me in my eyes and said that I do too much talking when I need just to sing and sit down. Which confused me because my senior leader encouraged me to flow and minister how the Lord directs me too. It was time for elevation and catechism. This was a big deal to me, only to have another leader tell me "Oh you will be elevated to Minister of music that's it. So, you don't have to study that much. That should be easy for you." Was there a "kick me" sign on my back or "She can't do all things through Christ" on my forehead?

My senior leader heard about the conversation because I was that one that kept the mess from them, he had to come to me. His words "Daughter you are called to preach the gospel not just sing. It is time." I said nope GOD didn't tell you that. I'm not called! He said you're right you were chosen. I am licensing you to preach the gospel, and nobody can take that from you, or they need to answer to me.

Why did I reject what GOD was saying through my leader? Why was I so sure that he made a mistake? It was an internal thing. Yes, people played a role. I will say this too, people who continuously insult your intelligence and confidence are very aware of the one thing you don't know. You have significant potential and are amazing, and they don't want you to figure it out.

That is the truth.

I just went on with life just figuring out how to live. There was a war within me that I had going on every day. The question is how long was I going to pretend to be okay and not be?

Almost 16 years later, I found myself facing all the words that were sent not to break my bones but break my spirit. They were uttered not just to hurt me but to destroy me. They were meant for evil; they were intended to cripple me. They were expected to paralyze me. They were designed to hold me back. Those words never wanted me to live, but to die. Those words tried to keep me bound up. How could I recover from years of these words?!

It was the fight back! The same battle I had to confront those bullies. The same struggle to walk away from a verbally abusive marriage. The same battle to stand up to the man that raped me. The same fight to stand up against spiritual injustice. I had to use that same fight to look at myself in the mirror and say "GIRL YOU ARE FULL OF HURT AND OPEN SORES! THE WORDS YOU KEEP HEARING ARE NOT EVEN FROM YOUR PAST RELATIONSHIPS, THEY ARE NOT FROM SATAN. MARKITA THEY ARE FROM YOU! STOP!"

I screamed and cried for hours. I could no longer blame them for the condition that I was in. I knew better. I had to repent. One might ask what does repent even mean?

Repent means

to turn from sin and dedicate oneself to the amendment of one's life

to feel regret

to change one's mind

The last part hit home for me. I had to change my mind. I had to turn away from the thing that had me bound up. As long as I pretended to be okay and no one could tell if I was hurting or not I was safe in my pain. Who would want to live in that condition?

Furthermore why? What did I have to lose by repenting? My old way of thinking. No more being a hero for others; it was time for me to surrender to GOD. It was time for me to be rescued by Him.

That meant for confronting every lie told on me that I had believed. I literally dismantled and nullified every curse and contrary word spoken over my life from a child to an adult. That meant fasting and praying... reading the word of the Lord and believing it. That meant reading books on self-esteem and confidence. That meant being around people who wouldn't allow me to talk negatively about myself. That meant me speaking the truth instead of repeating the lies.

Keep in mind, it wasn't just the devil. It wasn't just people. It was ME! I am sure you have done this to yourself as well and if you haven't PRAISE THE LORD!

There is a story that I am reminded of in the bible. The scripture reference is John 4:1-42.

It's one of my favorite stories, one that I can relate to so very well. The woman at the well. My God just thinking about it brings tears to my eyes. I can feel the love of God swooping down upon me right now. So, this woman that He met was rejected by her own community. Did you know that? The well in those days was the gathering place for women. Not just to draw water to drink and do laundry. They came to one another and drew strength. They swapped ideas and spent time with each. Oh, but they didn't have time for a confident woman. We don't know her name, but she was significant in many ways.

Our heavenly Father came through Samaria, He was tired from the traveling he was doing, and he sat down by the well. The woman began to get water, and He said to her, "Give me a drink." She said, "How is it that you a Jew can ask me for a drink I am a Samaritan." Jesus with his cool self said to her "If you knew the gift of GOD and who you're talking to you would be asking me for a drink, and what I have you'll never thirst again."

This woman came to know the Lord because of what He gave her and what he SPOKE into her life. She immediately dropped her water pots and ran into the city and told the people, the same people mind you that had nothing to do with her to come to Him. She said, "Come see a man who told me everything I ever did!" Because of that they also believed in God!

Now that's the power of words!

Just like that woman at the well I know how it feels to have people pre-judge and come up with preconceived notions. How do I know now that words may hurt me, but they will never wound me? Will they never kill me? Because I know a risen savior who came to restore my soul according to Psalms 23:3 "He restores my soul and God leads me in the path of righteousness for his namesake."

Presently I have come to know who I really am. As a wife, mother, entrepreneur, certified life coach, prophet, friend, sister, mentor, etc. I am no longer a broken crayon that still colors. I am whole. Challenges have come to take me out of my character, but I continue to stand on the word of God and not just the word, but great people who see the real me. I learned how to be open and trust again. That was hard for me because I dealt with so much internal emotional pain, I figured I couldn't let another person in. God said not so. I had to break down walls, and barricades. I had to cast that pain and brokenness to the Lord. Let me tell you something, when you really want to be free you will do whatever it takes.

- Fasting (from food and socializing)
- Reading the Bible, Christian books on healing
- Confession and declarations
- Listening to powerful teachings (visual or audio)
- Worship and praise
- Be around people who carry the LOVE of GOD
- Surround yourself with people who will value you and appreciate you.
- Go to places where you are appreciated and not overlooked and tolerated.

I did all that and continued to because I've seen the results. I GOT FRUIT HONEY! So, will you. It works if you work it! I'm going to say that again - IT WORKS IF YOU WORK IT!

The love that I feel from the Father is so amazing. You can feel that love too.

The same God that restored me can and will restore you too! Now I can't control what people say or think about me. The same goes for you. However, we can live in truth and teach people how to treat us by how we treat ourselves. It's time to reintroduce yourself anyway don't ya think?

Yes! It's time that people no longer take you for granted! It's time that you be free from words that GOD isn't even thinking about saying about you. I love the word of the Lord. The Bible had become my safe place. Just to read and repeat what the scripture says about how God feels about me has freed me from the words others said.

Here are some you can use - I know these words will bless you as they have blessed.

- Psalms 36:7 How precious is your unfailing LOVE, O God!
- Psalms 136:26 Give thanks to the GOD of heaven, for his steadfast LOVE endures forever.

In my personal time with God and learning how to let go of evil words spoken over me, I had become familiar with his voice. The things he would say indeed lifted burdens from the heart. Let me tell you somethings He said concerning me, and I am sure this will encourage and bless you as it has blessed me.

God calls me:
- Daughter
- Beloved
- Precious
- Friend
- Overcomer
- Conquer
- Fearfully and wonderfully
- Wealthy
- Wise
- Adorned
- Blessed
- Anointed
- Chosen and Called

- Powerful

That's just to name a few. What God is not calling me is:
- Orphan
- Bastard
- Cast way
- Foolish
- Silly
- Unlovable
- Heathen
- Sinful
- Stupid
- Unlearned

Check this out. Even in the times, I was the things I just listed above, He never once said that to me. That brings tears to my eyes right now. GOD is never calling his beloved anything but his beloved.

He loves us so much that He gave us his only begotten son. Yes, His son came to live and be called everything but who he was. But he never stops saying who he knew he was and that was the savior.

Never stop saying who you are. Don't believe another lie. Believe the truth! Believe that you can and will be everything God predestined for you to be. I understand that might be easier said than done...wait a minute...THAT'S A LIE TOO! I prophesy from this day forward, it will not be hard, it will be easy!

Easy to believe and trust GOD
Easy to trust in the Lord with all your heart and lean not to your own understanding.
Easy to walk by faith and not by sight,
Easy to forgive people.
Easy to live a God-driven life
Easy to love again.
Easy to move ahead.

Come on. Even while you are reading this, I want you to open your mouth and declare

"This is EASY for me. This will be a year of ease!" repeat it! And again! Say it until you shake off the spirit of heaviness and put on the garment of praise.

I speak words of LIFE and LOVE over you right now while you are reading! You will LIVE and not die! You will run and not faint. You will endure. Strength is coming to you right now in the name of our God.

You are not what they called you. You might be cast down, but you're not destroyed. Glory to GOD. Do you feel that release? It feels wonderful. That's the joy of the Lord.

Another hard thing I had to do was forgiving not just the offenders. Nope, that wasn't the hardest thing at all. I had to forgive myself too. You should forgive yourself for teaching people that it was okay for them to talk you any kinda away and mishandle you. It's crucial that you do that. Come on girl! (I am not sure if men are reading this too if so, COME ON MAN)

Hug yourself if you must. It's quite alright. Don't be ashamed and please don't beat you up. This is a good thing. Yeah. That's it. You got it! The spirit of the Lord is healing you even as you are reading.

I pray in the name of God that you get up and face yourself. This enemy you're fighting is not just the enemy of this world. But the old mentality that you must release.

Remember GOD loves you with an everlasting love. He wants you to LIVE and not die. Don't be the walking dead. Don't just exist. You are not what negative things you said you are. You are the opposite.

I am a woman who didn't graduate from college. I don't have letters behind my name. Yes, learning was difficult for me. I cried for many days. Sometimes I still cry. The thing is I'm reminding myself daily through the eyes of God that I am great! I am Great in the kingdom. Yes, a Bestseller 2x, Certified Life Coach, Entrepreneur, Ordained Prophet, Licensed Minister, Instructor, and so much more. Not to bad for a girl from Upstate NY who was told I was just right for doing hair and singing because I couldn't do anything else.

I sit back and laugh out loud (to myself not in front of people lol) when I think about how the devil wanted me to suffer. Although GOD had and has a plan for my life, satan also has a plan. He wants to kill, steal, and destroy according to John 10:10. He wants to steal your joy, kill your love for yourself and others. He wants to ruin your relationship with your heavenly father. I want to make an announcement, he may try, but he always loses. That's the good news. Why? I'll tell you why. Greater is He that's in us then he that's in the world. 1 John 4:4.

No weapon (words) formed against you shall prosper and every tongue that rises against you in judgment you shall condemn. Isaiah 54:17

You are seated in heavenly places with God. Ephesians 2:6

You have favor with God and man. Proverbs 3:4

Those awful negative words, my friend you have the authority and legal right to cast them down. Pull down the stronghold. Cast down every vain imagination.

You have power to change your world with the words you say. You are stronger than what you give yourself credit for.

I have faith in GOD that words are pulling uprooted from for your heart even know.

You have the same 24 hours in a day that I have. Start using some of that time to remind yourself who and whose you are.

Start writing it down, leave voice notes, use a tissue and write on that if you must. Get it out and hear your own voice say it.

I remember when I was told nobody would ever love me the way I need them because I was dirty and unclean. Respect was a thing of the past due to mistakes and choices I made. All of that was a lie. I am still here. This very day, this hour, this moment. I am here living my best life. I took the same sticks and stones and made books, cookies, classes, conferences, webinars, tours, and more out of it. Glory to GOD.

You see Faith comes by hearing and hearing by the word of GOD. I also say fear comes by hearing the wrong thing that's not from GOD. We are going to be who and what God calls us. No matter what comes up, I am not, and you are not backing down. We are to rise. The only way we get down is if we are bowing at the feet of our Lord. That's the only way. If we fall, we are going to get right back up and follow the steps again. Pray, fast, worship, etc.

We will not succumb to the lies that we were told. No more. It's over!

So yes, sticks and stone may break your bones, words can harm you...or HEAL YOU.

I choose life.

Markita D. Collins is a lady, wife, mother, published best selling author of "I'm still old fashioned!"), entrepreneur – President & Founder of Kita's Kookies, worship pastor, licensed minister, prophetess, certified life coach, international motivational speaker, visionary and leader of GIRL TALK WITH KITA and Co-Founder of The Unbreakable Experience Conference. Currently Markita resides in Pennsylvania with husband Ali Shaun Collins and

their four children. Through the power of social media, She has the ability to reach thousands of people every day and speak life to their situation(s). The world as we once knew it is no more; it is now in a constant state of chaos. Consequently, some people are prone to encounter life stressors. Markita's great passion and purpose is to help pull people out of dark places, remind them of who they are and yet to become. Girl TALK WITH KITA is a safe place where men, women, and teens' lives are transformed. She have received countless testimonials from individuals professing the positive impact GIRL TALK WITH KITA had on their lives; changes were emotional, mental, and spiritual. "Let me help you by serving in a capacity that will shift the way you see and love yourself. Let me help you heal and recover from past and present trauma and life stressors. It would be my pleasure to show you how to release the things that are preventing you from progressing in the following areas of your life: • personal • business • ministry • relationships" It all starts with one experience that can literally change your whole world. How can I serve you? I am here and waiting.
Markita D. Collins
www.markitadcollins.com
www.unbexp.com

ABOUT FUMI HANCOCK

Dr. Princess Fumi Stephanie Hancock, DNP., M.A., BSN, B.A.

Bestselling Author, NAFCA African Oscar & Indiefest Film Award Winner, TEDx Talk Int'l. Speaker, African Heritage Leadership Recipient, TV Personality, DR. FUMI: The Doctor of Nurse Practice™ Show &Transformation Interventionist, Philanthropist

D r. Hancock with her love for the literary arts and behavioral health sciences, she has managed to strike a balance between the two, through her TV /Radio shows, documentaries, feature films, books, and her mental health-wellness presentations. To date, she has written over 21 books, 11 of which have become bestsellers and on the heels of releasing other books in the success development, health & wealth arena. Her book series, Your Vision Torch™ has been received by organizations, ministries, and colleges, in Africa, USA, Pakistan and other countries as a success strategy tool. Quit Your Job in 90 Days as equally allowed her to speak in front of Moslem women from all over the world, who converged in London, United Kingdom. In 2018, she got an incredible opportunity to be the first black woman to grace the stage of TEDx Talk-Al Anjal National Schools in Saudi Arabia.

When she is not writing or making movies, she is a sought after International Public Speaker, (a member National Speakers' Bureau & Women's Speakers Bureau-USA), with interesting topics ranging from spirituality, mental health, & wellness, self-help development, personal & success growth. She has been invited to train traditional and political leaders in Africa on Innovative Leadership as well as be a keynote speaker in some African Universities during their convocation ceremonies. Her doctoral dissertation, *using mobile application as an adjunct in treating patients with anorexia nervosa (AN) in communities that regard AN as taboo* earned her invitation to speak at the Sigma Theta Tau International Convention in United States of America.

Some say she is a Social Changer; others say a Transformation Catalyst seeking to extend the hand & heart of social justice, and many, call her a Story weaver who strives to bridge the gap between Africa and America.

Dr. Fumi Stephanie Hancock, DNP, M.A., BSN, an African Princess living in Diaspora is an Advanced Nurse Practitioner turned Screenwriter, President of The Princess of Suburbia® LLC (Cambium Break Pictures), and the host of a nominated NAFCA African Oscar Lifestyle & Health Talk Show, The Doctor of Nurse Practice Show with Dr. FUMI broadcasted by The Princess in Suburbia®. She was a columnist for over two years at The New American Times, Tennessee where she wrote on "Mental Health & the Media" and has been featured in several newspapers such as the Princeton Packet, The Advertisers' News, Tennessean Tribune. Recently, she launched International Diaspora Network and an Online Virtual Incubator for Professionals in Transition & Emerging Creative Entrepreneur.

Her accolades span from Africa to the US, as the most recent NAFCA African Oscar Peoples' Choice Award Winner~ as Favorite Screenwriter, Indiefest & Accolade Global Films Merit Award Winner, and Depth of Field International Film Festival, Woman of Excellence in Films Award Winner. On the heels of her recently released award-winning movie, Of Sentimental Value, she launched a woman-centric radio show, The Southern Warrior Sister-Tribe which is gaining grounds globally from her homestead, Nashville Tennessee.

Her greatest achievement besides her husband, Dr. David Hancock & their 4 grown children is her philanthropic work in Africa (The Princess of Suburbia Foundation). Dr. Hancock's ultimate mission is to inspire, motivate, empower, and equip others; helping them to value themselves, connect/reconnect with their true calling, and live a well-balanced life. Her desire is to create platforms for others who have not had the opportunity to be heard by telling their stories, one woman at a time. September 2015 alongside a Nobel Prize winner, Dr. Wole Soyinka is being honored by the NAFCA Africa Oscar Film Critic Association in Hollywood, California for their contribution to Literary Arts Globally.

AWARDS OF DISTINCTION:

NAFCA (Nollywood Films Critics Association, Hollywood, CA) NAFCA *African Oscar* Peoples' Choice Favorite Screenwriter

Indiefest Films Merit Awards for *Women in Films*

Accolade Global Films Merit Award: *Women in Films*

African Heritage Award: Contributions in Films, Writing, & philanthropic work in Africa (African Heritage Festival Nashville, TN).

Depth of Field International Film Festival: Merit Award, Screenwriter

Doctor of Nurse Practice (DNP) in Mental Health with Areas of interest: Self-Image, Eating Disorders in silent cultures, Mood Disorders.

2015 Prestigious Honorary Award by NAFCA *African Oscar* Organization, Hollywood, California.

www.drfumihancock.com

www.princessinsuburbia.com

www.storytellerbistro.com

MORE RESOURCES

Other Books
www.drfumihancock.com
http://www.theprincessofsuburbia.com/

For information on booking Dr. Princess Fumi S. Hancock BSN, MA, DNP to your next event, please log in to:
www.worldoffumihancock.com / www.theprincessofsuburbia.com

My Blog
www.yourinneryou.com

My Podcast: Storyteller Bistro
https://www.spreaker.com/show/storyteller-bistro-podcast

My Film Production Company
Cambium Break Pictures/ The Princess of Suburbia Films
For details on her upcoming movies, please log on to:
www.cambiumbreakpictures.com
http://ofsentimentalvaluemovies.com

E-Learning Masterclasses
www.storytellerbistro.com

DR. PRINCESS FUMI STEPHANIE HANCOCK, DNP, MA, BSN.

The Princess of Suburbia® Brand
www.theprincessofsuburbia.com
www.drfumihancock.com
*LITERARY ARTS *FILM/TV/RADIO PRODUCTION
*SPEAKER/COACH
(Psychiatric Mental Health-Wellness Expert for the
Entertainment Industry)

&

Find out about
The Princess of Suburbia® Foundation, Inc.
The Adassa Adumori Project

DR. FUMI STEPHANIE HANCOCK, DNP, M.A., BSN, B.A.

Manufactured in Africa….
Assembled in United States of America….
Dispatched to the World.

This is just the Beginning….
One Event Can Change Your Life Forever!
Be the CHAMPION in your own Story.

MORE PRAISES FOR PRINCESS FUMI'S BOOKS

Dr. Fumi Hancock is an incredible woman with an incredible passion to see people, women and men alike fulfill their purpose on this earth. She has witnessed first-hand in her own life, and in the lives of friends and family, huge circumstances and challenges that have come to distract and derail them from the plan and purpose that Creator has created them for.

As you read, I believe you will be freed to dream once again. You will gain a heart-felt determination to become all YOU are intended to be and be moved to action to finish your race despite all odds."

~Snr. Pastor Janet Conley – Cottonwood Christian Center, Los Alamitos, California.

Your Vision Torch is just that, like a light down a dimly lit path, a bright, beautiful, and bold wisdom packed life manual for successful and very soon to be successful individuals.

I challenge anyone to read Your Vision Torch from cover to cover and not be inspired! Truly this has impacted me, and I know many others, to achieve your dreams and goals not just for the sake of oneself, but for us all! Thank You Dr. Princess Fumi Hancock, for all the good you pour into others!

~Interior Designer/Stager

"With hopes of healing herself and helping others, Fumi writes these words of inspiration to others"

~Lynn Miller, West Windsor & Plainsboro Newspaper

"Fumi shares the message of hope in the midst of tragedy."

~ **Star Ledger**

"Dr. Fumi is a breath of fresh air to those who cannot see their way out and have lost hope. She is a modern-day Esther understanding her past, recognizing her season and Creator's timing, while embracing her future. She reigns supreme as a communicator, a visionary, a spiritual giant that the world is about to discover, only we knew it all along."

~ **Dr. Phyllis Carter Pole, Author: Temperament – Your Spiritual DNA.**

Spring Hill resident Princess Fumi Hancock has been riding a wave of success since her new book, The Adventures of Jewel Cardwell: Hydra's Nest hit the shelves in September 2012

~**The Advertisers' News- Spring Hill**

PRAISES FOR DR. PRINCESS FUMI HANCOCK'S U.S.-BASED TV SHOW
THE PRINCESS IN SUBURBIA® TV
(AN INNOVATIVE & INSPIRATIONAL MENTAL HEALTH & LIFESTYLE TALK SHOW)
WWW.PRINCESSINSUBURBIA.COM
CHECK OUT WHERE IT IS BEING AIRED

Welcome to
The Princess of Suburbia's Haven

Snicker or Cry as this Suburbia Goddess Shares Her Life Story & Dishes Out Spicy Recipes for Life, Love, Family & Everything Inbetween!

www.twitter.com/PrincessinSub; www.theprincessinsuburbia.blogspot.com
http://www.youtube.com/user/PrincessinSuburbia

Despite our bad international image, some Nigerians, like Dr. Princess Fumi Hancock, still believe in promoting our image and African culture through her online TV Show. Bravo! ~ **Prince AF**

OMG just realized you have lots of videos, before and after this. I am off to watch them all ~**CY**

I really enjoyed one of your videos some minutes ago online. Keep the fire of good work you are doing burning, you are a source of inspiration to me and my family, Creator will increase your knowledge ~ **SO**

I am a new fan of the Princess in Suburbia Show! ~ **FL**

Didn't realize you had other episodes. Just got back you're your channel. I am a new fan! ~**LS**

I don't know how to thank you for your activities and your online TV programming. Creator will continue to strengthen your ability, provide more grease to your elbow ~ **OB**

You are so funny princess. You make me laugh so much ~ **RV**

I love your laughter and the way you approach life, Princess ~ **EB**

More grease to your elbow, Princess in Suburbia. I will keep watching ~ **GL**

Just found your video and I loved it. I am off to watch others on your channel ~**JL**

I came across your channel, Princess in Suburbia USA and found the content to be quite engaging and empowering. Thank you for making us laugh ~**YS**

Your show and the Let's Go Innovate Africa group online is quite inspiring. I am happy to be a part of this movement ~ **KC**

CPSIA information can be obtained
at www.ICGtesting.com
Printed in the USA
FFHW020827100319
50957545-56372FF

9 781732 889842